My Three Successful Escapes

Author: Antonín Moťovič

Translated from Czech by: George Jiři Grosman

JewishGen
מרכז עולמי לגנאלוגיה יהודית
The Global Home for Jewish Genealogy

A Publication of JewishGen, Inc.
Edmond J. Safra Plaza, 36 Battery Place, New York, NY 10280
646.494.5972 | info@JewishGen.org | www.jewishgen.org

MUSEUM OF JEWISH HERITAGE
A LIVING MEMORIAL TO THE HOLOCAUST

Published by JewishGen Inc.
First Printing: August 2022, Av 5782

Author: Antonín Moťovič
Translated by: George Jiři Grosman
Cover Design: Jan R. Fine

Printed in the United States of America by Lightning Source, Inc.

Library of Congress Control Number (LCCN): 2022941584

ISBN: 978-1-954176-54-6 (hard cover: 272 pages, alk. paper)

About JewishGen.org

JewishGen, an affiliate of the Museum of Jewish Heritage - A Living Memorial to the Holocaust, serves as the global home for Jewish genealogy.

Featuring unparalleled access to 30+ million records, it offers unique search tools, along with opportunities for researchers to connect with others who share similar interests. Award winning resources such as the Family Finder, Discussion Groups, and ViewMate, are relied upon by thousands each day.

In addition, JewishGen's extensive informational, educational and historical offerings, such as the Jewish Communities Database, Yizkor Book translations, InfoFiles, Family Tree of the Jewish People, and KehilaLinks, provide critical insights, first-hand accounts, and context about Jewish communal and familial life throughout the world.

Offered as a free resource, JewishGen.org has facilitated thousands of family connections and success stories, and is currently engaged in an intensive expansion effort that will bring many more records, tools, and resources to its collections.

Please visit https://www.jewishgen.org/ to learn more.

Executive Director: Avraham Groll

About JewishGen Press

JewishGen Press (formerly the Yizkor Books-in-Print Project) is the publishing division of JewishGen.org, and provides a venue for the publication of non-fiction books pertaining to Jewish genealogy, history, culture, and heritage.

In addition to the Yizkor Book category, publications in the Other Non-Fiction category include Shoah memoirs and research, genealogical research, collections of genealogical and historical materials, biographies, diaries and letters, studies of Jewish experience and cultural life in the past, academic theses, and other books of interest to the Jewish community.

Please visit https://www.jewishgen.org/Yizkor/ybip.html to learn more.

Director of JewishGen Press: Joel Alpert
Managing Editor - Jessica Feinstein
Publications Manager - Susan Rosin

My Three Successful Escapes

by Antonín Moťovič

With love
to my daughters Ivana and Zuzana,
their husbands Zeev and Hagai,
my grandchildren Nov Jonathan and Maya
...who will be hearing these ugly things for the first time.

To my sister Šarlota.

In Memoriam:
to my wife Alizka, who supported me in every step of our life together,
to my Mother, whose remains rest in the Holy Land,
and to my Father, whose remains in a nameless mass grave in Ebensee gaze upon the gorgeous scenery of the Austrian Alps, and
to my brother Natan.

Table of Contents

4

6

1   My Little County Town

Sometimes, even the driest-sounding official document can evoke a forgotten, albeit tragic, event that happened to a fourteen-year-old boy during summer vacation in 1941. He was a student between the tertia and quarta at a local gymnasium (third and fourth grade of high school) in Khust, in Subcarpathian Ruthenia. This would have been about three years before the massive, real calamity – the deportation of Khust Jews and their annihilation in concentration camps. It happened two years and four months after the 1939 Hungarian "liberation" of this region.

The Hungarian writer Béla Illés (*Carpathian Rhapsody*) and the Czech writer Ivan Olbracht celebrated its beauty. This region was poor, unique, and romantic but was also in the midst of a stormy flowering. I am borrowing the title of Olbracht's book "Mountains and Centuries" to describe the character of Khust – though it is in the foothills of the Carpathian Mountains, on bright days the peaks are visible and are sometimes covered in snow, even in June and July. Khust lies on a flatland, in the right angle of the confluence of the lesser-known Rika (in the parlance of local Ruthenians, and Nagyág in Hungarian) which flowed from north to south, and the better-known Tisa (Tisza in Hungarian), which flowed from east to west.

The town was dominated by a hill – it had a castle with the characteristic silhouette of a ruin, visible from any point in town and its three approaches. It was a favorite spot for walks by old and young alike. Students would have picnics there and due to its elevation, it was well liked in the winter by folks on skis and sleds. Around All Saints Day the place was quite busy as our Catholic fellow citizens and neighbors visited the graves of their loved ones, bringing bouquets of local wildflowers. The starting point for wintertime sledders was at the permanently open iron cemetery gate adorned by a slogan in Latin, Hungarian and Czech, a slogan that was incomprehensible and mystical to a young boy: "We were like you and you will be like us!" After World War I, the region became the easternmost part of the new Czechoslovakia and many of those born there kept a warm and never forgotten spot in their hearts for that place and that time. Khust lay on the Yasinia-Aš line, which spanned the length of the Czechoslovak Republic from its easternmost to its westernmost point. One would reach Uzhhorod (Ungvár in Hungarian) in three hours and then a further fifteen hours would get one to Prague via Košice, Brno and Jihlava.

I was born in Khust. It was my home for 17 years. It no longer is. Let me tell you my story as it unfolds from my memory very many years later.

The main approach was on the western side of town and it was quite impressive. Right beside the hill, known as Red Hill (the earth was really red), aka *Piros domb* in Hungarian for those who remember this version of its name, one got onto an iron bridge with three arches spanning the river Rika. Or had it only two? Such is my memory after more than half a century later! But that is the thing, all those places stand out in the memory as huge, towering dimensions. Were those iron arches not impressive? Moreover, about a hundred yards south of there, a railway bridge spanned the Rika, parallel to the iron bridge and on it the express train from Aš via Prague to Yasinia would zoom by. Those two points always served our math teachers as examples when they tried to explain the notion of a thousand kilometers. Our geography teacher used the railway line to demonstrate the length of our republic. Also, once a day, and in both directions, a Romanian express train zoomed by. That one could not be ignored, not even from a distance, seeing the black smoke billowing from its engine. If one came close, it was clear which train was which: on the Romanian one the lettering was CFR instead of ČSD. There, by the iron bridge we would have our first dates, and adjacent to the railway bridge there was one of our river beaches; we would jump from the railway bridge into the river headfirst when we noticed the girls' eyes fixed on us. The other beach was further up north, against the stream, where stone embankments protected little fields that stretched along the river.

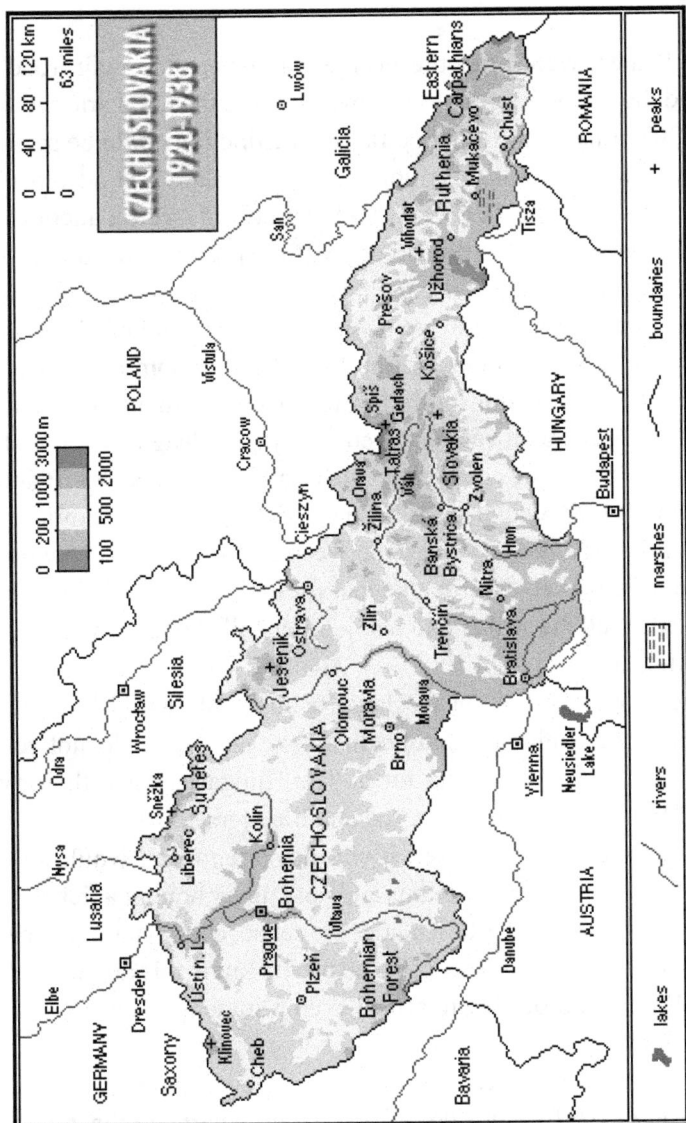

Map of Czechoslovakia between the two World Wars (source: Mariusz Pazdziora,
https://commons.wikimedia.org/wiki/File:Czechoslovakia1920-38.jpg).

Well then, right after the bridge was where the main road began. It crossed the whole length of our town and was the main artery that bisected all of Subcarpathian Ruthenia. Its first distinction could be seen right as it entered the town. On the right side of the road, behind old Hartsteins' house there was a large plot of land that hosted a cattle auction on certain days. In the distance, in the direction of the railway line, one could see the wooden stands of the soccer club SK Rus Khust (green jerseys), the younger sister of the more renowned SK Rus Uzhhorod, known as 'the flying teachers'. This description hinted at the composition of the team and their means of transportation to far-off destinations when the team played in Czechoslovakia's premier soccer league. I am sure every supporter knew the goaltender Bokšay who, next to Plánička, was considered the second-best keeper of the First Republic (the usual designation of Czechoslovakia between 1918 – 1938). If memory serves, for a time he was also the goalkeeper for Prague's famed club, Slavia. Fans may also recall the striker and ball juggler called Čančinov. He also played for both teams.

One more word about the local team of SK Rus Khust. It, too, was comprised of Ruthenian intellectuals exclusively: I do not remember a Hungarian or a Jew playing for it. The Hungarians had their own club – HSE (*Huszti Sport Egyesulet*, red and blue jerseys) at the other end of the town. Let me reveal a secret: it was not often that I would miss a home match of either of the two teams and yet I never bought a ticket. Like every other boy, I knew every hole under the fence, every tear in the barbed wire on top of the fence but I suspect the ushers knew this and looked the other way. Who would be able to afford even a student ticket?

My passion for soccer never left me, even later in Prague. I would switch night shifts with colleagues when Sparta Praha played a home game and there were definitely not many games during those twenty years (1945–1965) that I missed – though at that point tickets were honestly purchased, obtained as needed by my "court barber", a diehard Sparta fan like myself.

But let us go back to the main street. Its name during the First Republic was Zhatkovich Street (named after Gregory Zhatkovich, an American Ruthenian, a lawyer for General Motors domiciled in Pittsburgh). Along with Woodrow Wilson and Tomáš Garrigue Masaryk, Zhatkovich was a signatory of the agreement that incorporated Subcarpathian Ruthenia into the nascent republic of Czechoslovakia, and he became its first Governor. During the time of Hungarian control (1939–45), the street was called *Vámhíd* – possibly because there used to be a Customs house (*vám* in Hungarian) on the bridge (*híd*). In Yiddish it was called *Maikhesgasse* (from Hebrew *mekhes* – customs). The street was famous for three things: firstly, I was born there, at number 9, on January 17, 1927 and lived there till the age of 14. Secondly, two houses further west there was a Greek Orthodox boarding school for Khust High School students – and I mention it only because the headmaster of said boarding school, the spiritual leader of that community, Father Ivan Popovič, played quite an important role in events described later in my story. The last noteworthy denizen was the only taxi driver. His cab, a *Tatra*, was parked outside beside a ditch, not far from where we lived, on the corner of a street that led to the "little" train station where some slow trains used to stop, mostly ferrying high school students from nearby villages.

According to some recent eyewitnesses, our house is no longer there, and I only have a hazy memory of a long yard. We lived on its left, my parents with their three kids – my brother two years older and my sister two years younger than me –, as well as my grandmother and grandfather from my father's side along with my dad's four younger siblings. On the right side of the yard lived my grandmother's sister and her family. At the end of the yard there was a "garage" – possibly a former cow shed, the remnant of a farm. I vaguely recall that behind this rickety structure there was a long plot of land with a garden, stretched out to the edge of a small river near the high school. I was three or four years old when this plot was used to build a street with a row of nice low houses occupied, as I remember, almost exclusively by Jews. Across the river stood the tidy little modern homes of the "Czech colony".

Let us continue our walk towards the center of town. We cross a little concrete bridge over a stream called Mill Creek. I remember it being built. It replaced a wooden bridge that would be washed away every year to a bigger watercourse called Khustice/Husztvíz (probably the origin of the town name). On the other side of the bridge, on the left, stood the group of buildings that formed the elementary school. That was where Mr. Fedor (my first grade) and later Father Popovič (grades two through five) were my teachers. I barely recall the first teacher but the second one remains lodged in my memory as an excellent teacher and a good man. That is where I learned to read and write and all the other basics one needs throughout one's life. It was Father Popovič who prepared me for my high school entrance exams. He had planned to do it right after fourth grade but because only one student could be accepted directly from the fourth grade it had to be the best one. That title belonged to me but the student who was accepted was Mitrovič – a teacher's son and a Catholic.

This was in September 1937, I was then ten, and a brand new, un-Masaryk wind had started blowing in from the west across Sudetenland. (Masaryk was the first president of Czechoslovakia and a national symbol of liberty and tolerance.) No one said it out loud but a *numerus clausus* (a limit on the number of students accepted based on their race) was put into effect in a semi-official way. I spent one more year in elementary school and in September 1938 I entered the *prima*, the first grade of the gymnasium (high school). By then the atmosphere was totally changed. Seven months later the First Czechoslovak Republic ceased to exist.

But let us leave the school now and continue our walk in two different ways. We can either keep walking straight ahead, where on our left we would see the *Heder Talmud Torah* (school for boys dedicated purely to Jewish learning). Abutting it there was the sports complex of *Sokol* (a Czech patriotic social and gymnastics club), where preparations for rallies would take place. Handball and basketball were played, and in the winter, there was hockey on natural ice. *Sokol* was used mostly by the parents and kids of the "Czech colony". A bit further down we would come upon a square with a Greek Orthodox church, and to its left there were horse-drawn carriages for hire to carry merchandise to the surrounding villages.

Or we can walk down Barracks Street which would have been a long walk all the way to the barracks of the 45th Infantry Regiment (known as the Romanian) where my dad, Private Martin Moťovič had served. As I have no photograph from his service, all that floats up in my mind is a picture of a Czechoslovak Army soldier during the 1938 mobilization. The barracks were under the command of Staff Captain Netuka whose manservant would bring a horse to his house, whereupon His Highness the Staff Captain would mount the horse and ride it with an air of puffed-up decorum along our street to the barracks. The manservant ran behind him on foot.

Behind the barracks, on the edge of the town, was the Jewish cemetery. The only member of my family who found a place of eternal peace there was my grandfather. Thus, he barely avoided the catastrophe to come.

But let us go back to the schoolhouse. To the back of it we could visit the Czech kindergarten. I remember my sister attending. I suspect that instead of kindergarten, my parents sent me to the *heder*. I do not know anyone who could shed light on this, but it is not necessary. I have decided to write only what I remember directly or what comes to mind as I write (and that happens often).

Back to the main street. A gentle turn to the left and after walking about two hundred meters we reach the main square. The square lacked nothing: on the left, the city hall and in its yard a fire station. Deeper inside the structure – various city workshops, stables for the city stallion and the city bull. The boys who were able to find a small crack in the wooden fence would holler and whistle, reacting to what they saw. Personally, I never got to find one of those cracks and so had no idea what provoked their excitement. On the other side, in the corner of the square itself there was a wide entrance to the courtyard of our second, new movie theater and cultural center. On the opposite corner of that side was a gas pump. The square was wide (both in that time and in my present fantasy in which everything looms large). It was mostly empty and desolate, with a sporadic market or the Kludský Circus setting up shop once every few years. It also served as the location for military parades and the place to celebrate national holidays and occasions – October 28th during the First Republic and March 15th during Hungarian rule.

Across the square, on the left-hand side we saw the first proof that the city's few thousand Jews played a role in this narrative. This is where the "big" synagogue was, a gloomy old rectangle of a building, where the pious went to pray twice a day. It never lacked the necessary ten men over *bar mitzva* age – thirteen years old – to get a *minyan* as prescribed by Jewish law. This is where my father went on Saturdays and holidays, and this is where I stood before the Tora ark when I reached the age of thirteen. My ceremony was not completely smooth because a certain number of our co-religionists could not stomach the fact that I attended school – the second grade of the gymnasium – on Saturdays. And God have mercy – maybe I was even breaking one of the basic laws of the Torah, God forbid, and I had to WRITE at school on Saturdays; in other words, I was working! And Saturday, the Shabbat, as is well known is the holiest day of the week for a pious Jew and any work is strictly forbidden. I can now reveal a secret: I still have in my files a special dispensation from the Gymnasium headmaster which states I was not to be compelled to write on Saturdays. But what was I – nuts? To not write and to risk the possibility of being de-throned as the best student in my class? And so, if one of the Orthodox attendees wanted to see proof I did not write on Saturdays, I had it.

I will come back to the gymnasium but in the meantime, we should not turn right, into Krásná (Beautiful) Street but continue straight ahead where, on the left, facing the synagogue, there was the wholesale corn store of Mr. Wolf. He had three sons. The youngest, Rudi, was the owner of the Main Street pharmacy. (I almost wrote the owner of *The Shop on Main Street* and I have no doubt that my friend, the late Ladislav Grosman, may his memory be blessed, the author of the Oscar winning film of the same name, would understand if I did.) Rudi's partner was the pharmacist, Elek – they ran the pharmacy together. I remember the Wolf family well because my father worked for them for a time and because the Wolfs always urged me to study and to be an excellent student. I will write more about this later.

Now we find ourselves at the market – there were vegetable stalls there every day but every Wednesday we could buy whatever our heart wished for in the market. This brings me to Judaism again. On the left-hand side, before we reached the second, more modern synagogue, was the yard of famous Rabbi Dushinsky, as well as the offices of the Jewish community with a school, a *heder*, a *yeshiva*, a *mikveh* – the ritual bath in which every woman had to immerse herself after her monthly cycle ended, to be "kosher" for her husband after their Shabbat meal. There was another corner in the yard, untidy, even dirty where prior to the Shabbat or holidays the ritual slaughterers (*shokhets*) cut the throats of chickens, ducks and geese in accordance with biblical laws. That meant that every good Jewish mother and housewife could prepare not just a *cholent* but a full Shabbat or holiday feast. Naturally, I speak of those who could afford such an extravagance. There were many who had to make do with a bone or two and a bit of meat clinging to it.

There is no point in walking further in that direction. We would reach the wooden bridge over the river Khustice and then the soccer field of the local HSE club (the Hungarian football club). However, if we turned left after the bridge, we would pass Dunkel's furniture factory and get onto a side road to the rail station – but we would do that via the Main Street. We left it when we visited the square. So, let us continue straight ahead from the gas pump. The true heart of the city began here on the right, with a two-story building. On the ground floor there were shops of all kinds as well as the Schönfeld's pharmacy. On the second floor was the dance hall of the *Koruna* hotel, where the cream of our county society met three times a year. People came from far and wide for the Hanukah, New Year's Eve and Purim balls. A little further along if we turned right we would reach the first synagogue again, but on our left we would espy the *Central* – the building housing a restaurant, dance hall and hotel. If we do not turn right, on the left we would come upon another little square which served as a parking lot for the luxurious coaches of *Čedok* (Czech tourist agency) – or the *Ibusz* company during Hungarian rule. From here the tourists went either to the *Koruna* or the *Central* to have a meal and to rest after their wanderings through the deep, mysterious forests of Subcarpathian Ruthenia, through country virtually untouched by civilization.

The same location also served as a station for public buses on regularly scheduled routes: mostly northbound to Volove and Torun and, to a lesser degree, eastern routes. If you wanted to travel east, you took the train and a horse-drawn carriage would take you from your train stop to your native village. The only city bus also had a depot at the same location. It only had one route: to the train station and back. Once a day to the express train Aš – Yasinia and once a day to the same express train in the opposite direction. The bus line also served slow local trains that came through the railway station. And I must not forget horse drawn coaches and sleds in the winter. There was a whole row, perhaps fifteen cabs or sleds during wintertime, their horses hitched, standing straight and proud, waiting for a client but I cannot recall them ever being used for any other route but a trip to the train station. They stood on the side of the square in the corner where Rosenbaum had his shop. It was there that I first saw a radio receiver.

This is where the *korzo* (promenade) began. Before we walk down its path, let us visit the first street to the right. Here was Auslander's beautiful bookshop, the popular pastry and bakery shop of Mr. Bernstein who made the best cream puffs I have ever tasted. And soon we would begin "promenading" on the sidewalks on both sides of the street. The one on the right found more favor – that is where I would meet friends and acquaintances, teachers and professors from the gymnasium and mainly, in those good times, we would cast our glances at the girls, and they would cast theirs right back. Your stock was pretty high if you wore a hat of a military cut with the gymnasium insignia, and each year you would gain a silver stripe as you progressed: one through four stripes signifying you were a *prima, secunda, tertia* or *quarta* student (the first four grades of high school). Once you entered the fifth grade (*quinta*), the stripes colors changed to gold till you reached four gold stripes, meaning you were in the final year – *octava* (the eighth, or last, grade of high school). In my case, I was only able to reach the first gold stripe. I never got through *sexta* (sixth grade).

We passed Baťa's shoe store and one look at the prices in the window display showed that no pair of shoes was ever 20 or 30 crowns. The price was always set as 19.99 or 29.99 crowns. Did one heller make any difference (1 koruna / crown was 100 hellers)? No, but ten hellers was the price of an egg. I clearly remember the peasant women at the market shouting in four languages (Czech, Hungarian, Ruthenian and Yiddish) "Ten for one", meaning ten eggs for one crown. A sad memory comes to my mind of seeing the portrait of Tomáš Baťa in the store display window, framed in black to commemorate his death in an air crash in 1935.

But we are still in the middle of the *korzo*. On the right-hand side there was the front entrance to Rabbi Dushinsky's residence and kitty corner, on the other side, there was the Catholic church with its clock that chimed every fifteen minutes. One remark here: during holidays, or days when there was no school, I accompanied and helped my best friend Šuli (Alex) Treiber, who was a watchmaker's son, to wind the clock and make sure it was always accurate. Otherwise, services would be delayed or rushed by a few seconds, and we did not want that on our consciences. Alex's dad fulfilled all sorts of non-Jewish functions and tasks. He was a member of the local fire brigade, maybe even the chief. Beside his shop there was a little HSE display cabinet where we used to go every Thursday to see the following Sunday line-up and, naturally, this was a place of much critiquing and grumbling: why was this or that player going to be benched? We were only happy if we could all agree that the line-up was good enough to assure victory on Sunday.

Anyway, we leave the Catholic sanctuary, look at the post office on a little side street, return to the left sidewalk, pass the nice county courthouse building and jail, and reach the end of the promenade. Around the corner was the Heimfeld's department store, with the old movie theater across it. And if we turn left a bit further down, we are on the street where I was imprisoned in a ghetto before being dragged away to a concentration camp.

And now back to the promenade...at the end of the right sidewalk, we turn right, walk a few meters and are in front of a thin white tower with no cross at the top – the Protestant church. Back to the main street and to the right – is a schoolhouse, and a few steps farther, a street leading left and up to the Castle. A bit further left were the County Offices and the police station. A hop and a skip and we are under the Castle, and if we want to continue all the way to the railway station there is no need to turn back, just continue below the Castle and on the right we find ourselves back on the main road. Take a left turn and we are in Station Street. About a kilometer down, we see a tangle of rail lines – first the freight yard, then the passenger station. (I mention the rail station so many times! I guess it must have been the main focus of the town.) A few hundred meters further, on the left, was the warehouse for gasoline and oil that belonged to the South Carpathian Refinery, with its head office in Mukachevo. The warehouse was managed by my Mom's brother, and on our visits, we squeezed every last bit of gasoline out of the empty drums, literally drops, collecting them in cans, and then we would be able to have an oil lamp burning at home for a few days for free.

On the same side, a few steps further, "the kiln of sad repute". That is where they gathered us and squeezed us into cattle cars in the spring of 1944, like sardines, standing room only. They made sure rail cars were ready on a siding leading to the kiln and gasoline warehouses. But that puts us in 1944 and there is a lot to be told about the intervening years, especially 1941.

In other times and other rail cars, thousands of young people started their journey west to study, seek culture and enlightenment. They came back as teachers, lawyers, and doctors to bring some of the new world into our old one. And it had started working. And then the blow. For some it had already come in 1941. For the others after the German occupation of

Hungary, which up till that point was its faithful ally. This was March 19, 1944 and the Hungarians instantly began implementing the recommendations of the January 1942 Wannsee conference – the Final Solution of the Jewish Question.

2 Retrograde Amnesia is Reversible

I am writing these lines at the start of 1997. I have just celebrated my 70th birthday, I have put aside the first printed pages and started doubting that I really wrote them. As I write, my memory floods with places and events that occurred more than half a century ago – places I left and have never visited again, if I discount the one short week in 1945 when I returned to Khust and realized that everything I had known was gone, never to be again. One took mental stock – who was still there and more importantly who was not and never would be again? One saw Russian soldiers in the streets nabbing "suspicious" elements and "parasites" – both words could well be ascribed to those who had so very recently walked out of gates adorned with the slogan ARBEIT MACHT FREI – and the soldiers were pushing them to work on a landing strip for small planes where, a few years before, the SS had driven people out of the ghetto as an *Arbeitscommando*. They could have been the very same people! What a strange twist of fate! *O tempora! O mores!* (Oh, what times! Oh, what customs!) is what an ancient Roman would probably say. Moreover, I certainly did not feel that the local populace was too excited to see the wrecks of their former neighbors re-appear. Aside from my father (mass grave in Ebensee, Austria) we all survived: my mother and the three kids. My brother had left by then, on route to Palestine via Italy (only to be apprehended by the British and shipped to Cyprus). And so, my mother, my sister and I ventured into the unknown. We crossed over the new border between Czechoslovakia and the Soviet Union, a border that was never recognized by the rest of the world. This was not the first escape under my brave mother's command. More about that later.

And so, memories return. And I remember clearly, and will witness according to my memory, that in our town of approximately thirty thousand inhabitants, of whom about six thousand were Jews, all lived together in harmony: Ruthenians, Hungarians, Jews, Czechs, and a few Germans. Perhaps the co-existence was not idyllic but there was definitely tolerance. There was tolerance on the street, in the workplace, in shops and in schools. People of all faiths mingled: Greek Orthodox, Catholic, Russian Orthodox, Protestant and Jewish. Each had their place of worship, they all prayed to the same God. Each had one temple – only the Jews had two main ones, one Orthodox and one Reform, plus a few small prayer rooms. A supporter of a certain Rabbi or congregation would refuse to pray to the same God in another Rabbi's temple.

There was a full division of labor among the varying faiths and national groupings – almost all commerce and most physicians and lawyers were Jews. State and county employees, including the police force were in the Czech domain. Hungarians were mostly farmers but also worked in the trades and owned some shops. The Ruthenians were peasants and manual laborers (not a few Jews were among those as well). Many young people would leave to study in specialized schools and universities not only in Uzhhorod but in measurable numbers in Slovakia and the Czech lands as well. Each group had its elementary and middle schools. Gymnasiums were Russian or Czech, later Hungarian with the Hungarian language being the language of instruction – all depending on what years we are talking about. The Jews were an exception to all this. During the times of the First Republic, a substantial amount of the student body in Czech schools was Jewish and I remember that Jewish students tutored some Czech students in the Czech language.

The Jews were cosmopolitan: almost all of them spoke all the other languages. The parents had grown up in the Austro-Hungarian Empire and remained under its influence in terms of language dexterity. The Masaryk regime, fully open and democratic, also helped with its language, and cultural and religious liberty. Naturally, a large number of Jews also spoke Yiddish and were raised in the traditional Jewish spirit.

But there was the new generation, the generation born in the 1920's and those who had come of age as the new Czechoslovakia came into being. Without betraying their home values and traditions, this was a generation educated in Czech schools. In the villages, Czech schools were attended by Jews almost exclusively. This generation spoke perfect Czech and later became conscripts in the Czechoslovak army and Svoboda's Army (Czechoslovak military units on the Eastern Front, led by General Ludvík Svoboda, later president of Czechoslovakia). There was a custom for Czech teachers, police officers or administrators, who passed through the villages, to billet with Jewish families. About twenty-four kilometers from Khust in the small village of Zlatáry (Zolotarevo in Ukrainian) my mother's older well-to-do brother built a one room schoolhouse. He did this solely so that his four kids plus two Czech children, one belonging to the teacher and one to the customs officer, would avoid the daily commute to the neighboring village of Drahovo or to the county seat of Khust. And he added a small apartment for the teacher behind the school, all at his own expense. In another village, Sekernice (Szeklence), about ten kilometers east of Khust, my mother's family ran a grocery shop. The house in their yard was used by the teacher at the Czech elementary school, a kindergarten teacher, and, if I remember correctly, also a by tax office clerk. This did not escape the attention of our subsequent Hungarian "liberators". With the voluntary help of the local Ruthenian intelligentsia, the teachers, having shed the essence of Masaryk's democracy, had become nationally radicalized and openly anti-Semitic. They demonstrated this very clearly through persecution, harassment, and deportations – of which, more later. Still, the same cannot be said about the simple folk.

I do not want this to sound pathetic, so I will give you a simple explanation. It was a way of saying thanks for the idea of Czechoslovakism, that after centuries of persecution Masaryk's Czechoslovakia had brought full freedom and equality to Jews. Jews and everyone else in

Czechoslovakia were then able to enjoy the fruits of a full democracy. It was clear why this minority endorsed in the general, non-political sense the Czechoslovak nation and cause. And this is the case till this very day, despite all the geopolitical upheavals and changes in that part of the world. No one ever asked the few thousand survivors if they had wanted these changes. You can call the region what you will: Subcarpathian Russia, Subcarpathian Ruthenia, Carpathian Ukraine, Kárpátalja, Ruthenia – every single survivor without exception will list "Czechoslovakia" as their place of birth in their passport or ID card. Not Czechia, not Slovakia, not PKR (*Podkarpatská Rus*, Subcarpathian Russia) – simply Czechoslovakia and of Czechoslovak nationality. And "everyone in the know" would perceive that he is not dealing with a Czech or a Slovak but with a Jew from Subcarpathian Ruthenia. Until recently, this was never an issue.

Until the fall of the Soviet Union and the communist regimes in Eastern Europe, in western countries, including America and Israel, the place of birth of those people in official documents was always listed as Czechoslovakia (let us recall that Subcarpathian Ruthenia was broken away from the republic illegally). Recently, though, official documents in America but also in the Czech Republic will list Ukraine as the place of birth. I have heard of people who would return their passport saying they had not been born in Ukraine and had never lived there. I was told that the issue was litigated, and it had been decided by the courts that a citizen who objects to Ukraine being listed as his or her place of birth will henceforth bear a passport that lists the town of birth and not the country.

And what does the Czech Republic think of this? Many people like me were born in Czechoslovakia, not in Ukraine. We have never lived in Ukraine, never knew its culture, and never spoke its language (Ruthenian is not identical to Ukrainian). Is it a sensitive diplomatic question? I know the young republic at the end of the twentieth century has other problems, but this is a question of the truth, of a right, an emotional issue for many people who may or may not be citizens of the Czech Republic today.

To end this contemplation in a less serious spirit and on a lighter note, let me quote from a thin book by Karel Poláček, *Jewish Jokes*: "A Jew from Subcarpathian Ruthenia arrives in Paris in a kaftan, boots, long sidelocks and a strange hat. A group of boys run after him, teasing. He ignores them at first but after a while he gets mad, spreads his arms and yells at the kids: "What are you staring at? Have you never seen a Czechoslovak before?"

The purpose of my narrative so far has been to portray the location of my youth. I am not a writer, nor a poet and I beg your indulgence and understanding. It is simply a monologue and therefore it is very difficult to avoid being subjective. Furthermore, as I have already said, I write everything as I remember it and as it floats up to my conscious mind during writing.

3   The World is Changing or *Sic Transit Gloria Mundi*

Simply stated – my memory is coming back. But let us leave the earliest memories, say till the age of ten or eleven, aside, as they are hazy and imprecise. Today I know that it is not by coincidence that the beginning of my clear memory dates to a September day in 1937. I can clearly see the tall figure of teacher Father Popovič announcing to us, the students of the fifth grade of our elementary school, that the President of the Republic, the "old father of ours" Tomáš Garrigue Masaryk had passed away. I can clearly see before me the president's photograph in a black frame both in our classroom and in shop display windows. I remember the memorial services and people's sad faces but mostly I remember people whispering that his death meant the end of a great era, even for the ethnically diverse people of our town but mainly for the Jews.

And the whispers soon turned into screams of fear and despair. Within a few months I remember fat headlines on the title page of the daily A-Zet: SCHUSCHNIG WITH HITLER, followed by the Anschluss and just one year after Masaryk's death, Chamberlain flew to meet Hitler and I see before me the image of him waving a piece of paper, declaring he had just secured eternal peace for Europe and the world – and the Sudetenland for the Germans. He and other politicians were not bothered by the fabrications of Henlein and his cronies in the Sudetendeutsche Partei about the atrocities committed by the local Czechs, fabrications used to justify their rallying cry *Heim ins Reich* (Back home into the German *Reich*)!

Wise folks knew already then that the end of free and democratic Czechoslovakia was at hand, and it did indeed happen within a year. At the same time, Monsignor Jozef Tiso of Slovakia added fuel to the fire by becoming in 1938 the head of an autonomous Slovak government and later the president of Slovakia. And to make sure that no ravenous wolf is left hungry, the Poles took a good bite out of the Republic in the Těšín (Cieszyn) region. The Hungarians used the opportunity to pounce on the victim and annulled the Trianon Agreement of 1920, which was known in Hungary as the Trianon Dictate or Ultimatum. The agreement had decreed that Slovakia be taken away from Hungary and become, through Masaryk's and Štefánik's efforts, a part of the new Republic of Czechoslovakia. Transylvania was assigned to Romania and Vojvodina was incorporated into Yugoslavia. That seemed to give validity to the old Horthy slogan *Csonka Magyarország nem ország, Nagy Magyarország mennyország* which loosely translates as "A truncated Hungary is not Hungary, a big Hungary is paradise on earth". The original rhymes nicely. And so, in 1938, a part of Slovakia and a part of Subcarpathian Ruthenia returned to the bosom of the Crown of St. Stephan, the one-thousand-year Hungarian kingdom, ruled by Regent Admiral Miklós Horthy (the plan was for the king to return once ALL of Hungary was united).

On March 16, 1939, Hungarian mechanized armies (on bicycles) ran over the remainder of Subcarpathian Ruthenia. It remains a historical curiosity that the region was part of three different states on three consecutive days: an autonomous part of Czechoslovakia on March 14, the next day it became the free Carpathian Ukraine led by president Augustin Vološin. Khust was declared the capital and there was one single stamp printed with the legend "Carpathian Ukraine" on it. A country, a president, a yellow and blue flag, a state seal – identical to the present one for Ukraine – a militia...and all of this in one day!

One historical period had ended, and a new page of history was turned. A tragic and sorrowful history. Immediately in the first few days after the "liberation", the heroic soldiers showed us who was the boss. A neighbor from across the street, Mr. Šlomovich, slowly walked to his synagogue one Saturday morning, dressed in his kaftan and wearing his round fur hat, the *shtreiml*. The pious Jew had no idea that his presence on the sidewalk and his best Shabbat garments would rouse the natural instincts of our "liberators" who dismounted the bicycles, shouting and hollering cries of battle, beat the poor man so terribly that he had to retreat back to his home to nurse his wounds, never made it to the synagogue and never again walked on the street in his Shabbat attire and his *shtreiml*. While this was going on, another military unit was marching into the town center and their manly throats quivered with the battle cry: *Zsidó, zsidó, jaj te büdos zsidó, mit csinálsz te itt, az anyád istenit.* Freely translated without rhymes: "Jew, Jew, you dirty Jew, what the hell are you doing here?" I was incredibly sad and at the age of twelve I felt deeply offended and humiliated. Yet all of this was nothing compared with what was to come.

4   Slaps in the Face replace Courtesy

In March 1939 I was the student in the *prima* (first grade) of the Khust Gymnasium, and it did not take long before I got my first clear lesson about the new regime and the new order. I do not recall if there was a long break in our studies following March 16th. Probably not, even though I remember I earned my first paycheck during those days. The new currency was called *pengő* and I made a few *pengős* re-painting store and workshop signs in the new language. I was moonlighting in the afternoons, after school. New teachers-professors appeared. The new Principal's name was Béla Gável, and he took the ostentatious new title "Supreme Education Councilor". During the First Republic the gymnasium was bilingual: classes were taught in Czech and in Russian and there was complete harmony between them. Naturally, the Czech classes were cancelled immediately, and the Czech professors were let go overnight. New classes were set up: one group to be taught in Hungarian, the other in a language they called "Ugro-Russian". Do not ask me what it is. All I know is I found myself somehow in the "Ugro-Russian" class (*numerus clausus*?) – for which naturally no books were available. All the books and teaching materials were in Hungarian and the professor was lecturing chemistry or physics in Hungarian, and your humble servant was translating to the rest of the class into the above-mentioned language which I had not really mastered. Moreover, my Hungarian was even worse at that time – just the words I would learn by listening to neighbors as a kid!

About a year later no one paid attention to such trifles and everything was taught in the language of the Masters. One day they told us the Principal would visit our classroom in the coming days. It was supposed to be an introductory visit of sorts. We were given strict instructions on how to behave and what to do. First, when he entered the classroom, the student closest to the door was supposed to yell "Attention!" in his loudest, strongest voice (he practiced this for several days with our home room teacher). Then the class was instructed to jump up and stand at taut attention as outlined in the strictest military manuals (that, too, was practiced for several days). Then we were to sit back down but only after the command "At ease, sit!" This command was only to be given after "His Excellency Supreme Education Councilor" gestured to the teacher to give it. (I do not use the term "Excellency" ironically – that was how he wanted to be addressed). If this important personage were to address a specific student, he (the student) immediately had to spring to attention with his fingers stretched down along his trouser leg (that too was practiced) and answer shortly, clearly, and precisely. Each reply had to begin with the sentence: "May I humbly report, your Excellency Supreme Education Councilor!" And when his Excellency replied with some pearl of wisdom, you were permitted to reply "Yes" but again, with the full title. The whole ritual was like a passage from the Good Soldier Švejk but I doubt the "Supreme Education Councilor" had ever heard of this classic of Czech literature!

After some tense days of waiting, the great visit was upon us. In the morning, the class underwent a thorough inspection of our fingernails, and dirt was looked for in our ears as well. Attention was paid to our gym shoes (street shoes were not allowed in the class) to make sure there was no hole through which a dirty sock, or worse, a student's big toe was peeking. Our shirt collars were inspected, and God forbid if a little speck of dirt or a crumpled spot was discovered.

Then, suddenly, a thunderous "Attention!" The whole classed jumped up as practiced, as if pricked in our butts by a sewing pin. Anyone sitting in the back benches would have had difficulty seeing the person entering the class. His Excellency was an inch or two short of even average height. It was only when he stepped behind the lectern that we could see a short, slick man with an evil look and an obvious Napoleon complex. How else could one explain his conduct and his demands for precise titles? And then it began. After the command "At ease, sit", the little man barked: "Those of the Catholic faith, stand up!" A bunch of students stood up. We heard "At ease and sit". Next came the Greek Orthodox group, then the Russian Orthodox one and the Protestants. Then His Excellency, who was jotting down the numbers, apparently saw a discrepancy and one student's faith had not been registered. He tallied it all twice, then barked: "Is there a student here of a different faith?" I jumped up in the well-rehearsed routine and I stood to attention. The little man spat out the question: "Which faith?" And, as disoriented as I was in this serious situation, I answered quietly: "Jewish". God Almighty, I had forgotten to recite the "Your Excellency" mantra. I saw the little man marching towards me slowly and solemnly through rows of desks and despite being of only average height, I saw the man was a head shorter than me once he came close. He started yelling: "So, your Jewish pride will not let you reply to your Principal, your Supreme Education Councilor, an officer in the Hungarian Army, in accordance with the prescribed rules and principles?" I was unable to do anything but continue standing at attention and shrugged my shoulders. Suddenly the little man's color changed from puffy red to deathly pale and he began screaming at the top of his lungs saying I must stand at attention when he is talking to me. He jumped up and slapped me in the face so hard, I lost my balance. I straightened up immediately which gave him an opportunity to repeat the deed. Right after that he left our classroom, but he did not just leave, he shot out, without barking orders and without going through the rehearsed procedure. Muffled laughter echoed in the classroom but not a single classmate offered one word of sympathy to me. Clearly, their laughter was not aimed at the unbecoming behavior of the man, of the "Supreme Education Councilor", a man of small stature and smaller soul. Quite the opposite: what he did had found favor with some of my classmates. I did glance at the professor whose eyes seemed to show a little sympathy. Oh, how it hurt. Not the face slaps. The whole situation, the whole sad scene. I felt alone: abandoned and humiliated.

Even today when I remember that day, my pulse quickens (classic paroxysmal tachycardia due to excitement) and just like back then, I feel a sharp physical pain – humiliation, and like that day, a profound abyss of hopelessness. It was the first time in my life that I had been physically punished; punished in such circumstances by that little man – little in all meanings of the word. What a difference when compared with the recent past: we, the students of the *prima*, had been addressed by our professors with the utmost courtesy and by our surnames. It had been a different time, a different regime. But times had changed. We were no longer students of a Czechoslovak gymnasium but rather of the Hungarian Royal State Gymnasium. All well expressed by the Latin saying *O tempora, o mores,* to which we can only add *Sic transit gloria mundi*!

In the year of our "liberation", 1939, my whole life began changing. A massive Hungarization and suppression of everything that reminded us of twenty years of freedom, democracy, and of Czechoslovakia, was taboo. Aside from the external signs, such as changed street names, store signs and the Hungarian versions of all names, there appeared officers in Austro-Hungarian type uniforms and policemen in similarly archaic costumes, with a feather in their helmets. Schools put into action precise plans for changing the souls and brains of students and youths. I can give examples from my Gymnasium. Each morning, prior to the beginning of the school day, instead of the day's date, a designated student had to write in the upper right corner of the blackboard: "Trianon…" plus the number of years, months and days since the signing of the agreement. Before the first period of the day, students had to pray Our Father and as the only Jew, I just stood silently. Then the whole class recited as one: *Hiszek egy Istenben, hiszek egy hazában, hiszek egy isteni örök igazságban, hiszek Magyarország feltámadásában!* which translates as: "I believe in one God, I believe in one homeland, I believe in God's eternal truth, I believe in the resurrection of Hungary". We also occasionally had to sing: "*Hazádnak rendületlenül légy híve, ó Magyar*" – a song exhorting you to love your homeland. And to satisfy the majority shareholder, we had to recite the following prior to every German class: "*Treue, Liebe bis zum Grabe, schwör Ich dir mit Herz und Hand, was ich bin und was ich habe, dank ich Dir mein Vaterland*". The poor students of all faiths and nationalities had to swear allegiance to the German motherland!

Perhaps it is heresy, and it may be in bad taste to compare the situation I just described to the one that existed in Czechoslovakia prior to the Velvet Revolution – when the Soviet flag always flew next to the Czechoslovakian one and when we had to sing *Soyuz nerushimiy respublik svobodnych* (the opening words to the Soviet national anthem) right after *Kde domov můj* and *Nad Tatrou sa blýská* (the first lines of the Czech and Slovak national anthems always sung together before the dissolution of Czechoslovakia), but it is unavoidable. In both cases, we are talking about the worst form of brainwashing. A thousand apologies for seeing the situations as being parallel. There was not much that one could do back in the early 1940s, as one lived with a feeling that perhaps it is all temporary. I do remember that among good friends, we repeated the well crammed Latin phrase *Quo usque tandem abutere, Béla Gável patientia nostra* (replacing the original "Catalina"). Behind closed doors we asked our Principal, His Excellency Supreme Education Councilor, how much longer he intended to abuse our patience. Some heroes we were!

Any hope we might have had that our salvation would come from the east, disappeared quickly in August of that historic year of 1939. Germany and the Soviet Union signed a non-aggression pact by Messrs. Ribbentrop and Molotov. People, including us twelve-year olds, felt a sense of despair. Conversely, in the Hungarian and German rags, *Magyar Nemzet* and *Völkischer Beobachter* – read with several days' delay – there was palpable euphoria. Not a single word about the two superpowers agreeing to split Poland between them, as came to pass a few months later. World War II had actually begun and less than two years later the *Drang nach Osten* was visited upon us.

As for the treatment of the local Jews, the principle of *numerus clausus* was strictly enforced. Jews were harassed, humiliated, persecuted and subjected to violence. People would disappear without a trace. But I attended school and my movements were not restricted. Young people got married, children were born, Jews were still able to serve in the armed services and Jewish youth attended *Levente* (Hungarian pre-military courses) along with everyone else. We were even permitted to continue our participation in various Zionist organizations – from the right wing *Betar* to the left wing *Shomer Ha-Tzair*. And because there was not a whole lot to do after school, we would go to the gatherings of both clubs. Beginning in 1941 Jewish soldiers found themselves serving in labor units of the army – they were the "Black Barons" – not for political but rather for racial reasons. Unlike in the Czechoslovak army in previous years, "our boys" did not work on construction sites or in agriculture but were seconded to units that dug trenches or cleared mines on eastern battlefields. A few "Barons" saved their lives by running east across the line, some of them disappeared in Russian Gulags. The minority that saved themselves later became the kernel of the army of General Ludvík Svoboda.

All of this, of course, was after Germany had attacked the Soviet Union on June 22, 1941. And Hungary stood by Germany's side.

High school in 1940: My fellow students and me: we are now Hungarians!

5   Robbed of All Human Rights

This is a whole different chapter: one that has to do with the "driest sounding official document" mentioned in the opening sentence of this memoir.

The document contains two separate decisions of the Czech Social Security office. One, from July 1995, which awarded me a onetime sum of money as a citizen who had been the victim of Nazi persecution. The relevant date on the decision is July 15, 1941. The second decision is from November 1996, which awarded me an Old Age pension for the 22 years and 68 days of work in the Czechoslovak Republic. It included time prior to my 18th birthday and that date is, again, July 15, 1941. What can I say? Being persecuted is included in your work time for calculating the height of your pension!

So, what actually happened, on that July 15, 1941 to a fourteen-year-old student at the local gymnasium, between his *tercia* and *quarta*? What actually happened 23 days after the assault on the Soviet Union by Germany and its faithful ally, Hungary? War effort this, war effort that — the regime could always find the time, resources and opportunity to "solve" the Jewish problem. There was already the example set by Germany, even before concentration camps, on how to deal with the so called "Ostjuden" and citizens without citizenship. Let us deport them! Where? No problem: freshly occupied parts of Soviet Ukraine (previously Poland) were lawless territories, perfect for such deportations. Those places were ruled by local thugs and deserters from the defeated units of the Soviet army who were enthusiastic helpers to the victorious German and Hungarian Jew killers.

I do not know why, but my family did not have Hungarian citizenship. Perhaps we had never applied for it or maybe we had not gotten it, even though all my ancestors were born there back during the Russian emperors' rules and the Hungarian kings' rule and later in Czechoslovakia. Nevertheless, and despite this, during the days of July 1941 my father found himself in a labor unit of the Hungarian army. For that, one did not need to have citizenship!

We were asleep on that night of July 15: my mother, my older brother, my younger sister and myself. We had no idea what the Hungarian Alien police had in store for us. Banging on the door and coarse voices shouting,

"Open the door!" My frightened mother and three kids, 16, 14 and 12 years old, stood there in our pajamas. The gendarme asked in a rough voice "Where is the head of the family?" He was told that the head of the family was a member of a work unit of the Royal Hungarian army. The statement had no effect on the uniformed official. While a few civilians were standing on the side, the official started reading from a document: "You can pack 20 kilograms per person, food for 48 hours, and line up in front of the house in 15 minutes." We followed the order without saying a word and without protest. Outside in the yard we saw some members of my grandmother's family. We learned later that some other members of her family had been able to hide and disappear. Later, as the day broke, surrounded by the gendarmes, we started marching towards the railway station. We saw similar groups of people emerging from all corners of the town and when we reached the station several hundred others were crowding the platform in front of a special train. Towards evening, as the platform filled, we were pushed, yelled at, kicked, and squeezed into railroad cars. In the morning, through the mewling of infants, the crying of toddlers and other children and the frightened eyes of adults, we saw that we had arrived at the Yasinia train station, on the border of what used to be Poland and the last stop on the Prague – Yasinia line. In the east, above the Carpathian mountaintops, the summer sun started peeking out and despite it only being not more than five in the morning, it was already warm outside. Inside the train cars, behind locked doors, it was stuffy and dirty and the stench that grew worse with the rising temperature made the situation desperate.

Our gendarme escort began alighting from their special train car onto the platform, soldiers and civilians started opening the doors and pulling us out while yelling at the top of their lungs. We started marching towards a nearby schoolhouse. Hundreds of old men, youths and children were shoved onto a dusty yard, surrounded by a barbed wire fence beyond which soldiers and policemen stood guard, bayonets set on their rifles. I must add one more thing to draw the full picture: in one corner of the yard, beside a high wall there was a functioning pump. Scenes of despair were playing out all around it...who would be able to fill a jar or a pot with water...and whoever was able to fill it, would have very little left after fighting his way out of the crowd.

In the yard itself, other fights were going on: trying to grab even a little bit of shade for an old person or for babies who suffered diarrhea and vomiting. In one corner, behind an improvised curtain, people went to pee and defecate. The stench was unbearable. A volunteer stood at the "entrance" to this "latrine", letting in one group of men or women at a time. It appeared that the whole situation was very amusing to the guards outside. They probably told jokes but more than anything they derived pleasure from what they were hearing and seeing. For all I know, maybe even their sense of smell added to their elevated mood. Around noon, as hopelessness rose along with the temperature, a back gate of the schoolhouse opened, and several men and women emerged. Soon we learned these were members of the local Jewish community. In their hands they carried pots, baskets, boxes, jugs and bottles – our salvation. They gestured to tell us they were not allowed to talk to us, but they began distributing delicacies to eat and drink – dishes my mother had routinely served to us just a day earlier. It seemed like an eternity had passed.

During the rest of the day no other person appeared. None of us knew why we were there and where we would be that night or the following day. All we knew was that we were helpless and homeless. But not even in our wildest fantasies did we imagine we would soon be fair game for anyone and anything. This gaggle of people spent their last calm and not so calm night sleeping – or awake – under the warm skies, on the tamped down earth of a schoolyard. As dawn broke, a convoy of army trucks appeared behind the barbed wire. Two gendarmes got out of each vehicle. Inside the fence a quiet unease was felt, even the children stopped crying and every frightened staring eye was fixed on the gates. A few dozen policemen and soldiers burst in, surrounded the standing crowd, each pair of uniforms took a group of people (likely pre-selected), and group after group then walked to the trucks. In total silence and completely resigned to their fate, people climbed onto the trucks. Some could do this unaided, some with the help of family. The trucks were filled to a point where some could literally only stand on one foot. Children would have suffocated in the crush, so they had to be carried by their parents or older siblings. Two policemen climbed up to the driver's cab. One all-terrain vehicle in the front, one in the rear, eight armed soldiers in each, and the convoy moved forward.

Army trucks with a load of scared civilians, ranging from toddlers to old men and women, began their journey. People were hungry, thirsty, dirty and sweaty, wearing their everyday clothes; some dressed in traditional kaftans, like the Jew in the Poláček's joke mentioned earlier. There were poor people but also people who had until very recently been considered well-to-do. The convoy was cumbersome and slow, the way military vehicles are. We all made our way on a narrow winding road, deep valleys at the side, through a pass (Jablunický pass perhaps) in the tall Carpathian Mountains. The lead car came to a stop next to a column of the type one sees at a border crossing. The trucks were catching up and stopping too. As we came to a halt at a bend in the road, I was able to see two soldiers in grey uniforms get out of a sidecar of a motorcycle – the grey uniforms meant only one thing: Germans. From the other side of the narrow road, two Hungarian soldiers appeared. I was not able to hear what they were saying but after less than a minute both the Germans and the Hungarians stepped aside and the space between the columns opened up. We started moving again, very slowly. I was standing on the left side and I saw the Germans sit back down on their motorcycles. Both soldiers stared ahead, bored, and indifferent. It was clear that what they had just seen was nothing new, they had seen such convoys before. Why get excited? They knew what awaited the people in the trucks.

Basic knowledge of geography and a bit of imagination was enough for me to know we had just crossed the border into former Poland, that is Poland before it was divided between Germany and Soviet Union in the Molotov–Ribbentrop non-aggression agreement of 1939, – a border that a mere 27 days prior had been the border of the Soviet Union. Crossing over to Poland before that was simple, and during the First Republic one did not even need a visa. Once the Soviets took over, the border was strictly watched and guarded. But now, there was only a remnant of a former border barrier – the barrier itself was gone. It was as if they knew there was never going to be a border there again. Not even after 1945, which was when the great Soviet empire moved westward to the border of Slovakia and Subcarpathian Ruthenia changed into Carpathian Ukraine. I never heard or read anything that explained what this geographical change had been based on.

After about five minutes of further movement, we witnessed a whole different border and a whole different show. On both sides of what used to be a road, the forest suddenly disappeared. High barbed wire fences, seemingly without end, framed both sides of the road, interspersed by watchtowers at regular intervals. A couple of the larger and higher towers stood right beside the road. Between the fences, as well as on both sides, there was about ten meters of freshly ploughed and turned up earth. There were no guards or soldiers on watch. We reached a spot where "our" trucks had to force and zigzag their way through concrete roadblocks, possibly there for tanks. There were signs posted on both sides, warning about mine fields. The road entered a deep forest again but there were reminders all around us that war had passed through here – admittedly a blitz but really a war? Overturned cars and trucks were visibly damaged, as were occasional tanks, but there were no signs of scorching warfare. There were scattered remnants of uniforms and broken helmets and in one spot we saw the carcass of a horse. The number of collapsed and mangled trees was horrific. The damage to the forest was beyond description, as if a hurricane had blown through. Here and there a small village would appear; I recall the name Vorokhta (a town in Ukraine, about 20 miles to the east of Yasiniya). There were a few farms and more and more road signs as we traveled. Arrows and signs stating the distance to places, with numbers, slogans, and graphic symbols. The text was always in German. I noticed a specific sign that appeared more and more often: a white goose (or duck) with a bright red beak on a grey background. It turned out to be the symbol of an army unit which would play a very serious role in my and my family's life. More about that later.

The names of the larger settlements and towns, written with a clumsy hand in the Latin alphabet, remain lodged in my mind without having to look at a map: Nadvorna, Kolomea, Horodenko. Oddly enough, now and again we would see civilians in the streets but always old women and men, occasionally a child – no young people at all. On the other hand, men in German or Hungarian uniforms stood or sat on every corner and on road curbs. Interspersed among them were young men in civilian clothing with a military style cap on their heads and a yellow band on their left arm that said: *Polizei* – it was quite clear who they were. It did not seem that a convoy of trucks loaded with Jewish families made any kind of special impression on them.

6   The River Dniester Flows behind your Backs

Judging by the position of the sun that beat down mercilessly, it had to be noon when the convoy left the road. It lined up in front of a pontoon bridge that spanned a wide river. Guarded by many German soldiers, the convoy moved forward and slowly crossed to the other side. Once on the opposite banks, on a field strewn with the remnants of trampled grain, the convoy stopped in disarray and an order rang out: "Off the trucks and line up". Most people started looking for a bush or some trees – they needed to empty their bladder after the long ride. Our uniformed guard had already formed a live fence around us, their weapons ready to fire and so most people forgot what they were about to do or did it in their pants. Human dignity and minimal privacy were squashed and stomped on. After a few minutes, a Hungarian police officer hopped up on one of the trucks, accompanied by another policeman. The cop yelled "Silence! Line up beside the trucks" We lined up and the officer spoke:

"THE RIVER DNIESTER IS FLOWING BEHIND YOUR BACKS. FROM NOW ON, THE RIVER IS YOUR BORDER. YOU CAN CONTINUE FROM HERE TO WHEREVER YOU WANT BUT ANYONE TRYING TO CROSS THE RIVER WILL BE SHOT ON THE SPOT!"

Aided by the policeman he jumped off the truck and disappeared. The remaining cops immediately ordered us to hand over all our valuables – money, jewelry, watches. They tossed everything into shoe boxes they had prepared previously and because they felt the spoils were insufficient, they started threatening us with their weapons. A few poor souls dug out the odd valuable or money from under their clothing. The uniformed men were still unsatisfied and right there, in the middle of the field, they ordered everyone to undress, men and women. The women were crying heart-rending sobs, trying to cover up the bodies in front of the men and before the lewd stares of the cops. One of them, an especially fat and revolting specimen hissed at a pretty young woman: "You Jewish whore! No use hiding your body, you will be rotting in some ditch in a few days anyway!"

I do not believe that in that terrible, hopeless situation anyone actually realized that man had just told them what the real intentions of the Hungarian Crown were and where the road that had begun only four days previously, actually led. From a more-or-less normal life into what was later named the HOLOCAUST. For a few tens of thousands of Jews, the Holocaust had begun here – not in 1944, when Hungarian Jews were dragged into concentration camps *en masse*, in a short span of time.

Another scene that remains stuck in my mind is that of the cops divvying up the loot a few steps away from us. Then they jumped into their vehicles, and I saw them cross the Dniester via the pontoon bridge and disappear in the distance, towards the west. We were given free passage eastward. For a minority, the passage led to a few years of suffering and death lurking at the end of it. For the majority, the last journey of their life loomed in the near future.

I have taken a few weeks' break in writing to sort out my thoughts and my memories. The situation I am writing about was so beyond belief, so beyond comprehension for the human mind, so unlike any conceivable reality, that I simply could not go on. To make sure that I remember all the main events, I talked to my brother who remembers them exactly as I do. As I contemplate and reminisce, the image of my mother becomes clearer and stronger. She deserves to be immortalized – and not just in connection with these events. There should be a whole thick book written about this beautiful, simple, and noble woman in order to keep her in the hearts of her loved ones. I will never write such a book; I am not capable of that because it is not just enough to remember. One must be able to formulate one's thoughts and properly get to the heart of the matter and that is beyond my abilities. But I will keep in my heart and in my mind everything that happened to us that fateful summer of 1941 because the fact that I and my two siblings did not end up as part of the statistic of those whose path ended there, or a few kilometers to the north-east in Kamianets-Podilskyi (Kamieniec Podolski in Polish)...that is only thanks to my mother. If I have sufficient fortitude to write further chapters of my life, my mother will most definitely have a place of honor in it.

No one had a watch anymore. We could tell by the position of the sun and the lengthening shadows, that the afternoon had progressed. Even though a July afternoon is long, my mother sensed that the most immediate danger, if we tarried and once the dark night descended, would be finding ourselves in an open field. The local populace was concentrated nearby. None of us really thought of actual physical dangers; it seemed they too, had not yet awakened from the shock of the hurricane of war that had recently blown through here. But the few bags, small sacks and the occasional small suitcase drew their attention. People started forming small family groups. My mother's eyes espied the roofs of some small houses not too far from us, she took my fragile little twelve-year-old sister's hand and divided the few items that had not been stolen from us. She appealed to us, insisted to stay by her side and we set out into the ravaged field. Some instinct had told her not to take the road. We were told later that those that did were immediately robbed of everything, including all their clothing, and had to continue their trek into the unknown in their underwear. Along with a few other families, we made our way to a small town.

Somehow, and I do not recall how and with whose help, we found ourselves in a small two room house before sunset. It may have been the remaining Jews who had not managed to escape before the Germans arrived, or a secret Jewish organization – since local Jews would already have known about the deportations – that aided us. It most certainly was not the local Ukrainians, Poles or Russians! An old Jewish couple lived in one of the two rooms. We found shelter in the other room, behind a small kitchen. There was no furniture, just some rags on the floor and we fell asleep totally exhausted. We had just gone through a journey into the deepest darkness, a journey a few centuries backward. We slept deep and long but when we awoke, we found out that our mother was already hard at work doing laundry and organizing our first breakfast from the crumbs that were still left over in one of our bags. And yes, we also discovered that during the night she had sewn a white sleeve band for each of us with a blue star of David on it. "God forbid you should leave the house without it" was the first instruction mother got from the old couple. Mother explained to us what the potential punishment was for disregarding this ordinance. A beating to the point of loss of consciousness, twenty-five lashes on your bare bottom (with the same result). Frequently, the guilty party, the "criminal" would simply disappear without a trace inside the bowels of the local police station, which in these parts was mixed German-Hungarian-local. But no one dared to leave the house in the coming days anyway. We all knew soon enough that there were daily, even hourly raids, and the victims who got caught were sent farther on to Chortkov – those in the know suspected something even worse. We heard the name Kamianets-Podilskyi more and more often (I will write about this later). We heard it from the mouths of random escapees and from the mouths of the thuggish local gendarmes – rough, coarse, bloodthirsty individuals who would tell you after beating you like a dog – just for sport, out of boredom: "We will send you Jew to Kamianets-Podilskyi!" In our hopeless situation we hardly even asked ourselves what they meant. What could be worse than what we were already experiencing?

Still...medieval ghettos, the inquisition, the pogroms, centuries of persecution and oppression, centuries of spiritual and physical annihilation...they had all taken root and solidified in people in the form of an exquisite sense of self-preservation. That sense kicked in right from the first minutes of our deportation. Being deported meant being exposed to the cruelty of any criminal, being deprived of all rights and all justice. "I can now do whatever I want to you, I can even kill you". Nothing is off limits, nothing is punishable, in fact, much of it is praiseworthy and prizeworthy.

We found out quickly that the neighboring fields – a former kolkhoz? – contained potatoes, cucumbers, tomatoes and other vegetables. There was also the odd chicken, and so one would stand watch and one would steal, despite public notices on the walls that proclaimed the harvest and all agricultural produce, including fowl and cattle, to be the property of the German Reich, and whosoever should be found stealing these products was guilty of sabotage and would be executed. That made all of us equals. Bullets did not ask for ID. If you were seen in the vicinity of a potato field, you could have been a Ukrainian, a Pole or a Jew, bullets would start whistling around you immediately. And the bullets found what they were looking for quite often – a live target. Everything would be forgotten by morning. Just the act of leaving the house exposed you to dangers that lurked on every corner. Not that staying at home gave you a feeling of security. The Germans did not yet have lists of the "new" Jews, the *Judenrat* had not drawn them up yet and so there were random raids. Those that ran were shot at; a job the local militia performed with some enthusiasm.

The hot days of July and August dragged on through hunger, fear, and hopelessness. Death of individuals and reports of mass murder spread among the local Jewry, especially among the recent additions. It was not just rumoring but actual actions that occurred more and more often – groups were sent farther east to Kamianets-Podilskyi. And now, it was not just whispered about, it was being mentioned out loud: that is where they murdered Jews in large numbers. Eyewitnesses – Hungarian soldiers and the local populace spoke about thousands...mostly with satisfaction, rarely with sorrow. There were some who claimed they could hear noises that sounded like machine gun fire at a time when the front had already long passed much further east. And as it happens in these cases, some believed, some dismissed it with a wave of the hand, but no one could deny that something evil was afoot. One could not ignore the rapidly decreasing number of Jewish inhabitants of Tluste. This constantly decreasing number was busy drying bread or baking various pastries made of flour hidden since better times. They hoarded it for a future they assumed would be even worse but really, they knew that the future was already here and now – they had to get ready for yet another journey. They believed there was going to be work to be done at the end of that journey and if you are working, you are going to get fed. In other words, it is just the journey itself they felt they needed to be ready for. The Reich would take care of the rest. And boy, did it ever!

Now, as I write, I have decided, for the first time, to open an official publication. In the *Encyclopedia of the Holocaust*, published in collaboration with *Yad Vashem* and *Sifriat Ha-Poalim* (Israeli publishing house), we can read on page 1099 that according to German sources, 23,600 Jews were murdered by the SS on August 27 and 28, 1941. Of those 14,000 to 18,000 were individuals deported by the Hungarians, the rest were local Jews. It is doubtful they ate much of their dried bread and pastries. Those who managed to avoid Kamianets-Podilskyi, as did mother's brother Natan and his family – my mother had literally dragged them out of the transport with the help of some Hungarian soldiers – met the same fate in the following days and months. Uncle Natan and his family managed to get back across the Dniester, but the family was killed by the Germans and their local abettors in the vicinity of Nadvorna.

A few kilometers from the killing grounds, I lived through those days just like thousands of others, searching for someone or something to hold on to, like a drowning man fumbling for a straw: anything, anyone that could lend a helping hand, a little hope, some advice – salvation. These are things that in such desperate straits can only be given by the ONE. Someone or something mystical, supernatural. And so, it became a daily occurrence that I would sit on our hosts' stoop each morning and piously read the psalms cover to cover and over again as many times as I could squeeze in between sunrise and sunset. As you know, August days are long. I became a target of ridicule for some, of admiration for others. It did not take long for the rapidly changing village to dub me "the sunrise to sunset praying boy".

7   A White Duck with a Fiery Beak

Help arrived locally in an unbelievable manner. As I sat on that stoop during my long praying sessions, I noticed something unusual. A group of Hungarian blue and grey army trucks would pass by every couple of days. The trucks had a logo of a white duck (or goose?) with a red beak painted on both sides and the top. Every time they passed, one would stop on the road, close to the houses occupied by folks like us. The driver would change a tire, or he would look busy fiddling with the engine, but it seemed to me like he was conversing with the poor folks and occasionally I would notice one of them quickly put something under their jacket or shirt and quickly run back into the house. And what do you know: the following day, sugar cubes, flour, dried fruit, and cigarettes would appear on the local "market". Curiosity got the better of me and I began lurking behind a nearby bush for hours on end, close to where I had seen the trucks stop. And my patience was rewarded. One day a convoy of dark trucks pulled up and I noticed figures emerging from ditches on both sides of the road. The last truck came to a stop not far from me and the driver hopped down from the cab. When I saw he was alone, I approached him. He was a short soldier in a Hungarian uniform, and my head started spinning – could this be true? Was I dreaming? Perhaps he just looked familiar! It could not be! But it was! It was my mother's cousin Joseph who had been a cab driver and who used to come to Khust in his taxi. Our eyes met and a few seconds later we were sitting under a bush in the ditch and he was telling me that Jewish drivers still served in the Hungarian army, that he had been looking for us for a month and that on his last trip from Yasinia to the retreating front he had been told by folks that a woman with three kids was billeted in a house here. At the time he could not stop since any leak about his activity meant a bullet to the head. This time the "repair" took longer. A small box of sugar cubes, flour and cigarettes was suddenly "lost" and found its way into a secret hiding place in our hosts' house. Joseph also managed to let us know that shortly after we were dragged away, the deportations of those whose family head, like my dad, served in labor units of the Hungarian army, were halted. He also told us that many people had returned home illegally, and he spoke of what had recently taken place in Kamianets-Podilskyi. Finally, he said this: we could sell what he gave us and make a few rubles that were still the local currency. Or we could use the sugar and the cigarettes to hire local people who would get us back across the Dniester at night. By night we could then walk all the way to the border, and there, again either in exchange for the money or the goods, smugglers would take us across the line into Subcarpathian Ruthenia territory. He insisted this had to be done immediately, no delay whatsoever. This was a matter of life and death. In our case, it was literally *to be or not to be*.

I am continuing now, after a few days' pause. I used my short hiatus to try and recall as precisely as possible the course of the dramatic events that followed. What I do remember will suffice.

It might have been days later or perhaps just a few hours but one cool September night we stood, little bundles in our hands, in some barn we had reached having walked for four hours through fields and forest paths accompanied by a man I did not know. My mother's sister was with us as well, with her handsome thirty-year-old husband. They were childless. We could see nothing though a muffled cough, a sigh, a distant whisper told us we were not alone there. When dawn broke, we understood the night sounds had come from just one other family – unfortunately, I do not recall how many they were or how old. They must have gotten there before us because we had not heard any door or gate opening throughout that sleepless night. I saw through a crack that we were in the middle of a forest, nothing around us but trees – pines, I think – and birdsong was the only sound cutting through that beautiful autumn morning.

8   The Dniester is again Behind our Backs

As I have alluded to, there is a gap in my memory. I recall events in broad outlines. The details have evaporated from my brain cells but that does not detract from the authenticity of my narrative. I remember we found ourselves on the banks of the river Dniester after hiking through rough terrain all day. I do not know how the river flowed normally but it seemed turbulent, and the current was very strong. It was night, so I do not know if the water was clear or muddy or how deep it was. In my mind's eye I see a group of about three or four locals and about three adults from our group. They were engaged in a lively discussion. Items were changing hands – cigarettes perhaps, or money. At that point I noticed three or four little wooden boats tied to tree trunks on the bank of the river. We hurriedly got into the boats, all jumbled, families were not necessarily together. Basically, we were tossed in, the knots were loosened after some effort and the current carried us away. One of the boats reached the other bank – just barely. Another was being hopelessly carried downstream and one of the smugglers just about managed to push and turn it in the direction of the opposite bank. We reached a spot that would not enable docking, so we waded through water that reached our waist, we reached the bank, wet and desperate because we could not see our whole families. The missing ones were carried downriver by the powerful current but – and I do not recall how – we did manage to find each other during the night, and we were united with my uncle and aunt again. Soaked, frightened, and exhausted we snuggled close to each other on the wet ground for a feeling of warmth and security. Starting a fire to warm up and dry out was out of the question, of course. The smugglers had disappeared into the night but, as it turned out, not for long.

Maybe we napped for a while but were woken up by rocks and large pieces of wood raining down on us. We felt invisible hands pulling our bundles from under our bodies and our heads. They even ripped some clothing off us and tried to get our shoes which they could not do as the shoes were wet and likely stuck to our soles. My sister has a lifelong memento of that night: an ugly scar on her left temple, close to her eye. When the first autumn light broke, we saw the ugly deep wound after mom rinsed my sister's face with some water from the river. A doctor, stitches for the ugly gash, a bandage, a tetanus shot? HA! Don't make me laugh. All we could do was a fast inventory to check and see what the nighttime uninvited guests might have forgotten to grab. It turned out that a few bundles containing things that later came in handy had been left behind by the robbers.

It was a clear, chilly autumn night and I can say that the night and the morning hours that followed were physically the most difficult trial we had thus far been subjected to. Beaten up, wet, exhausted, most of us suffering a cold with a fever, hungry...and that swollen bleeding face of my little fragile, skinny, tiny twelve-year-old sister – it all brought us to the very edge of human endurance. That is how we felt, as any semblance of a human image vanished from the wrecks we had become. Yet we knew we could not stay put. Moreover, we had no means of drying out and warming up what remained of our clothes and shoes. The disappearance of a couple of members of our second group lowered the morale even further. They were lost crossing the river and I cannot shake the sad feeling about the fact that they were not even mourned out loud; their family's tears were silent and reserved. Our senses were completely dulled.

The moon was still up when each of us was given a few gulps of cold "tea" by my mother, that wonderful mother of ours. She also gave us a slice of dried bread each and a pancake baked out of corn flour. When the first rays of the rising sun appeared, we started slowly, heavy footed, towards the Carpathian Mountains. Our exact route was unclear, but we knew we had to leave the River Dniester behind as soon and as quickly as possible. We walked on rough footpaths through the fields and we only stopped when we reached a large forest. It was not very dense, allowing the sun's rays that penetrated the canopy to dry our shoes and socks, and the heat of our bodies dried our underwear and clothing. We also had to rest a bit and pay close attention to my sister, who was running a high fever, her face crimson and swollen. Her wound started bleeding as soon as we touched it while trying to clean it with a rag dipped into a creek. Even today, after more than half a century, I see before me the image of that poor little girl whom I loved so much – and still do. Here I must say a few words about my older brother. He was sixteen at the time, quiet and humble, just as he is till this day. He was a great support for my mother, taking on the role of the father in everything: helping us, his younger siblings and helping everyone who needed it. Mature before his time, he was serious and steadfast in any situation, his presence inspired confidence. We greatly needed him back then and were lucky to have him. It is hard to imagine a better brother or a better son.

Our physical and mental exhaustion was such that our brains refused to absorb any further impulses or excitation. Everything seemed to happen in a haze of semi-consciousness. Therefore, I do not remember how and when we suddenly found ourselves in the presence of a local smuggler on what used to be the Polish-Czechoslovak (and later Hungarian-Soviet) border. It turned out that he knew the border region like the palm of his hand and smuggling was his lifetime profession, as it had been his father's before him, under all political regimes. These professionals could not be deterred by anything: a system of electrified barbed wire or the wide strips of ploughed land where the forest had been cleared. The Soviets had built the strict border zone right after occupying eastern Poland (or western Ukraine if you prefer) to stop escapees (from where? to where?). It was also apparent that the smuggler was not a thief of the type that had ferried us across the river but a professional who exposed himself to the threat of immediate death penalty if caught: first by the Soviets, now by the occupying Germans. During Soviet times, the reasons were political. Now, the sin was even greater: helping Jews escape a certain death...for now! The smugglers did it for monetary or material gain, of course, but there was something else there, too. Something humane. I came to that conclusion because we were served a warm meal for the first time in a long while, we were able to wash a little bit and for a few hours we could tend to my little sister's temple injury. The wound appeared to be infected and festering and the one day's rest we were afforded really helped. It probably helped regenerate my brain cells too, since that moment on I remember the course of events clearly.

It goes without saying that not all escapes, not all border crossings are the same. The reason I am saying this is because as I am about to describe crossing a border where the enemy lurked on both sides, I am recalling another escape, the Hollywood kind. I am talking about the film depicting a crossing of the Austrian-Swiss border by that singing patriotic, aristocratic Austrian family. A bitter smile crosses my lips when I remember the musical *Sound of Music*, when I recall those well-fed folks, those Hollywood actors in modern, sturdy hiking boots and pretty clothes that would not look out of place at a fashion show or on fashionable Alpine ski slopes. There were beautiful shots of the giant mountains and before you knew it, the refugees' faces brightened in a well-directed, understated scene...and voila: good job everybody – a true happy end for all concerned.

No doubt a good writer would know how to utilize the cinematic fade-out technique in a literary form. The screen would darken, then slowly brighten again, only this time the light bears no resemblance to the previous light. In the gloom, the viewer would now see a dense, moonlit forest and on a narrow, barely navigable path a gaggle of adults and kids, wearing torn up, dirty rags I would have rolled up and used as a soccer ball in happier times. On their feet most wore what used to be sandals or some other summer shoes, tied to a sockless foot by a piece of wire or twine. All of that because of the theft, or a forced sale and the passage of time since the summer. Everyone looked small and skinny in the moonlight (they really were!), shivering with cold and famished. The smuggler/guide whom I only saw now in the clear moonlight stood out: a strapping man, looming larger wearing his sheep skin, something like a staff in his hand and a burlap sack on his back. The sack did not look too full. He stood to the side, the adults were grouped around him talking in what sounded like a mixture of Polish and Ukrainian. When the adults came back, they lined us up with the mysterious man up ahead, the older kids behind him, meaning my brother and me, followed by my mother who held my sister's hand with my aunt and uncle in the rear.

And we started walking – slowly, carefully. It was late evening now, night perhaps, the cold light of the full moon above us, the dense and foreboding forest all around us. From time to time a gust of wind through the trees would make sounds that filled me with dread and despair. Was it something more than just the wind? A wild animal? Truth be told, even the guide would stop from time to time, gather us around him and listen intently for a minute or so. We must have lost our way at least once because after an hour's hike we found ourselves in a spot we had already passed. I am not sure how we knew but it must have been true: we talked about it later and the adults looked animated and frightened, and there was talk of the guide having betrayed us, leading us not across the border but into the hands of the Germans, or the local gendarmerie or highway robbers and who knows what else. We were used to living with rumors, with wild imaginings, hopes and news - good and bad, whispers and grapevine rumbles.

Looking back, it seemed suspicious when, in a wood clearing, the guide told us to sit in a tight row between massive tree trunks. We were so tired and frightened that nothing could stop us from falling asleep, not even the wet grass and rotting leaves. Mom woke us up by gently shaking us and letting us drink some mildly sweet liquid from a glass bottle. We calmed down when we saw the guide pull out a large loaf of corn bread and a herring from his sack. He used his pocketknife to slice off a piece of the herring, about a third of the corn bread and then wrapped the rest up reverently and carefully and put it back in the sack. He then uncorked a bottle, put it to his lips and two or three gulps of homemade plum brandy flowed down the gullet into his large belly. I believe I even heard a good burp in between wind gusts. Our guy corked the bottle up again, put it back in his sack, tied it up carefully and threw it over his shoulder. He gestured to show rest time was over, lined us up and we slowly walked on. The pain from our blistered feet in worn out shoes and with no socks, was unbearable. Wet trousers stuck to the skin of our naked behinds. Even the shorts I had on instead of underwear had become tattered and useless. I do not know and do not recall if the "small detail" of actually crossing the border and making it back was even on my mind as we marched through the second half of the night.

9 After Friendly Greetings – a Betrayal

It was still dark when we suddenly found ourselves in front of a ten-meter-wide strip of ploughed earth. We saw the barbed wire fence in the moonlight. The famous Soviet border. The human brain is inscrutable. In this case, the brain of a high school student who not long ago had finished a school year with honors in every subject. In that moment I started calculating how many tens of thousands of kilometers this fence must be traversing from the Far East, going southwest to this frontier and farther north to the Baltic Sea, and back east all the way to Vladivostok and the Sea of Japan. But I returned to reality soon enough. Here we were, in the Poloninski Carpathian Mountains, two parallel barbed wire fences in front of us, freshly ploughed earth which made human footprints clearly visible between the fences, and on the outside a watchtower every couple of hundred meters, and we were quite sure we could hear loud drunken men's voices from the distance – Germans? Hungarians? Local police? Forest workers on the Hungarian side?

It was hard to imagine that on the other side the defenseless were not yet being murdered, that the deportations had likely stopped, that perhaps our father was carrying rocks or polishing door handles in Hungarian army facilities, where he might have found snippets of information about his family. Hard to imagine that there existed a semblance of a normal life under the prevailing circumstances. Our smuggler-guide ordered us to remain sitting on some rocks and logs at the edge of the forest and he turned away, walking back towards the tree line. After a few minutes he returned and put all our doubts and worries to rest. He stood us up and in confident strides he took us to a spot in the fence, where he could lift the barbed wire just enough for us to crawl to the other side and when we were all through and gathered, he ordered us to run to the second fence where he repeated the same maneuver except he did not crawl under with us, he remained standing, and motioned with his hand to show us the general direction in which to keep walking – without him. We saw his silhouette quickly retreating to the first fence and that was that.

Luckily, or perhaps unluckily, light started appearing on the eastern horizon and it caught us at a spot that would have been heavily forested not long ago. Now, thick trunks were lying on the ground and large stumps stuck out, showing signs of being tended to by human hands. We began descending into a valley and soon we arrived at a forest path that widened as we walked. We began seeing hoof traces and tire prints as well as footprints that look like they were made by *poštols* – homemade shoes worn by the mountain folks. As the morning fog lifted and the autumn sun appeared over the thick treetops, we saw groups of the local mountain men, the *Hutsuls*, a local ethnic group, on the hillsides. They were wearing their traditional garb: wide grey trousers made of rough cloth and embroidered coats. They were already hard at work. Horses hitched by a rough-hewn rope pulled tree trunks to a wooden trough. Eight to ten workers, using their special pickaxes would heave the trunk into the trough and the trunk would slide, gaining speed, down to a narrow river which spilled into a nearby lake. A second group of workers would tie a few tree trunks together and float the stack on the lake which emptied out into another, wider river and from there the bundle glided to the mouth of the Rika. At that point individual bundles were tied into rafts (called *bokor*). Each raft had a team of two men (*bokorás*) – one at each end. They took turns maneuvering a long oar in the shape of a spoon fastened to the end of the raft as a lever. Equipped with a small sack of home-made leather or burlap which contained modest provisions, plus a bottle of hooch – that was all the modest, hardworking mountain men needed – they sailed down the river. Their passage always depended on the amount of rain or melted snow since the river needed to be deep enough. They sailed all the way to the river Tisa and from there, the wood would continue to various sawmills scattered along the river. From where we were, I saw the start of the trees' journey – the rest was supplied by my imagination, based on what I had seen in better times. I was so immersed in thought that I hardly noticed the occasional cyclist that passed, an axe and a small saw on his back, as well as folks on foot carrying the same implements. They were all rushing to work, oblivious to our presence. I am sure we were not the first such group they had seen. They all greeted us in a friendly way and the men in the distance who worked bent over the hundreds of years old logs, would raise their heads and smile, waving their calloused hands. At this point we were walking on a wide road and saw little village houses not far away. We could discern barns near some of the houses as well, but the best sign that we had reached the end of this portion of our journey was the smoke coming out of the chimneys.

The mountain border village was called Torun (or was it Olbracht's Kolochava, *Nikola Šuhaj*'s headquarters?). My uncle who was now leading our group seemed to know the area because he confidently took us to one of the larger houses, opened the creaking gate and we found ourselves in a small yard. A stout woman, around fifty years old appeared in the doorway. She was wearing a headscarf the way religious married women did – whether in villages or in the cities. She glanced at our little ragged, battered group, obviously not surprised to see us, and pointed to a ladder leading up to the attic. Except for my uncle and my brother, we all climbed up and gathered around the warm bricks of the chimney. I found out later that my brother had earlier joined a group of villagers carrying chickens, ducks, cucumbers, and potatoes to the weekly market in Khust. If I remember correctly, market day was Wednesday which made sense: Tuesday would have been too far from Shabbat for the Jewish housewives and too close to Sundays for the Catholic ones. And Thursday would have been too late. I am sure the villagers welcomed the strong new boy who could help carry their packs and they asked no questions. And I learned later that my brother had reached Khust exactly at the time when the *Levente* unit, the youth military training group, was assembled in the main square. The Christian boys were issued a wooden gun, the Jewish boys, in special teams, were issued a hoe. My brother attached himself to the group at the right time. The commanding officer doing the roll call read his name in that official martial manner, he yelled "here" ...and he was home!

My uncle climbed up to the attic with a large pot of boiled potatoes and a jug of warm milk, fresh from the cowshed. It all disappeared in minutes and then my uncle spoke with seriousness. He said that we must keep completely silent and start walking again as soon as darkness fell. Many groups like ours had reached this village, but most were caught and returned back across the border. Just one of those friendly forest workers was enough; perhaps one of the bosses, a Hungarian rather than a Rusyn, could denounce us to the local gendarmerie – every suspicious movement, especially groups like us, made us an easy target. It was obvious who we were.

We took a short nap and were woken up by loud, gruff men's voices. One look through a crack and our hopeless reality was immediately apparent. The yard was swarming with police and local gendarmes, among them there were a few civilians and one villager. They were all yelling at the lady of the house. One of the gendarmes climbed up the very same ladder we had previously used and bashed the little door in with the butt of his rifle. First, we saw the feather on his hat, then the uniformed torso of the man who shouted down triumphantly: "The Jewish scum is here".

We climbed down the ladder, right into the hands of the uniforms and the civilians. The lady of the house was standing nearby, shaking with fear, and the villager who had come with the policemen was now asked to have a good look at us and confirm we were the ones he had seen walking from the border to the village. He nodded his head but was asked sternly how come he had mentioned six people and there were only five. The man said he did not understand Hungarian and perhaps he had not understood what he was being asked or he could have miscounted in the morning mist. Oddly enough, they asked no more questions – not of the man, and not of us. The villager trotted out on the double and a few seconds later they let the housewife go and told her to get back into the house.

At this point I must state that the officials were not mean to us and they had little enthusiasm for their dirty work. They even asked us if we wanted to go back to the attic to retrieve personal belongings. They looked away when the lady of the house gave us a loaf of bread. I do not believe that these men had suddenly become people lovers, or should I say Jew lovers. They simply let us have our last meal before our second journey to a certain death. When we told them no personal effects were left behind in the attic, they escorted us, mere shadows of human beings, out of the yard. A military truck stood outside, a couple of the policemen jumped into the cab and a couple loaded us up and stayed with us. We started moving. The canvas was tied down tightly and we had no idea which direction we were traveling in. In my mind, I was going over the possibilities: jail or an internment camp, of which we had heard in the past? In less than an hour we had our answer – and it was the most brutal of all.

10 Second Deportation and Becoming Wiser

Judging by the slow speed and frequent gear changes, it was obvious we were climbing, and the tiny bit we could see through a small opening in the canvas between the two seated guards confirmed that we were indeed going up the mountain, not driving inland. A few minutes later we stopped and were ordered to jump off. A quick look around and we knew where we were: back across the border again. A few meters behind us, once again the barbed wire fence, an abandoned guard booth, the border barrier lifted and a warning from one of the gendarmes not to try and come back again because the next time, the result would be worse. He said it all very matter-of-factly, no excitement in his voice, just calm authority. He got back into the cab (the other cops had never even gotten out), a few difficult maneuvers, they turned around and headed back.

We remained at a loss, silent. The despair! The hopelessness! No one said a word, a large question mark hung in the air and so I will never know what the three adults thought about in that moment. As for my little sister, I cannot for the life of me imagine what she must have been thinking: sick, her face swollen, the gash on her temple still open. As far as my own thought process went – I lost any faith in the future and I vaguely remember wanting to lie down under a tree, go to sleep and never wake up.

I was still pondering this when I heard the voices of my mother, my aunt and my uncle. After the long silence, the fact they began speaking was at least something. The troika decided to get back across the nearby border once again. But our tactics would be different. This time the flight would take place only during nighttime, without eyewitnesses such as yesterday's forest workers – even though the location was different. We were not in the midst of the woods now, on narrow forest paths; we were in the middle of a paved road reachable by army trucks. We proceeded to find a spot in the woods for the rest of the day, a bit further away from the border line and because the day was quite warm, our bellies full of the homemade bread and warm milk from the good Jewish village lady from Torun, we collapsed from exhaustion and fell asleep. We were woken up by a strange stampede and we saw a herd of about fifteen wild boars, black, threatening, large –terrifying! The boars ran past us, about twenty feet away. Our blood ran cold, but the boars disappeared, and we were fine.

We knew the locals went to sleep at sunset as they had to wake up before sunrise to labor in the forest or work the tiny fields around their ramshackle houses. Others would leave for the market while it was still dark. They hitched their horses to wagons loaded with produce and headed for town, where they would sell the produce and buy corn, flour, oil, and various implements needed for their households or for resale. By the time they would head back, the sun would be setting, and they would reach home during the night. For a small fee, sometimes for free, a rider could perch atop their produce for a lift to town or back home. The chance rider would usually be a person coming back from some official business in town, a visit to the court, or to his lawyer to discuss his mortgage – in some cases receivership – on the house, the little field, the cow, and the horse. The debt kept on growing – not just to the bank but to the lawyer too, and the peasant found himself not owning anything anymore. Still, he would go to plead with the lawyer to defer the next payment, as the dry summer had reduced the farm income and a few weeks of labor in the forest would not even cover the pigs' feed or a couple of pairs of shoes for the kids for the coming winter.

We found just one such good man after we crossed the border at night. After three hours of walking and waiting in ditches on the side of the road we saw a horse-drawn cart approach around four in the morning. The driver got a scare when a dark figure jumped out of the gloom to stop him. The villager negotiated for a short while, then asked us to come out of our hiding place. My sister and I sat on some burlap sacks right next to shoeboxes filled with eggs. The adults grabbed onto the wooden sides of the hay wagon, and we set out. The villager was possibly the silent type or more likely, did not want to start chatting to a bunch of strangers whom he must have suspected of being border crossers. He wanted to avoid the attention of the wagon drivers and foot traffic that grew all around us as we rode on to Khust through the darkness. The town had lost its title of county seat long ago and now bore the ostentatious title "Royal City" (Huszt Koronaváros). It was still the most important town in the county, though now in the Kingdom of Hungary. We rode through the sleeping villages of Horinchovo and Iza and it was still dark, though almost morning, when we reached the outskirts of town. I am sure that no one had given a single thought to what we were going to do and where we were going to find shelter if we actually succeeded in our second attempt to flee hell...hell where nothing but certain death was going to be our fate.

At the end of Iza street, from a square dominated by a Greek Orthodox church, another street – mentioned before in this narrative – led to the barracks of the former 45th Czechoslovak Infantry Regiment and that street bore the same name under the new regime: Barracks Street. My mother's uncle, Moshe Davidovič, known in the family as "Uncle Moishe" lived on that very street.

I guess it was spontaneous and partly out of fear of daylight: the driver told us to alight quickly, and we jogged down the street till we reached an empty storefront. Through the door, we entered the bowels of the building which was home to a lonely elderly couple. Three grown sons had long ago left the house of their birth. One of them, an avowed Zionist had left for Palestine in the 30's, the middle son had a dental practice somewhere and the youngest was a rabbinical seminary student in Budapest (yes, in 1941 and all the way till 1944 – in Hungary! A fact that should be commended). This was the very same Emil Davidovič who was later, in the 1950's Assistant Rabbi to Rabbi Dr. Sicher in Prague and even later, till his death, held a rabbinical function in Dortmund, West Germany. In other words, there was plenty of room in the household.

It seemed like an hour but in reality it was barely half a minute between our knock on the door and the appearance of my mother's sleepy aunt opening up for us. She was too surprised to say a single word. Time was of the essence, as the sun had started rising and the streets started filling up. Only God knows what would have happened if someone had seen or recognized us. There was no doubt about it: a quick look at our ragtag group and anyone would have known immediately what was going on.

Ivan Olbracht's epic novel, *Golet in the Valley,* about that place and its people, that town and those ancient mountains and valleys, had been written in a totally different – though not too distant – time. His artistic talent would truly be needed to write about the series of events and experiences of that little group of ours. Scorned, cast out, yet during our escape from the claws of certain death that early autumn of 1941, we demonstrated the most basic desire of a human being: the desire to stay alive. And when your right to life is denied and when you are given even the tiniest chance – grab it! The actions of my uncle and my heroic mother showed that this was not an empty phrase.

Warmed up after our long night march, we ran across the room that used to be the store and found ourselves in a roomy kitchen with a large, massive rectangular table in the middle of it. We thought the heat of the kitchen unbearable but judging by the fact that "auntie" was wearing a warm sweater and "uncle", who had just returned from morning prayers was not wearing summer clothing, it was clear that the cool autumn days had arrived. And it was Friday morning, the eve of the Saturday-Shabbos holiday. An easy guess in any Jewish family, going by the dizzying smells of holiday delicacies being prepared. That night and the following day the dishes would be served on a beautifully set table. My nostrils smelled the classic fragrance of the famous Jewish *cholent*. Two items that could never be absent from a Shabbat table, a pair of white *halla* loaves, also known as *barkhes*, lay on a small serving table next to a glass cabinet, like two soldiers in their parade uniforms. Naturally, they were baked at home, in a clay oven out in the yard in which the holiday cholent was now cooking, for a full 24 hours, to be served on Saturday at noon.

My hungry gaze was fixed on auntie's slow movements. She took out a long kitchen knife from a drawer, cut an inch-thick slice from each loaf, spread a thick layer of homemade jelly on them, poured some boiled milk along with its crust into large mugs and put it all in front of us. Then she sat down and started sobbing. Only at that point did I notice my uncle. He sat at the head of the table and interrupted the silence by telling us that our father had been released from the army labor unit and that he had returned home with my brother two days ago. All done completely legally. That was too much even for my mother, despite her being toughened up by our experiences. Wordlessly, streams of tears started pouring down her cheeks as she tried to dab her eyes on the sleeves of what used to be a sweater. My sister just stared, and I was not able to find relief in tears. You could describe my mental and physical state as one of complete and utter apathy. Auntie took everything off the table quietly and I fell into a deep sleep – probably sitting down or perhaps even standing – a sleep that lasted at least twenty-four hours.

I was woken up by voices from the adjoining room and my mom came in, roused my sister, and told us that in the laundry room next door there was a wooden tub full of hot water, with more coming soon from the boiler, and she sent us to take a bath. What a divine experience – this was the first bath in a very long time, and I have never forgotten it. We stayed in our bedroom for a long time and when Uncle came back from Saturday worship we were asked to come to the kitchen, sat down and ate our breakfast and lunch in one. My aunt and uncle who had made the journey with us had left in the meantime. I never learned where they went. I wanted to see my father and brother terribly but someone decided that they should stay away for now and so we spent several days, including the Jewish New Year eating and sleeping. Mother told us one day that we needed to find another place to stay, saying there was danger here: it was a busy spot, not far from the barracks. Additionally, there was always the risk of being denounced by the neighbors who shared a backyard fence with "our" house. Mom told us our next hiding place would be a secluded house at the edge of town owned by her brother Alexander, who was the manager of a gasoline and diesel storage facility. I have mentioned him before. The house was a modest, one-story structure adjacent to a warehouse full of empty metal barrels. There was no shortage of room. His two older sons had done what many other young men had done: when the Soviet Union occupied eastern Poland (the Soviets called it western Ukraine) and suddenly became Subcarpathian Ruthenia's (now Hungary's) immediate neighbors, young people crossed the border into that land of equality and plenty in droves.

The following is not really a part of my narrative and so I will be brief: The younger of my two cousins, Antonín, used to give Czech lessons to students in the higher grades of the Czech gymnasium in Khust – that was during the 1930's under the Czechoslovak regime. He was also a champion high school skier. He was just about to graduate from the gymnasium when he, his older brother and many others, crossed into the Soviet Union. They all were all jailed, interrogated, branded as spies, and interned for a long period of time. Some of those interned were released eventually and joined General Svoboda's Army. Others, like cousin Antonín, spent the rest of the war in labor camps in the Urals. Some perished. Very few came back. Antonín was one of the lucky ones. Long after the war was over, he was still in Vorkuta in the Urals. His appeals to Czechoslovak authorities were falling on deaf ears, his pleas for repatriation were ignored despite the Soviets not recognizing him as a citizen even though he had been born on territory that now belonged to them. The Soviets simply said that he had been born on what was then Czechoslovak land and washed their hands of his case. I know cases like his and I guess that the Czechoslovak authorities must have had a serious reason for not wanting anything to do with these folks, who once upon a time used to be their citizens. He was finally released with the help of the Hungarian government, which did not abrogate its responsibility – even if Antonín and people like him had only been Hungarian citizens for a scant few years. He traveled to Hungary but did not feel a sense of belonging, so he crossed to Czechoslovakia where he was exposed to the imminent danger of being deported, possibly back to the USSR. In 1947 he packed his bags and left for Palestine, today Israel, where he recently died.

11 Return from Illegality

In uncle Alexander's house we were given the room that used to belong to the two young men whom everyone assumed lived in socialist paradise. Two more sons still lived in the house (both perished in a concentration camp). There, in that secluded spot on the outskirts, we finally relaxed a little. Our reunion with Father and brother was joyous and soaked in happy tears. Because our new home was so inconspicuous, even some friends began to visit me. It must be said that the authorities adopted a somewhat laxer attitude to people like us who had been deported before when the heads of their families were in the army (there were a few families like ours). Nevertheless, the situation was complicated. We had to maintain contact with the border police (a euphemism for the police and other government departments that dealt with the Jewish population). We found a good contact through the Menčel family whose kids and cousins were our friends. It so happened that an official of this border police – I think his name was Molnár – was renting rooms in the Menčels' house, adjacent to the post office. I do not know what went on behind the scenes, or maybe I have forgotten, but be that as it may, we were able to return to our old house on the condition that father had to report to the police once a week.

After a few months of life at the edge of an abyss we found ourselves in a situation that beggared belief. Normal life went on all around us. No trace or echo of what was happening to Jewish people only about a hundred kilometers away. Yes, there were professions that were closed to the Jews. *Numerus clausus* was practiced in all high schools but that problem was solved by establishing Jewish schools. I do not know who financed them, but attendance was compulsory for Jewish students and if you were barred from a local school, you had to commute to Jewish high schools to Mukachevo, Uzhhorod (Hebrew high schools in former Czechoslovakia), Debrecen or even Budapest, where a Jewish rabbinical seminary was also still functioning. You could go to the cinema, you could travel anywhere in Hungary, people were getting married, children were being born. Boys chased girls, fell in love, had rendezvous outside of town or the surrounding villages. There were picnics, and guileless plans were being hatched. No yellow Star of David on your chest. Yes, there was open anti-Semitism, young people died in army labor units on the eastern front, some from barbaric treatment, some while clearing mines or building anti-tank barriers and trenches with their bare hands – hungry, dirty, inadequately dressed in the cruel Russian winter. Only a few returned and those who did were, as I said previously, as members of Svoboda's Army. Still and all: let it be objectively said in the Hungarian government's favor that while in Germany and Austria and everywhere else, where the Wehrmacht and Gestapo boot had come down, the "solution of the Jewish question" was in full swing. While in Slovakia the same was being done by the Hlinka guards and the Tiso regime – life in Hungary was relatively bearable.

Let me remind you, we are now at the end of 1941 / beginning of 1942, and I suddenly find that life goes on and I am possessed with a desire to continue where my life was forcibly interrupted about six months previously. In my case, that meant continuing my high school study. And because my family was not able to finance one of the previously mentioned institutions, the tuition and accommodation away from home. the only remaining possibility was a return to my local high school. That really seemed like an unattainable dream to me. Let us remember I was still only "semi-legal", plus I had gotten the news of a new Jewish student in my former class. This was Alex Pikkel, more about him shortly. His parents had moved to town from the Hungarian inland, so the question was – had this student taken my place in the system that strictly limited the percentage of Jews in any school? My parents knew my unquenchable desire for knowledge and study, but it was my mother again, my forward looking, initiative grabbing mother, who acted.

12 A Good Word about a Greek Orthodox Priest

Exactly what and how she did it I only learned later but things began to move at warp speed. I had been dreaming about starting school again in September which would have meant the loss of one school year, but I was told one fine day that I should begin preparing for an entrance exam as an external student of "my" grade – grade four of the gymnasium. I still remember that the very same students who guffawed and did not have an encouraging word for me when I was slapped in front of the class by the principal Béla Gável, were now competing in helping me prepare for the external exams. One would bring notebooks, another textbooks, another would sit with me for hours, cramming and explaining material. The exam was set to take place at the end of June 1942 in the principal's office.

I found out on the day of the exams that the chairman of the examination committee was Father Popovič, the principal of the Greek-Orthodox church boarding school and our neighbor. His wife came from my mother's birthplace, Zoloterevo. (It is worth noting that married Greek Orthodox men can be ordained as priests.) The two women were probably not friends in childhood but there were warm neighborly relations between the families. I learned that mother paid a friendly visit to Mrs. Popovič. She persuaded her husband, who taught religious studies at our elementary school, that since I used to be an excellent student who served as an example to many of the most influential and important gentlemen's children, I should be given a chance to continue my studies. Without losing a school year! The impossible became reality. My entrance exam report card was not as unblemished as it had been before when A's were my only grade in all subjects. Now there were quite a few B's and C's but still, the only important thing was a remark at the bottom of the page: "May continue to 5th Grade". I immediately bought myself the high school hat, which was part of our uniform, I found a gold stripe for my sleeve that served as a clear symbol of me being a *kvinta* (5th Grade) student and I was back in the gymnasium! This was during the summer vacation of 1942, exactly a year after our deportation but I was the happiest boy under the sun because despite everything – I would continue my studies and I had not even lost a year!

13 A Regular Grade Five Gymnasium Student

The welcome I received from my classmates in the beginning of the school year 1942/43 was lukewarm, except for about five or six close friends who were happy to see me. Those were the ones that had been encouraging and helping me prepare for the external exams. Among them was one Alexander Pikkel, the only other Jewish student, whose parents had moved to Khust from Hungary in the previous year.

At the start of the school year, we all received a yearbook, as was the custom then. The book contained a list of all the students of the gymnasium, all the classes, each student's grades in all the subjects, with the names of the top students in bold print. A short time ago, after 55 to 57 years, I got hold of the yearbooks for 1940/41, 1941/42 and 1942/43. After more than half a century it was finally possible to visit Subcarpathian Ruthenia and one of the descendants of the above mentioned Menčel family was able to travel there and bring the yearbooks. In fact, he got them from one of the sons of Dr. Klein, a well-known doctor in Khust, who still lived there. I have leafed through the yellowing pages, now almost six decades old, and every time I find something new, memories float up in my mind – beautiful boyhood memories but also many sad ones.

First off, it was very odd to look at the year 1941/42 where I see my name taken off the list as someone who had dropped out and yet the next line mentions my passing the external exams. As for the names of other students, I mostly remember the names of the tolerant ones whose number increased after 1939, students who were two or three years older and able to compare the situation prior to '39 and afterwards. On the other hand, the stubborn ones became even more stubborn as time went on. Some of the girls' names remind me how the levels of my testosterone began increasing in those years and with the increase came my first secret loves.

But mainly I need to stress that there were 26 Jewish boys and girls in the gymnasium back then. Of that number 19 never came back from the concentration camps and as far as I know, only seven survived. Jolana Schonfeld lives in Israel today, Alexander Pikkel never came back. Otto

Brandstein lives in Israel and Tibor Burián in France. One of the sons of Dr. Klein remained in the former Soviet Union. I found a mention about my cousin Antonín who disappeared like many others and is listed as having dropped out. There is another person there, an 8th Grade honors student by the name of Ervin Adlerstein, later known as Ervin Adam, MD, a physician at the Clinic of Infectious Diseases at Bulovka Hospital in Prague and afterwards in the USA. Or graduate Lieberman, later Libal who now runs a large accounting firm in Netanya, Israel. The others scattered through the world.

There is more interesting reading: the religion of each student is listed next to his or her name, but from 1942 you do not even have to make the effort to read the names – just look at the report cards and the timbre of the times becomes clear. Under the subject "Knowledge of Defense of Country", those whose names bear the suffix "izr" (denoting "israelite" religion) are not graded on that subject. And more: students who excelled academically – just like students of meager means – did not have to pay tuition. Tuition was expensive, in fact awfully expensive for folks like my family, and the only way we could afford it was by me tutoring weaker students and taking on odd jobs during the summer vacations.

There are some other items of note in the yearbook. It is noted that on August 20, 1942, Air Force First Lieutenant Istvan Horthy, a great martyr of battle, died a heroic death. He was the vice-regent and the son of the Regent of Hungary, Miklós Horthy. I guess that, too, belonged in our high school yearbook. But there are many other things – which noted personage visited the school, which professor attended which conference, who was being drafted, which events – mostly of a religious nature – were being organized, the worship on school premises and outside it, various *Levente* events, prizes awarded to students and professors, the state of health of both students and professors, and more. Excursions and field trips were also mentioned, as well as extracurricular activity but almost none of these had any Jewish participation. No mention in the yearbook about the existence of two categories of students. But that could be considered as positive. One is excluded from all extracurricular activity, but it is not made official and not mentioned. And I must stress categorically that there was no open anti-Jewish incitement, unlike outside the walls of the school. The headmaster, the Supreme Study Councilor, *Levente* Commander, His Excellency Béla Gável ignored Jewish students, which had the advantage of us being left in peace. He no longer slapped faces the way he did during his first year of employment at the Khust Royal Hungarian Gymnasium.

And what about the professors? What a wide palette of characters, personalities, and pedagogues. While reading their names, I am trying to recall some important details as well as their character. Elek Ban, physics and math professor – a gentle, slim, tall man. A pity that he was drafted into the army shortly after the attack on the Soviet Union, I never heard another word about him. He was an excellent teacher. Michael Griga, a Ruthenian, taught Russian and history. Always nattily dressed, always in a bad mood – apparently because he resented having been transferred from the gymnasium in Uzhhorod. Like most Ruthenian intellectuals, he had no affection for Jews, but I think he was aware that he himself, as a Ruthenian, was not exactly beloved by the rest of the faculty. Professor Iréne Hamza, who taught Hungarian, always tried to demonstrate – perhaps too eagerly – that she wanted nothing to do with racism of any kind. A pleasant lady, about 45 years old. We liked her. Mária Kudroň was our German teacher. Always bitter, expressionless. You never knew who she really was. Her husband, Emil Kudroň, shone next to her. He taught history, geography, and philosophy in other classes. In our class he only taught one lesson a week: defense of the homeland, which we, Jewish students, skipped. I never knew if he was a Russian, a Ruthenian or a Hungarian. His presence in the school did not seem to make any difference at all. Not exactly Mr. Personality. At least his wife, Mrs. Kudroň, initiated us into the secrets of Heine, Goethe, and Schiller. I can still recite a few verses of Lorelei till this day. And yes, there was the main *Levente* instructor (did I mention that Jewish students were equipped with a wooden shovel and the others with a wooden rifle?), Tibor Semsey, physical education instructor. Always drunk and I could tell even then that his heavy breath, hoarse from constant yelling of military orders, was infused with cheap, throat burning hooch. His whole appearance was really the exact opposite of the sportsmanlike image of a Phys-ed teacher. I guess he compensated for it by being vulgar, yelling and displaying open racism and not just towards Jews. Ruthenians also felt his wrath. He was always dirty, like all chronic winos. And his Phys-ed teaching? The occasional run around the gym or the schoolyard, otherwise just barking orders, marching and martial exercises. On my mid-term report card, I always got a B. It did not matter as it was not included in the overall average, but he simply would not have it in his heart to give me an A. For some unknown reason he did not do this on the final report card and so he never managed to spoil my A average. Singing and art classes also did not count in the average tally, so the teachers of those subjects also employed the same trick of marking down in the mid-term. Still, I need to stress again: most professors treated us justly, save for the principals, Griga and Semsey. One more teacher should be added to this small group: Professor Petronella Üvegeš, who taught history and geography. Apparently, she wanted to go beyond the call of "duty". She was a Hungarized Ruthenian and the combination of being a Ruthenian intellectual and her desire to be a true-blue Hungarian created a great recipe for intolerance and a personality full of hate. Moreover, she was a middle-aged woman and not exactly a beauty queen…

14 A Keyhole and Saved Virginity

And how could I forget our external religion teachers! The first one was a red-haired gentleman by the name of Alfred Friedmann, later Mr. Leopold Adler. I do not recall their level of erudition, nor how they filled that one lesson a week, which was after the end of the ordinary school-day, attended by all the Jewish students at our school, no matter what grade they were in. What I do recall is that we skipped that lesson often. Instead, we would organize a little group and visit a certain house under the castle and there, for a small fee (group discount), one could get a lesson in the female anatomy and be shown what it was that the adults did when they locked themselves up in their darkened bedroom. No darkness in the room we were in. The point was to see what one was supposed to do or to be shown by the madam what needed to be done when one's turn came. That is where taking turns at the keyhole came in. I will admit right here and now that when they first talked me into joining – I was about fifteen – I fumbled in my pocket for the larger coins and marched into town, head bowed, with a group of about five boys. I was convinced that every passer-by knew where our group of high school students was headed. As we approached the street where the deed was to take place, our student caps disappeared in our deepest pockets, and we found ourselves in a gloomy narrow hallway. It was shabby and stuffy and was devoid of all furniture The more experienced boys, the ones who had already visited the house and gained plenty of experience, demonstrated the technique of peeking through the larger-than-normal keyhole. The order of entry was set without objections – there was no need to draw lots: the more experienced ones went in first and a battle for a spot at the keyhole began among the rest of us.

I dreaded my turn. Profuse sweat on my brow and the crimson color of my cheeks told me the episode would not end well. Through that keyhole I suddenly saw a fat, aging woman with enormous breasts that hung down to her navel and the guy who was in there, naked, his head between the fat, short, raised thighs. All of that and the vibe of the house had an immediate effect on me: I puked right there on the spot, then ran out to the yard where I must have thrown up even food I had eaten a week before. I do not remember how I found myself back at school, with my schoolbag and my books. I felt ashamed, nauseous, and almost threw up every time when I recalled the scene I would see through the keyhole. I was in total shock, sitting at my desk in an empty classroom at least an hour before I was able to slowly amble home. I felt sorry for myself all the way – not sure if it was because I gave hard-to-come-by money to "that person" (she got paid for the group, not for each individual) or because I remained a virgin. Also, because of the anticipated mocking and teasing by my friends. They never actually did, not to my face. But they were boys, so I am sure they told the story behind my back to whoever was interested about what went on in that house. For me – nothing had happened at all! So that is what we did during our religion period – but most importantly, I always got an "A" in that subject.

15 Professor Lesev – an Exceptionally Good Man

I have left T. Lesev, our home room teacher and professor of Latin for the end of this part of my story. Unlike the rest of the faculty, about whom I write based on fleeting, vague memories, making their characters only superficially drawn, the memory of Professor Lesev remains lodged deep in my heart. I am speaking of the years 1942–1943, when nothing extraordinary was happening in our lives. If not for the full-bore conscription of young men into labor units, you would not have known that rivers of blood were being spilled in the east. Various rumors, some proven, some not, would bring daily hope and daily despair. As I gather my thoughts, I must state here that our situation was completely different to anywhere else in German-occupied Europe. Of course, we did not know that then. No Jew anywhere in Europe lived in the kind of relative comfort that we enjoyed. We also did not know that Admiral Horthy, the Hungarian Regent, had undergone a transformation. When he took power after World War I, after two thirds of former Hungary – a part of the Austro-Hungarian Empire – were taken away, Horthy was a charismatic man. He had been the commander of the Austro-Hungarian navy and he had commenced a fight against the Treaty of Trianon, which he vehemently opposed. That did not stop him from openly displaying his anti-Semitism. Back in 1920 he started implementing a *numerus clausus* at Hungarian universities. Between 1938 – 1943 he instituted various anti-Jewish laws but at the same time, in 1942 and 1943, he fiercely resisted tough and heavy pressure by the Germans to solve the Jewish question using the German recipe. He never gave in to the demand to brand Jews with a yellow star or any other distinguishing symbol. The only exception were the ID cards and military cards of the "black squads". The authorities printed the letters *Zs* (*Zsidó*, Jew) in large print on those documents.

This more or less stable situation lasted until the spring of 1944 – March 19, 1944 to be exact. That is when the German armies occupied Hungary and an ally had turned into a vanquished enemy. The reason was an alleged intention of Hungary to "betray" Germany and to join what was fast becoming the obvious winning side. For us, this meant a rapid and immediate change. A yellow star of David adorned everyone's chest within days – and I mean everyone, from newborns to moribund elders. Signs were posted everywhere telling the marked, stigmatized segment of the population what they could or could not do. The one thing still permitted was to breathe; everything else was forbidden.

What we had learned from our deportation in 1941, meant we were the only ones who really knew what was to follow. Even today I do not know if our prognosis and our experience had really made a deep impression on anyone, though we recounted it often. Soon, we had to do forced labor, mainly building a small emergency airport not far from town. People would return after 12–14 hours, beaten, hungry and dirty, only to start the routine again while it was still dark. The first wounded, the first dead came quickly. Some simply could not take the physical strain, combined with the barbaric treatment and the beatings. A ghetto was organized swiftly, using just two streets. Every room in every house was crammed with tens of people of all ages and genders, each with the permitted ten (possibly twenty) kilograms of personal belongings. The ghetto was guarded by Hungarian cops, who realized quickly they could do what many of them had been wanting to do and what I had personally witnessed three years previously. Still, the police and the authorities did not want to dirty their hands with everything. They nominated some folks to a *Judenrat* which tasked boys of my age (I was seventeen) with patrolling the ghetto. That gave me the advantage of being able to move freely, unlike the others. We would use this freedom to visit a bakery on the edge of the ghetto, they would give us fresh hot pancakes made from bread dough. We were also able to steal away and visit places where our girlfriends "lived". Once I was patrolling with my friend Alex, the watchmaker's son, and I snuck away to the Kahans' house where my platonic love resided. When I came back out after five minutes, Alex told me the *bugrish* (policemen) asked him where his partner was. One of them overheard the pejorative title (*bugrish*), they dragged him into a yard and beat him bloody. You could hear his cries throughout the whole neighborhood, and I have always felt guilty about it. Still do. But Alex visited me from the United States a few months ago and we recalled the episode with sarcastic humor.

16 *Aurea Prima Sata Est*

The day the German armies rolled into town, they immediately commandeered all schools and turned them into barracks. Our school suffered the same fate and we moved into the building of the county court, turning small courtrooms into classrooms. In one of these "classrooms" we were just being taught Latin by Professor Lesev, who was our home room teacher at the time as well (called the "class professor"). We were learning how to recite the famous hexameter *Aurea prima sata est* ("Golden was that first age" verses from Ovid's Metamorphosis) and I was asked to stand up and recite the part I had been assigned to learn by heart for the lesson. I memorized more than just the first seven assigned lines and so I stood, yellow star on my chest, for the first time during my student years without self-confidence. I felt degraded, and I knew from experience what was to come in my life now, and so I began, for the first time in my life, in a voice that trembled with uncertainty...*Aurea prima sata est*... and that was that! I blanked out! I could not say another word. The classroom/courtroom fell totally silent. You could hear the breath of each stunned student. The silence lasted about a minute. Professor Lesev came up to me, put his hand on my shoulder and told me in a quiet, fatherly voice to sit down. He closed the little book where he marked our grades – without writing a thing. He remained standing behind his lectern and looked at me with sad eyes, and I think I saw a tear glisten in his eye. He called for recess, even though the class had barely begun. The students left the room, I remained seated with my head bowed down to my arms, folded on my desk. I felt that kind man's soft hand on my head and then he left without saying a word. I managed to pull myself together and leave but I never went back there. Even the rest of the class, the whole school in fact, did not go back many more times because the school year ended at the beginning of April.

17 A Report Card with a Yellow Star on my Chest

Professor Lesev notified me not to come to school to pick up my report card (they called it an "index", a print-out of all my mid-term and year-end report cards for all my years at school). He asked me to come and pick it up in person from his house. This took place before the ghetto was set up and so I went. Before he handed my index over, this tall, dignified older gentleman put his head on my shoulder and started sobbing like an inconsolable toddler. It goes without saying, I started crying too. He asked me to wait for him to leave the room and without saying another word, he turned around and was gone. I opened the index as soon as I was outside. I was expecting a "B" at least in music, art or phys-ed – that seemed to be a faculty routine, to keep the average high but with a cosmetic blemish. The surprise was that the "B" was in the Russian language, by Professor Griga. He was not a *nyilas*, a member of the local fascist guard. He was a native, like me, only a Ruthenian who was eager to want to trump everyone in his anti-Semitic zeal. This was common, as I have said, among Ruthenian intellectuals. But even the infamous principal only demonstrated his attitudes in an official manner, not as a personal thing. And I knew that because there it was, clear as day, his signature at the bottom of the report card and his remark: "May continue to the seventh grade". Just like Griga, the principal knew of course that this was not going to happen, but he had held his personal racism in check. Not so the town native, Professor Griga.

After my return from the concentration camps, I looked for Professor Lesev in the house I had last seen him, where he had given me my report card. Someone whispered that he had been deported somewhere immediately after the arrival of the Red Army and never heard from again. To be clear: Professor Lesev was a "white" emigrant and that was not something the Communists would have let slide, not even a quarter of a century after the Revolution. His son, who had also been a student at the gymnasium, though in a higher grade, never again saw him or heard about him. In the late 1940's I bumped into him on Wenceslas Square in Prague, but he seemed very vague, did not want to speak openly. This was after the celebrated "Victorious February" (*Vítězný Únor* in Czech – a commonly used euphemism for the Communist Party *coup d'état* of 1948) and the slogan "With the Soviet Union till eternity" had become a daily affirmation.

The deportations started shortly after the ghetto was established. Rumors were flying. Some had been listening to the BBC, others to Radio Moscow and hopes were high that it all would be over soon. Moreover, others still, claimed they could hear the rumble of cannons from the approaching front (this was not far from the truth), that the Germans were packing up and preparing to bolt. I am not sure where they came from, but suddenly various messengers appeared in the ghetto and they started pulling out various blank documents from their deep pockets: birth certificates, citizenship certificates, blank ID documents, even passports, all of it signed and bearing official logos. We were told just to fill it out, write whatever Aryan name you could think of, your date of birth (your own, so you did not have to remember too many particulars). You could even keep your surname, assuming it sounded Aryan enough. I had a whole set of those documents in my hand, but they all ended up buried in the ground. I do not know that anyone ended up using them. People simply began believing that we were going inland or to the occupied territories to work, and everyone wanted to keep family groups together to help each other. In that desperate situation it was not difficult to convince oneself that somehow the Nazis' intentions toward us were good. Our unwillingness to run away and hide in the mountains was proven to be the correct course. The feather-capped policemen were bringing into the ghetto whole families caught and hauled in from some bunker in the Carpathian Mountains. Probably denounced by some locals up there...after all, we had experienced the very same thing. We knew the whole truth and we spread the truth far and wide, but the wheel had begun turning and the bitter end was approaching with lightning speed.

18 Overcrowded Trains Headed for the Unknown

Everyday transports reduced the ghetto population substantially. We were the last ones to be taken because my brother was by then a licensed auto mechanic. He was escorted daily by two cops to the Gestapo headquarters where he fixed their vehicles. They were eager to keep their free labor till the very end. I do not remember the day or the month when we finally found ourselves on that siding that led from the railway station to the fuel depot. We were herded and corralled there at nighttime. The cattle car doors opened. A group of men in German and Hungarian uniforms, as well as quite a few civilians, stood at the opening and pushed in as many people as possible. No place to sit, – standing room only. Some orders were given, the doors were bolted on the outside and that was that. I do not know how long the first portion of our journey lasted. Based on my knowledge of history it must have been June 6th when we saw the name of the station Košice (a city in Eastern Slovakia) through a small, barred window. We heard the typical railways station sounds of clanging metal, long hammers testing the wheels and the brakes. A man, possibly a railway employee, stole up to our wagon and between two loud hammer bangs he told us that the Americans had opened a second front. We also knew, as I have written, that the eastern front was literally over the hill and around the corner! Still, it was no secret the Germans insisted on rules and order, and a job, once begun, must be completed to the letter – no matter what. The train then stopped one more time on Polish territory (I knew it by the blue-grey insulators on electric and telegraph poles which I had remembered since 1941). Poland again. Like I said, not a journey into the unknown for me and my family. The doors of the cattle car flew open and two German soldiers entered, apparently not bothered by the foul stench inside. Two large barrels full of feces, plus the sweat, the filth, and a corpse in the corner – all the result of a few days ride in locked cattle wagons. None of it bothering these people of a superior race and lofty culture. They only cared about one thing: to fill their pockets and sacks with money and jewelry, robbed from us at gunpoint. Anyone trying to hide something risked an immediate bullet in the head. That, too, I had already experienced before.

The place was called Osvětim... Auschwitz... Oświęcim. It was the last alighting stop for the freight train and its cargo without hope and without a return ticket. Mauthausen and Ebensee were to follow.

I was liberated on May 7, 1945, when a jeep with four American soldiers appeared on the square of the Ebensee camp in Austria. The square that just yesterday had been the feared *Appelplatz* (roll call place) for all of us. A fellow sufferer told me that he had witnessed the death of my father. I had spent my whole time in the camp with my father until the moment he was taken away to the *Revier*, a so-called hospital from which almost no one returned. And because the crematorium was working over capacity and was not able to burn everyone, his body was tossed into a mass grave. According to the signage in the town of Ebensee, it is there till this day, in the *KZ Friedhoff* (concentration camp graveyard) where only a broken, crumbling old gate stands as a silent witness to the fact that surrounding this mass grave, on land that now boasts lovely new buildings, there used to be a horrific concentration camp.

I remember very little besides the jeep and the alive and the dead lying in their own runny waste on every step – people and half-people covered with white DDT dust. Later, as a medical student and a doctor I realized the terrible mistake the liberators made. They were obviously inexperienced and naïve, and thought that a goulash-type meal in large military barrels, would save those who could still be saved. What happened instead was a stampede. Those who could still move, rushed to the boiling barrels, stomped each other to death, burned or boiled themselves, and if they managed to grab a bite, later writhed with terrible stomach pain and even died from diarrhea resulting from this heavy, greasy meal. The American army apparently understood their mistake as the barrels disappeared the next day to be replaced with large tents marked with a red cross and many men and women wearing white coats over their uniforms. My medical record showed I weighed 28 kilograms (62 lb) and I remained alive only because I did not have the strength to reach those barrels. I awoke from a long coma in some hospital in Linz, from where I was discharged once I reached the weight of 40 kg (88 lb).

In the former barracks in Linz, trucks arrived daily with signs denoting their destinations as well as country flags. It was high summer when I climbed on one such truck, adorned with a Czechoslovak flag and a few hours later we reached České Budějovice, in Czechoslovakia – though only after having been harassed at the border by a Soviet soldier who scrutinized us with a piercing, hostile eye, apparently looking for Red Army deserters.

In Budějovice, we were taken care of by repatriation authorities. They fed us and clothed us, had us fill out long questionnaires and inquired about our destination. Without giving it any thought, I wrote down Khust, Subcarpathian Ruthenia as my destination. The region belonged to Czechoslovakia once more (albeit for a short time) and I was certain that only back home would I be able to learn the fate of my close and distant relatives and find out which friends had survived the cataclysm.

In Khust I found my mother and sister. They reported to me that my brother had also returned but stayed barely a few days and left again. He departed for Romania and was planning to reach Palestine from there. I kept my father's death from them for now. We also sat down to do the first reckoning, and the bottom line was that about fifty aunts, uncles and cousins would never be coming back. My mom was one of eleven siblings; my father one of eight. The married ones had children who were my cousins…

19 The Return and Good-bye to my Little County Town

Nothing resembled what had been there a year ago. I have described the Soviets' behavior elsewhere. I started school when the school year began but one visit convinced me that this was no longer a place for me. I had a long talk with my former elementary school teacher, Father Popovič with whom I had maintained contact and who used to insist I show him each new gymnasium report card. He told me, frankly, leaving was my only option. As I said, Professor Lesev was nowhere to be found – I certainly would have valued his advice. On the other hand, there were the Soviet officers, not a few Jewish men among them, and they were not afraid to warn us to get the hell out of there while we still could!

20 The Closely Watched New Border

It looked like we might have missed our opportunity! There were no newspapers, no radio, and the rumors circulating from mouth to mouth and ear to ear all stubbornly insisted changes were imminent. All the Czech institutions that re-opened after the war, started to close. Czech military personnel were leaving *en masse*. Suddenly one realized that Subcarpathian Ruthenia was no longer a part of Czechoslovakia and that the border was now closed.

This time, though, my mother, wiser and experienced from previous escapes, found a helper for herself. I was now eighteen years old and felt the need to take responsibility for the remaining three-member family.

The grapevine whispered that the Romanian border was not guarded yet and the recommendation was to hire an army truck with a driver. We paid the required sum, and the drunk driver took us on the ten-kilometer journey and across the river Tisa; I believe the border village on the other side of the river was called Veliatyno. A further short ride through a mountain road and we were at the border. And *voila*! The barrier was down, stern soldiers standing on the roadway, a command for all to alight, the driver's clothes and pockets were searched, and the money found went into one of the soldier's pockets. A search of our luggage followed. There was precious little to be found in them, a few months after returning from the camps. Nevertheless, the luggage was substantially lighter when it was returned to us. Then a quick "about turn!" and our third escape attempt since the war started, had failed. On the way back I realized that what had happened at the border was not completely "kosher". If those were indeed legitimate border guards, how come they let the driver go? After all, this was a soldier attempting to help people escape – an unforgivable transgression for the Soviets at that time. I could not shake the impression that our "hero" had, in fact, been one of the collaborators.

I do not know who was more stubborn – my mother or me. But once the decision to flee was taken, it was going to get done, come hell or high water. The fact that I had been born in Czechoslovakia and had never renounced its citizenship was all the more reason to get out. The actual city of birth was unimportant: in the year of my birth, one could be born anywhere between Aš in the west and Yasinia in the east, and anywhere along that line one could claim Czechoslovakian citizenship. No one had asked my opinion whether I wished for my birthplace to remain in or to be left out of Czechoslovakia.

I will leave it to the historians to answer the question why and how it came to be that Czechoslovakia, a country on the winning side of the world war, ended up losing territory following victory! I have never understood this and still do not till this very day.

21 A Dry Cleaners' Ticket Did the Trick

Rumors about possible repatriation back to Czechoslovakia spread like a flu virus during an epidemic. For instance, it was being claimed that there was some type of commission with its headquarters in Uzhhorod, whose task it was to decide who was permitted to leave and who had to remain in Subcarpathian Ruthenia, now Soviet territory. And so, we immediately took a train to Uzhhorod. We found a huge courtyard attached to a local military unit; simple office tables spread around it, and behind each table a Soviet officer. In the courtyard and outside of it, hundreds, perhaps thousands of people with every single person trying to convince the officers that his or her true home was over there, beyond the nearby border. Various pieces of information floated around, some true, some false. The common denominator was that one had to show an official document written in the Czech language. You would be showing to someone who did not understand a word anyway and you had to convince him that it was indeed in Czech. Various "advisors" circulated among the crowd. It turned out many were Jewish soldiers of Svoboda's Army who could still move across the now closed border freely, in or out of their Czechoslovak army uniform. The poor guys were crisscrossing the border, searching for surviving family members and friends. One of them approached us, gave my mother a piece of some crumpled paper and led us to one of the tables. As we approached the table, he managed to whisper, "that officer is one of ours". My mother approached the officer and handed the crumpled note to him, as my sister and I stood nearby. The man glanced at the paper absent-mindedly and asked in a muffled voice, in Yiddish, how many we were. He stealthily turned the note around, slapped a stamp on it in a ceremonious gesture, scribbled +2 in large letters and waved his hand as if to say – "get out of here"!

I do not remember how we reached the railway station in nearby Čop which was now a border crossing, and from which one could take a Czech Railways train. I also do not recall any difficulty crossing the border on foot, but I remember the station Čierna pri Čope. Sitting on a wooden bench, so typical for small railway stations, we finally breathed a sigh of relief. I took that fateful, all-important piece of paper from my mother and had I been in a lighter mood, I would have laughed so hard everyone would have thought me completely nuts. It was a note from a dry cleaner! But it was written in Czech and that was enough for that kind officer in Uzhhorod. I am convinced he was not stupid, and he knew very well what he was doing. As for us...we could put this down as our fourth escape and our second successful one.

Our journey in a slowly crawling post-war train which included long stops at every station and often in between stations led to Teplice Šanov (later Teplice the Spa in Czechoslovakia, later just Teplice). We knew an uncle of ours lived there. He was a "foreign soldier" (a Czech soldier who served abroad during World War II), still in uniform, wearing the stripes of a sergeant of the Czechoslovak army. A large apartment was turned over to him after a Sudetenland doctor had been removed and every member of my family who returned from the war automatically took up lodgings there. We joined about eight uncles, aunts, and cousins already there.

I think the name of the street was Sadová Street. I found out the very first morning that the town gymnasium was located atop a small hill, right across from the house. Let me say here that I was able to save my personal file with all my report cards. Across the ghetto fence there was a house belonging to the Ruthenian attorney, Stanek, whose son, Jaroslav was a classmate of mine. The night before our transport into the unknown I had snuck up to the fence and when Jaroslav approached, I threw the file to him. This was a very dangerous thing to do. Not so much for me – my fate had already been sealed but if he had been seen by a gendarme, his punishment would have been severe. (How I wished I would have been able to do the same with a family photo: today I would have a photograph of my father. My continuing search after the war to find a single memento, a single picture of him has been – and remains – fruitless till this day. A couple of years ago I even reached out to the Ministry of Defense in Dejvice, a Prague district, thinking that every soldier would have had to have been photographed for their military ID card, but I have not heard back from them.) Immediately after my return my classmate returned the file to me.

22 Temporary Gymnasium Student in Teplice – Grade Seven

Personal file in hand, I knocked on the door that said "Principal". A loud "come in" was the response and ten minutes later I was a student of the Teplice Gymnasium. It was morning and the school day was in full swing. The principal escorted me personally to my class where everyone stood up as we entered. He introduced me warmly to the teacher and the students, I was shown an empty spot at one of the desks and that was that: my third continuation of high school studies was now a reality.

The reality did not last long, as it turned out. The situation in my uncle's house was such that studying or preparing homework was well-nigh impossible and my low mood did not escape the attention of my home room teacher (a teacher of Russian language, as it happened). He asked to talk to me in private and when we found an empty classroom to talk, he asked directly what the problem was. He advised me that the gymnasium had a special counselor for students who had survived and returned from fighting, or from concentration camps. I explained my situation to the counselor in a few sentences. He thought for a moment and said he thought he might have a solution for me, and would I wait a few days for him to confirm a few things. Less than 48 hours later he divulged the solution to me: he would be sorry to see me leave and for the class to lose such a talented student but there was a better place for me. In Prague, in the Pankrác district there was what used to be a Russian gymnasium, closed after the war, and now re-opened as a regular gymnasium but also functioning as a boarding school. He had spoken to the principal, who expressed his willingness to accept me. He gave me a letter of reference to deliver to the boarding school, accompanied me to the principal's office (apparently, the principal had already been apprised of the situation), they wished me the best of success and I was out.

23 Slow Night Train to Prague

No one "at home" knew about my decision but it did not seem like the world came down crashing when they learned I was leaving. Packing up was easy, all my belongings fitted in a small suitcase and it was still half empty. One shirt, one pair of briefs/shorts, a pair of socks and a razor with a plastic handle, along with a brush and a few razor blades I had snagged somewhere in Germany. Also, a toothbrush and some toothpaste. I also packed my report cards, the reference letter from the Teplice Gymnasium professor, two slices of bread spread with margarine, and less than half an hour later I was at the train station. I did not have to wait long for the slow train to Ústí nad Labem, I had just enough time to buy my ticket and by late afternoon I was standing on the platform of the Ústí station, waiting for the Děčín–Prague train. I paid for my inexperience: after buying my ticket to Prague, I was told I could have bought a ticket in Teplice for the entire trip, as breaking it into two phases was more expensive. I had about twenty-five crowns plus some change in my pocket, but it did not matter... I had no idea if that was a lot or a little, likewise I did not know how far it was going to be from the railway station in Prague to the school in Pankrác and, naturally, I had no idea how to get there! I had plenty of time to ponder all this. The train was really slow, moving at a snail's pace from station to station, stopping at every one and in no rush to get to the next one. The engine also sounded like it needed the rest. I was almost alone in my rail car, my reverie interrupted only by the occasional traveler. It was cold outside, the calendar was showing October already, and night was falling. The heating was on inside the train, and I fell asleep after my eventful day in the pleasant warmth of the wagon.

I woke up to the touch of a hand in a coarse woolen glove. The conductor stood above me, telling me we had reached our destination. A passing glance outside the window showed a crowded train platform, with people rushing in all directions as well as small groups standing beside all types of luggage. When I raised my head higher, I saw the large, well-lit circular clock showing eleven p.m. Only when I stepped down to the platform could I see the large, dim sign: *Praha–Masarykovo nádraží* (Prague–Masaryk Station). This was history in the making – I stood for the first time on Prague's soil. For the next twenty years I did not leave it. During that period I grew strong roots. My longing for this beautiful and unique town grew deeper and stronger. This is where my "normal life" started. This is where my spiritual and physical transformation occurred. This is the place in which every important event that happened to me I will remember forever.

But I am getting ahead of myself. Here I am, now standing on the street in front of Masaryk Station. It is almost midnight. The street is deserted and I discover there are narrow islands on each side – tram stops. I have one piece of information: tram number 14 would take me to Pankrác. But in which direction? Do trams even operate this late in the evening? Do I have enough money left to buy a ticket? I am not going to write about that now, perhaps I will at some other time, when I write about other chapters of my life, more mundane chapters, about events that an average young Prague man would have experienced. With one difference: the first few years in Prague were full of the excitement and hard work needed for me to reach the level of that "average young man" in Prague.

Very briefly: high school graduation within two years (by 1947), the Faculty of Medicine at Charles University 1947–1953 and, before completion, marriage in 1952 at the Old City Hall to my Alizka, who heroically put up with me for 66 years. Two beautiful daughters followed: Ivana (1954) born at the Thomayer Hospital in Krč (a Prague district) and Zuzana (1960) born at the maternity hospital at Štvanice (that hospital no longer exists). She was also supposed to be born in Krč but, due to a quarantine that was in force there at the time, she could not be accepted and was almost born in a taxicab on the way to the Štvanice hospital. On December 1, 1953 I started working at the Pediatric Surgery department in Krč, first as a resident, then, as time went on, assistant to the head of the department and for a short time as deputy director of the Pediatric Ward. Further board certification exams (first degree) in surgery and board certification exams in pediatric surgery followed. In August 1965, a vacation in Bulgaria and on the way back, coming out of Yugoslavia, instead of heading for Hungary my little Fiat 600 changed direction, and after crisscrossing Bulgaria and Yugoslavia for a month we headed to Italy, and from Venice took the Israeli ship *Theodor Herzl* to the Promised Land. (As a consequence, in Czechoslovakia I was sentenced to one year in prison and my wife – who was the true initiator of the whole thing – only got eight months.) September 9, 1965 we docked in Haifa. On October 1, 1965, I started in the Meir Hospital in Kfar Saba (24 km north of Tel Aviv). Started from scratch as a resident, then went through board certifications again – in general and pediatric surgery. There were several long stays in England and the United States, then, beginning in 1977 I became Director of Pediatric Surgery within the Department of General Surgery. From 1987, pediatric surgery became an independent ward affiliated with the Medical Faculty of Tel Aviv University, where I became Senior Lecturer. I retired on July 1, 1992, at the age of 65, in accordance with the strict regulations governing heads of surgery departments. Today, I moonlight for small insurance co-operatives as a freelance pediatric surgeon, and I perform surgeries in private hospitals. I get paid by the insurance company. My Czechoslovak (later Czech!) citizenship was restored in 1990. I visit and stay in Prague often.

And now for the most important things: a grandson Jonathan (1992, Ivana's son) and two granddaughters – Nov (1989) and Maya (1993), Zuzana's daughters. They are the most beautiful in the world. Yes, I know, every grandfather and every grandmother say the same thing, but grandmas and grandpas...I don't know your grandkids; I do know mine...right?

24 You Speak my Soul, Mr. President

I am now about to close this chapter which consists of three periods: the time up to 1941, then 1941–1944 and finally 1944–1945. I have tried to write about the first two and will try to write about the next two, 1945–1965 and 1965 till the present, if circumstances allow and the muse favors me. But what about the missing period, from the spring of 1944 to the month of May, 1945? I will say it once more: I cannot write about that period...because I cannot. Instead of answering why, let me borrow the words of President Václav Havel, whom I greatly respect and admire. He spoke these words during the visit of the Israeli President Haim Herzog to Prague, in October 1991. I will quote the passage that clearly expresses that which I have been feeling for half a century: *"...whenever I come across Holocaust documents about concentration camps, about Hitler's mass annihilation of the Jews, about the race laws and the endless suffering of the Jewish nation during World War II, I feel a strange paralysis – I know I must say something, do something, reflect upon all of it somehow but at the same time I realize that any words of mine would be false, insufficient, incomplete, inaccurate and so I cannot but hold my words and remain silently uncomprehending. I know, of course, that one cannot remain silent, yet I am struck desperately dumb"*. I agree with Havel's every word, including the closing sentence of his speech: "One has to talk about the suffering of the Jewish nation in spite of this being hard." However, I am not capable of even that much:

The wound is too deep, and no word can heal it. Neither can time.

25 Retirement

I never really intended to write chronologically, to put together a kind of curriculum vitae, and so I can take the liberty of beginning this chapter by stating again that on July 1, 1992 I retired after a thirty-nine-year career as a pediatric surgeon.

Retirement did not catch me unprepared. Unlike other heads of departments, I never requested a six or twelve-month deferment "in order to..." This is where each one would write his or her reason for persuading even the most stubborn unbelieving boss to grant the requested deferment. An attentive reader would naturally understand that the requester, and only the requester alone, is the one person who is completely irreplaceable and without whom the department would not be able to function. I did not think that way about myself. Throughout my career as a pediatric surgeon, I never used the expression "I operated, I did it" but rather "we operated, we did it", and my cheeks turned red whenever I heard – at home or abroad – these kinds of expressions from other, supposedly "great" surgeons.

I feel a great amount of satisfaction having left a beautiful pediatric surgery ward behind. Due to the never-ending battles connected with building the facility and specialization that did not exist in Israel at the time of my arrival, I guess I did not make many friends and at first had no influential supporters among the decision makers in our profession. I simply was not a part of the clan. It was a tight clan of people who had attended school together, wielded a weapon in defense of the country together. I did not fight in any of their wars, I did not receive officer commissions like they did, nor did I serve in the reserve which in Israel means one month of active duty every year. I also was not able to remark casually at every opportunity "I saw this in New York, I operated in Boston, I lectured in San Francisco, I had lunch with John or Tom, or drinks in Los Angeles". I always had to chuckle because I remember that back in Prague, we used to say, "Keep your advice to yourself, man, you haven't been to Moscow". Here, in Israel, there was a new title: B.A. Not Bachelor of Arts, something much more important and precious: "Been to America"!

My God, I almost forgot about one detail – not the most important but something that definitely would have come in handy: Do you belong to the right political party? Back in the day, the party was *Mapai* (Israeli Labor Party) – which ruled all unions (including the General Union to which the hospital belonged), which would insure you, employ you and protect you. Although belonging to a political party did not influence anything, not even on whether I would or would not receive the necessary support for establishing the department of pediatric surgery, it would do no harm.

Well, my dear fellow citizens of the old motherland – does that remind you of something?

I have never been and am not now a member of any party. What are you going to do? I have been an immigrant, a refugee from an Iron Curtain country, meaning I had nowhere to go back to. I was made to feel that I had to be thankful to everyone (whom?) for even being here because... "would you have preferred Siberia?" Yes, that is how it was. Prague or Siberia was one and the same. The old generation who helped fight for Israel – incidentally with Czech weapons – did know the difference, and I do not mean just the geographical difference. But the younger generation has not matured enough to understand. Moreover, doctors burdened with a surplus of self-confidence and a feeling of invincibility, tried to get as big a piece of the action for themselves as they can. But let us leave it be.

It did not take long, and they understood that I had indeed brought something to the table, that I was someone who could contribute and that helped my confidence and determination. And all of this even before I became acquainted with the world's pediatric surgery departments.

As for the Prague–Siberia thing, after 1989 even the younger generation started discovering all the great and beautiful things that came from the old country. I frequently get stopped or called by those who have just visited Prague for the first time and ask my forgiveness for calling me a fibber when I first told them about my years in that city.

It is time to stop looking back and reminiscing about the difficulties faced by an immigrant. I will leave my grumbling aside – all's well that ends well, and all ended well thanks to my own efforts.

26 A Retiree

A large part of my easy transition into retirement was the fact I had prepared the ground years earlier. I tried being completely self-employed, but I was never able to learn the secrets and the tricks of working alone. I was simply never able to figure out what to charge people for an examination and for their surgery. I would start asking them about their profession and other details and I ended up coming up with an arbitrary sum, red in the face and ashamed that I even had to ask for remuneration. My fees were ridiculously small when compared with other surgeons. And so, not even having started a full freelance career, I found another solution. Private work but the patient did not pay. A few years prior to leaving the hospital, I had signed contracts with three small health insurance companies and based on those contracts, I became their consultant for pediatric surgery. Kids who needed surgery could be operated on in one of the very good small private hospitals, as these hospitals did not have their own insurance structures. The procedure for the patient was insured and the insurance company paid me as well as the hospital. This is officially called being an "independent surgeon".

This is how it worked in practice: I saw the child-patients in my office (in my case a specially designated part of our apartment with a tiny waiting room and toilet). I set the appointment time by phone – since the start of the computer era each patient got half an hour, which was longer than before. (No one was ever promised that working with computers would make things faster!) If surgery was indicated, I set the date and time right there and then. The necessary pre-op tests, usually a blood panel and urine, could be done in a local laboratory. Patients arrived about half an hour before the operation, on an empty stomach. During these 30 minutes, they were registered, examined by the anesthesiologist, and accompanied by one of the parents to the operating room. The parents left once their children were under anesthesia. Following surgery, the patients were taken to a recovery room and when they opened their eyes, the parents were there, so they never learnt the parents were not with them throughout the procedure. The patients went home after three or four hours. A week later, they came back to my office, we removed the dressings, and they could return to a normal routine. It should be added that during the post-op week the parents could pick up the phone and call me any time they felt they need advice or help.

Let me emphasize that I am talking about hernias or undescended testicles – the small stuff that can be dealt with quickly and discharged. For me it was easier this way because I have never underestimated even the smallest, simplest pediatric surgery. Even a seemingly very simple operation can get darn complicated when it comes to children, not to mention newborns and toddlers.

Let it be said: no one tells an independent surgeon not to perform complex operations if he / she so desires. These private hospitals are equipped to perform even the most complicated heart operations. They have perfect recovery wards, intensive care and comfortable patient rooms. All of that would not be covered by insurance companies though. These operations would be paid based on private patient contracts but even with discounts, hospitalization would always be substantially more expensive than in public hospitals. (The public hospitals would naturally accept all patients, including patients covered by small insurance companies, and they would pay all expenses, no matter whether the hospital was public, state or city operated. The one disadvantage for patients in a public hospital was that they could not choose the surgeon even though they were fully covered and taken care of under the terms of their insurance.) The advantage for independent surgeons like myself, who had the same type of contract, was a decent addition to my pension, the fact that I could continue "moonlighting" and last but not least, that I was permitted to work till the age of 75, assuming I was physically and mentally able to hold the scalpel in a steady hand.

My activity those days could be characterized as a modest dessert after a rich and filling main course. And the main course lasted 39 years. Twelve years in the Thomayer Hospital in Krč (Prague) and 27 years in the Meir Hospital. (No relation to the former Prime Minister of Israel, Golda Meir. The hospital is named after Dr. Josef Meir, a former functionary of a trade-union-owned health insurance company. It opened in 1956 as a hospital for tuberculosis.) The name of the facility today is Sapir Medical Center, and it is a part of the Tel Aviv University Faculty of Medicine. I need to add almost ten years of post-hospital activity to this resume: altogether 44 years with a scalpel in my hand. During this time, I performed about 16 thousand pediatric surgeries. Of that number, about 13 thousand performed solely by me and the rest, in the last ten years at the hospital, performed by surgeons who studied under me – in my presence, in cases of big operations such as premature babies and newborns.

I started compiling an exact statistic only after I started working as a pediatric surgeon within the auspices of the adult surgery department I had the ostentatious title "Assistant Director of Adult Surgery with Pediatric Board certification". In other words, I worked full time, with a full slate of regular surgery and on top of that, receiving no additional salary, I performed all the pediatric surgery cases. That was on January 1, 1973, seven years after disembarking in Haifa. Until June 30, 1992 (the date of my retirement, remember?) the number totaled 11,974 operations. I would estimate about 1,800 till the 1973 date, about 2,000 in Prague between 1953–1965 (under Dr. Štol in the hospital in Krč, no one did much operating apart from him!). I could add a not negligible number of surgeries during various study trips to the UK and the United States, plus a solid number for the above-mentioned insurance companies and a few privately. I am not including all the various operations I performed on adults before pediatric surgery started functioning independently. I coached three doctors who passed first and second board certification exams and I established a department recognized by the Science Council and the Tel-Aviv University – a department that started literally from nothing and took major battles to get going... All of that contributed to the fact that I could retire completely satisfied with my career, and that is the reason for writing about it in detail.

Surgical staff, Meir Hospital, Kfar-Saba, 1968. I am on the left.

27 Thomayer Hospital in Prague-Krč

My medical career began with a "distribution committee" of the Medical Faculty of Charles University deciding (or recommending?) that after receiving my Diploma of General Medicine on November 27, 1953, I should begin employment as resident in the Department of Pediatric Surgery and Orthopedics at the Thomayer Hospital in Prague-Krč commencing December 1, 1953. The hospital is named after Josef Thomayer, Professor of Internal Medicine.

I had a wee bit of knowledge in orthopedics due to some study during my eleventh semester. Pediatric surgeries were few in number, as was the custom then. The same situation existed at Prof. Hněvkovský's clinic – where the boss of my first workplace had come from. Add my own special interest in surgery that I had cultivated during the last semesters at university, especially pediatric surgery, and hours spent even outside of my official internship at the 2nd Surgery Clinic of the University Hospital, and I was incredibly happy on that December day when the head nurse handed me a brand-new white coat. The lining of the collar sported red embroidery, sewn in by some nurse just for me: *Antonín Moťovič, MD.*

The head of the ward was Dr. Josef Štol, a better singer of folk song, especially Slovak ones, than a teacher. Nevertheless, he was an able pediatric surgeon and orthopedist. He was also a good businessman which was highly unusual in those days. Apparently, his conscience was clear, as was that of his wife, Dr. Olga Štolová. She was the head of the Department for the Care of Mothers and Children at the Ministry of Health. The Minister was one Dr. H.C. Monsignor Josef Plojhar (the "H.C." signifies an honorary doctorate) who had been excommunicated from the Catholic church and who had gradually dropped the "HC" and insisted on signing and being addressed as "Dr". Plojhar was the head of the People's Party within the framework of a national coalition.

Aside from Štol, the physicians' staff consisted of three women. Within a short time one of them, Irena Kraftová and her husband Mirek became good friends of mine, along with Mirek's parents who lived in Nusle (a Prague district). Our friendship outlasted Irena's time on the ward. Mirek was a great guy and a great friend. He became disabled following a spine operation and made his living as a translator of technical literature from English to Czech. There is a very warm and special place in my heart for the Kraft family and I want to dedicate a whole chapter to these beautiful, rare people.

28 The Krafts

Back in those days, there was an acute shortage of accommodation and young couples squeezed into their parents' apartments. Irena had been lucky enough to snag a room at the hospital. The room was in Pavilion G2, on the second floor. The department of pediatric surgery and orthopedics was on the ground floor. The neighboring room was reserved for the surgeon on call and consequently, I was their neighbor ten or twelve days a month. Their apartment problem was solved, and I had gained, as it turned out, close and faithful friends. We shared the bathroom facilities for years, even after Irena left the surgical ward and got a job working on a rehab ward for kids with polio. After many years, they were assigned an apartment in a project in Pankrác. Their building was famous for having no chimney – some forgetful architect had omitted it from his blueprint which had the positive effect of saving on material and the builders were thus able to fulfill their socialist commitment. In those days buildings were built from what was designated "public money". There was no problem tearing down a part of the building, adding the chimney and the whole affair was hushed up. The big pooh-bahs wanted to keep things on the down low. Publicizing this sort of business in, say, *Večerní Praha* (Prague's evening newspaper) could have had the adverse effect of undermining people's "socialist enthusiasm" for new construction. In a normal world, someone would have paid dearly – literally – for a similar screw-up but back then it was all done on the sly, no one publicly admitting anything, and it became a subject of sarcastic mirth and jokes of the denizens of Prague...naturally behind closed doors and windows.

Local parents would take their kids there, as if going to a local fair, instead of going to the real one, Matthew's Fair in Dejvice (Prague district) on the well-known Big Circle (a Prague roundabout intersection), later the location of the Technical College with dorms and a commissary. And so, my dear Krafts had to wait another year to move, and I had the pleasure of their company for that much longer.

I would like to dedicate the next few lines to Mirek. I regret it is going to be a requiem for this beautiful man. Believe me, I am not writing this out some sense of duty, as expressed in the Latin *De mortuis nil nisi bene* (nothing but good words about the dead). I cannot remember now who had given me the bad news that Mirek had been killed in an automobile accident (possible in the *Poběda* – a Soviet car I knew of?). And I do not even know when in the years between 1965–1989 it happened, as we had no contact during those years. I am terribly sorry that I have not been able to find Irena during my frequent visits to Prague. There are many Krafts in the phone book but not a single Irena or David (their son's name). I did find a Daniel Kraft in the book, but he denied any connection to David Kraft or knowing someone called Dr. Irena Kraft. Not even mutual friends, for example Dr. Marie Šlégrova, could add anything.

Returning to Mirek while he was alive, living in a one room apartment on the second floor of Pavilion G2, a closed unit which included my on-call room. One room only but homey and cozy. Two L-shaped couches on one side, a table, and chairs in a corner, Mirek's "office" in the other corner – a small desk with a typewriter, a chair, and scattered all across the floor and the couch various Czech-English and English-Czech dictionaries, piles of typewritten pages in both Czech and English and on the side, stacked sheets of blank paper. Lording over his kingdom, Mirek's burly figure and smiling face, always wearing flannel trainer pants and a sleeveless T shirt in the summer, a bulky sweater in the winter. On the couch, there was Irena, deep into reading something, or possibly cooking something on the small gas stove in the hallway. Night shifts back then were not too strenuous. We received acute cases once a week and once every third weekend (the other days were covered by Professor Václav Kafka's clinic in the Children's Hospital, or the pediatric surgery clinic in the Bulovka hospital located in the Northern suburb of Prague of the same name). From my room next door, I could hear when the clacking of the typewriter would stop, and simultaneously I would hear the shuffle of Mirek's threadbare slippers on the floor, a door of their toilet opening and the toilet flushing. It was a sign that Mirek's post-surgery back still gave him trouble, magnified by constant sitting and that it needed a rest. That meant sitting down with a cup of fragrant black coffee or a tasty bite cooked on the above-mentioned hallway cooker. In such moments, even an on-call doctor from a different department would sometimes show up, and not a few non-hospital friends too.

Those discussions...politics was the main topic. Talking politics between four walls was called "anti-state talk". You could say it there and you buried it there. Those were the most interesting evenings I have ever experienced and many tidbits, many pieces of information have stayed with me and still form the source of my overall knowledge. Let me say this: that small group was a bottomless source of information, knowledge, and intelligence. I include Karel whose skirt-chasing stories were also told with intellectual flair. Those stories served to neutralize the danger of becoming too snobbish. Sometimes there was silence, mainly after the arrival of Dr. Václav Holub to our ward and his inclusion in our circle. I will speak of this later. We became very friendly with Mirek's mother who lived alone in a typical Prague apartment on Jaromírova Street, close to the railway line on the way to the Nusle bridge. We would often sit at her place, sipping tasty coffee and eating great Czech home-made cake. Mirek: those trips up to your cottage in the mountains, with a small lake nearby...I cannot recall the location...but I remember them clearly. I want you to know, up there where you are now, that Alizka and I are so terribly sorry we did not find you alive after renewing our Prague connection. We wanted to tell you these words in person. I want you to know, you were one of our closest friends and no one could ever replace you in our hearts. There is one specific story that illustrates your noble-mindedness and fidelity to me and my family, and which demonstrates your humanity and that of your family. My family has not forgotten and will never forget. We remember often and I would like the following words to be my eulogy for a friend and a real man.

29 "The Hungarian Events" of 1956

It was October 1956, and a revolution/counter-revolution (delete the unnecessary) was raging in Hungary. The anti-Semitic, progressive, and class-aware press and radio was shedding tears because the first victims of the counter-revolution, led by imperialists and their Zionist lackeys, were "citizens of Jewish origin". That is approximately what the twisted logic sounded like: a Zionist lackey pitched against a citizen of Jewish origin! People are stupid and they swallow it. Even during calm times, Jews were shunned, and it was perfectly fine to write any kind of bunk about those Zionist cosmopolitans. The more shameless the lie, the bolder the headline and the higher the esteem for the ideological maturity of the writer or speaker. It made the writer more acceptable with improved prospects for his or her professional future. It was generally known that this soil enabled the growth of the vilest anti-Semitism in Czechoslovakia, the worst kind among all the countries with Marxist-Leninist regimes. Not long ago when I was rhapsodizing about the old country to someone, he pointed out to me that the only court to sentence Jews to death while highlighting their Jewishness, all under strict Party and government instructions, was a Czechoslovak court. No other progressive or democratic socialist country had done that. This was a country that with Masaryk democratic tradition allowed you to correspond with people anywhere in the world, including the most despicable dictatorships, but absolutely not with your brother in Israel if you harbored any ambition for career growth and professional advancement. I speak here from my own experience and perhaps I will mention it again later. One cannot really be surprised. Whole generations were brought up in the spirit of the

Illustrated Encyclopedic Dictionary (published in 1980, by Academia, the main publisher for the Czechoslovak encyclopedia). Here is what I found on page 969: "*Israel – history...the state was established based on a UN resolution...the power in the Jewish country was seized by the bourgeoisie* (my comment: they must have brought their millions from the concentration camps) *which, aided by international imperialism (USA, Great Britain) and Zionism...etc.*" One more nugget: "*Israel prevented the creation of an Arab state by an act of aggression*".

Well, it was possible to bamboozle a younger reader, but the older ones knew the truth. The Arabs did not accept the UN resolution, they banded together to attack Israel, and Israel, thanks to a supply of weapons from Czechoslovakia, won the war. You gentlemen, who put these lies and fabrications in the encyclopedia, did you receive academic recognition for knowingly making up and distorting facts? I know the standards of Czech intellectuals and I do not believe you did it in the interests of ideology. You never imagined that someone outside of Czechoslovakia would one day read your calumny and would feel sorry for you!

Let us get back to Mirek and to Hungarian events. The end justifies the means and if some ideologue imagined that persecuting Jews would be useful, why not take advantage of it. To be perfectly honest, the news was broadcast during the night by the BBC and by the Radio Free Europe and Mirek, a faithful listener to both stations, heard it with his own ears. And because fear or hope (again, choose the one that fits better) had begun to spread, intimating that the tsunami of revolution/counter-revolution would soon roll across the Hungarian border into Czechoslovakia, Mirek, you, too began to fear for our safety, and along with Irena and your mother you decided to take preventive measures. We learned of this a few minutes later. First, we heard the doorbell in the cold, dark autumn night. That alone was frightening enough at that time of night, in those latitudes. At the time we had an apartment in Smíchov (a Prague district), on Janáček Quay. Soon we heard your friendly voice, Mirek, and soon saw your stout presence and we calmed down. We were not too surprised since our relationship was informal, and it was not all that unusual to just show up. We were always welcome in each other's houses and a sudden visit was common. Still, a visit that late at night was something out of the ordinary and we soon learned what a great, true friend stood before us. You were the messenger for the whole Kraft family and in its name, you came to tell us of your decision. You told us, Mirek, that the events in Hungary could have repercussions in our country and that, according to Radio Free Europe, there were already signs of disturbances in Slovakia. Apparently, the West feared that Jews might again be the first victims. As you were telling us this, you pulled two keys out of your leather jacket and gave them to us: "Here are the keys for the building gate and the apartment of my mother. She lives close to you. At the first hint of danger, grab Alizka and Ivana (Zuzana had not been born yet) without delay and get yourselves to my mom's place. You'll be safe there!" I see your serious face before me as I write. At the time, I realized that what you were saying could really come about. I knew that before me stood a real man, the truest of friends and when I close my eyes forever, it will be with that thought in my mind. Mirek, I am certain that your eternal rest is easy because of that show of kindness!

Here is an epilogue to this chapter: no revolution/counter-revolution came to Czechoslovakia. Soviet tanks that had rolled through Čop and Čierná pri Čope (now the Čierná nad Tisou, border crossing between Soviet Union and Czechoslovakia) on their way to Budapest were rehearsing for a similar crossing through the very same towns twelve years later. How vain were our hopes that the West would show – even without a full-out war – what it meant by "fighting for freedom and democracy in Europe"! It was clear that small nations were but pawns in the superpower games, as evidenced by Helsinki (*the Helsinki accord of 1975*). By that point, Western Europe was already stuffing its gullet from its horn of plenty and the average person there knew nothing of us, the "eastern barbarians". This fit the playbook of our "Party and Government", of course. No one in Western Europe cared a fig about what was happening in their backyard. It is absurd: at the end of the 80's and the beginning of the 90's, Eastern European countries fell into their laps without the least effort. This was "the devil's luck", if I may borrow again a title of the short story by my friend Ladislav Grosman. It happened without anybody having an inkling of what was about to come down, even a few months prior to the events.

I was talking about Krč – but I had to write what I just did, I had to repay that debt. I was at the spot where I began the long journey as a fresh young resident and ended it thirty-nine years later as the head of the department of pediatric surgery on the other side of the world.

30 Pediatric Surgery Ward

The pediatric surgery ward was opened about a year and a half before my arrival – apparently in a great hurry because shoddy workmanship was obvious everywhere. Consequently, even though the department was of a decent standard for the time, there was the quirk of transporting the children to the operating room in the small pavilion G4 which was about 50 meters away from the actual ward. No matter what the weather – summer, winter, rain, snow or baking sun. Infants and toddlers up to two years old had to be carried over from the gynecology and maternity ward, pavilion U, about 200 meters away! (Our older daughter Ivana was born there!) This was the premature infants' lot too, although most of those were treated in the Children's Hospital which was much better equipped and where the pediatric surgery was headed by Kafka, then Tošovský, then Kafka again. Another important section of the hospital, the out-patient department, was in pavilion K, in the basement, about halfway between us and the above-mentioned U.

Along with the outpatient department, pavilion K also contained a small X-ray lab. The only task of this X-ray lab was taking pictures of the hip joints of 3 to 4-month-old infants. It must be said: only Chief Physician Štol understood congenital hip dislocations; none of us – new residents – could even come near it. That is what the chief physician intended, and this is how he understood his role as leader and educator.

I remember two images vividly: The orderly, approximately seventy-year-old Mr. Josef Tůma – a well-liked character on whose shoulders lay the whole weight of our scattered ward. He carried kids to the operating room, to the out-patient department or X-rays, carrying various materials from one place to another and on and on. Another image I can still see in my mind's eye is a small group of two or three doctors walking uphill from the ward to the out-patient building, bundled up in winter overcoats.

Surgical staff in Krč Hospital, Prague. From the left me, Dr. Štol, Dr. Zdeněk Gottwald, Dr. Fany Dittrich

31 Head Nurse Horká

Head nurse Anežka Horká was a dominant personage on the ward. She was about fifty years old, single and, as was common, living in pavilion K. The department head just called her Horká. As mentioned, she had arrived at the ward with Štol from Hněvkovský's clinic and the relationship between the two defied description. To him, she was just "Horká" and she served him as a watchdog, protector, sister and mother. It is quite awkward for me to deal with the subject of this very complicated and distinctive individual. She was a very fine nurse who would not let almost any other nurse near her.

The head nurse excelled at anesthetic techniques for children of all ages using the Schimmelbusch mask for chinoform and the Ombredanne inhaler for ether. We tested the depth of anesthesia by the state of the pupils or the color of blood – an operation could proceed when the blood was pronounced as dark. She would remove the inhaler, let the child breathe a few breaths of the operating room air and simply say "You can continue". In 1955, when I had been at the ward a little over a year, Professor Knobloch, the chief physician of general surgery in Bulovka hospital (famous for a textbook on surgery and coincidentally a neighbor – we lived in the same building on the Janaček Quay) told me that his clinic had just obtained the new Chirana anesthesia machine. (Chirana was the Czechoslovak manufacturer of medical equipment.) The anesthetic was delivered in a closed cyclical system with a precise dosage of ether, nitrous oxide, and oxygen. They had a special machine for children with a smaller "dead zone", in other words narrower tubes and who knows what else. He invited me to his clinic for tutorials and even suggested I could ride with him on days when he was going to his clinic (rather than to the university or government offices).

The next morning, I told the boss about this and what do you know – apparently the very same machine had been sitting, unwrapped, down in the basement with Mr. Tůma! It turned out that nurse Horká had manipulated the situation so that the machine was never used. Nurses were permitted to operate dangerous and difficult to control machinery,

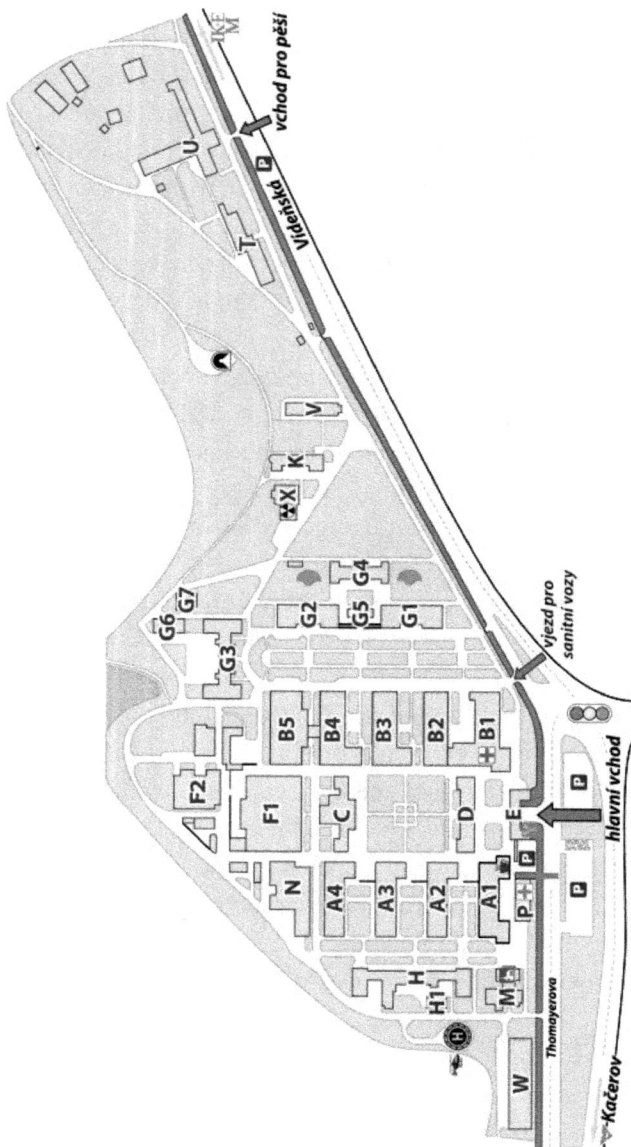

Map of Thomayer University Hospital. Not much has changed since I was there.
(Source: ftn.cz.)

delivering open anesthesia, yet were not permitted to work with a safe machine that enabled precise dosing of narcotics and oxygen! There was no one in the department who knew how to work with it (here it must be stated that the institute for specialized anesthesiology was still in its very initial stages and anesthesia was delivered by well trained nurses or residents – all of it, as mentioned, via the open mask method).

And so, I started visiting Bulovka hospital and came back with rudimentary but sufficient knowledge of the new machine and I was able to divulge its secrets to the other residents on the ward. Unknowingly and surely not on purpose – but I caused the dismissal of the head nurse from her essential operating room duties. She either could not or did not want to go back to her original duty as head nurse for the ward or scrub nurse. She occasionally assisted the head physician with some more complicated operations but the shadow of her "displacement" hung over our relationship, and it was never the same again.

Let it be stated here that I started working four days after graduation, with some basic theoretical knowledge. The few stitches or applying a cast under strict supervision during my internship and days spent at the 2nd Surgical Clinic of the University Hospital had not made me a surgeon. I knew how to scrub, put on my sterile surgical gown and comport myself in the operating room, but gaining some basic knowledge and experience, even as only the third assistant, was difficult. Head physician Josef Štol was in no hurry to initiate anyone into the secrets of surgery, not even residents older than myself. And so, I was left doing night shifts during which I had to stitch up wounds, prepare a cast or examine a child with a belly ache or a twisted hernia. We were assisted in this by our night shift operating room nurses but the main person there was nurse Horká. Pavilion K also housed our outpatient department, as I have said, and nurse Horká would usually come down from her apartment to each acute case and help me treat the child. I still lack words to express my gratitude to that somewhat bitter woman who always handed me the required instrument with quiet virtuosity so that the parents would not even notice. Everything she handed me she did in a way that clearly demonstrated how to handle it and use it, and practically guided my hand as I was stitching or performing any other task. I can declare here that it was she who taught me the most basic technique and I have never forgotten it. She did the same during emergency operations, such as appendectomies – she simply guided my hand. I was truly sorry when our relationship started deteriorating following the anesthesia machine fiasco. It got progressively worse between us even after I was no longer dependent on her help, and I never stopped being grateful and always thanking her for the assistance she had provided when I was learning my first surgical baby steps. Her help had been crucial, mostly because our boss might have been a nice man and a good surgeon, but he certainly was no teacher to any of us new doctors. Relations between me and nurse Horká got so bad that I would hear rumors about her telling other nurses not to be too cordial with "that Jew". I am sure it was not anti-Semitism. We knew each other well and respected each other but something had happened to her, something perhaps besides the events I have described. I have never learned what it was. She eventually left to become head nurse on a different ward and if it was because of me, even if unintentionally and unknowingly, I am sorry about it till this day. She was a good woman and a great nurse, and I am sure that had our collaboration continued to the days when I was assistant head of the ward and for a time assistant of the chief surgeon, we would have worked very well together. Well, it is too late to fix today, no matter what the cause of it all was.

Everybody on the ward made my beginning fairly easy. The only disadvantage was the frequent night shifts, but I have concluded that those were actually very useful for a young surgeon: you had to make instant, on-the-spot decisions. Everything was a learning experience: distinguishing between occasions when I could act on my own and ones where I had to call in an older, more experienced colleague. One could learn from his actions, his decisions, when to start additional, more complex tests and auxiliary examinations and when to use his accumulated experience and instincts and get the child to the theater without delay. If you had a good "senior", an on-call older doctor, and if you were able and ready to learn – those were the great teaching moments. You learned even if the decision was to admit the child for observation because then you could utilize all the laboratory and other advanced tests (the most advanced and modern test we had then was the x-ray...no ultrasound, CAT scans, MRI or the newest advances in nuclear medicine). And if you were prepared to learn from the very beginning, to fully dedicate your life to this difficult, physically and mentally exhausting profession, and if you were lucky enough and the elder surgeon was aware of his mission to teach and raise a new generation of doctors – you have won the battle!

As an aside – I see it as my duty to state that during my twelve years on the ward I never encountered a single anti-Semitic remark or any expression of anti-Semitism. I was glad to go back and visit once it became possible in 1989.

32 Chief Physician Štol

Chief Physician Štol, director of the pediatric ward, should have been just such a man but let me state here and now – he was not, not by a long shot. I have heard that things did not change after my departure. If I am to describe the character of this highly intelligent, cultured and mostly amiable Moravian Slovak, I need to do so from two points of view. As a person – easy to take. During our small ward parties, he was jovial, witty, fatherly and he just loved a good glass of wine which made him burst into song. He loved to sing the folk songs of Moravia and Slovakia, as well as Czech ones – mostly the sorrowful, melancholy ones. I can hear his *Oh, it's gone now, it's gone, Fly away, falcon, Good night, my love* ...the sound of sad taverns, ticking clocks, falling hearths (references to a famous Czech folk songs), dancing girls. His heart-felt *Oh my boy, my little boy, how you plowed the field* is hard to forget. He also knew how to use his mellifluous voice to sing whole arias from *Rusalka* and *The Bartered Bride*. He had tremendous fun when he sang *When you go back to your maidens, you'll have become a smelly force* (from Act II of Rusalka). We always corrected him "you'll have become a deadly force" (*deadly* and *smelly* sound very similar in Czech) but he would have none of it and say, "My force is smelly"! This used to happen when he was in a mood, after bolting from his family nest on London Street in Vinohrady.

Today I can reveal the secret. It happened frequently that before going home, he would inquire which doctor was staying on-call for the night shift. When the doctor was someone willing to co-operate, he asked to be telephoned at home that night and informed that a serious case had been admitted and it was imperative for him to see the child and decide on treatment. The situation would get complicated when Mrs. Štol picked up the phone. She immediately announced that "daddy" was not home, and she started interrogating the caller – what child, what is wrong with it. She was not trying to show off her detailed pediatric medical knowledge but rather decide whether to let "daddy" make the trek from Vinohrady to Krč. The medical details of the case were not necessarily the issue. Now and again, it would happen that the call was indeed necessary at which point you would be spending long minutes on the phone explaining to the chief's wife why he must see the child. Occasionally, she only "released" the chief after I threatened to send the child to Kafka's pediatric surgery clinic because I was not able to judge the seriousness of the case and the chief was not available. Suddenly "daddy" was home and about thirty minutes later his car (first *Škoda MB 1000*, later an *Octavia*) would pull up.

An awkward situation was created when he would show up accompanied by his wife, who was also a physician as I have stated before. When the call was genuine, there was no problem. However, if the call was fake, agreed upon before the boss had gone home for the night, and there was no emergency to treat, things got complicated. Nothing was left to chance. We had always been briefed about just this type of situation and there was no room for improvising. If there was a difficult case already on the ward, then that was the reason. Or there had been a call from an ambulance which was waiting for our decision and when it did not come, they took the child to the Children's Hospital. However, most nights, the chief came alone, almost always in a foul mood that he was not too good at covering. He would open a bottle of wine and only calmed down after a good few long gulps. His improved spirit was immediately evident as he burst into song – classical and folk music filled the ward. Our next assignment was to call his house and say that there were delays in the operating theater and therefore he was going to stay overnight and sleep in his office. In these circumstances, we were told not to get into a discussion, just state the facts and hang up. I must say, in those situations his demeanor was collegial, with no bossy affectations.

That should be enough to describe Štol the person, in rough outline. However, he was the head of our department and therefore it was not the social life of the ward but rather the professional running of it that was his main responsibility. The job parameters of a ward or department director are the same the world over. The job consists of three parts: clinical work, scientific work, and pedagogic work. Pediatric surgery and orthopedics in the Thomayer Hospital in Krč was new and its exact charter unclear when I began working there. It was clear that from the clinical point of view, it could have been a good ward but the main job, surgery, rested on the shoulders of one man. Almost without exception, the Chief Physician performed all surgeries by himself. The other doctors either administered anesthesia or were the designated "hook holders". I guess from a teaching point of view, this was supposed to be our theoretical training as future pediatric surgeons or students. But there were no students there at the time – those came much later. We were already qualified physicians and I do not recall a single seminar, a single lecture or even a single discussion of a case. This changed in later years but that is how things ran when I arrived. I also do not remember being asked to participate in a conference, seminar, or congress outside the ward, not to mention any kind of professional conference outside of Prague or abroad ("abroad" would have been only in other "progressive democratic people's republics"). Only one person participated in such outings: Chief Physician Štol. There was a period when there was talk of meetings dedicated to overviews of professional literature. It started nicely: each doctor was supposed to follow a specific journal. *Aspects of Surgery, Acta Chirurgica Orthopaedica, The Czech Physician Newsletter* or *Family Physician*. And yes, we had one foreign journal...a Russian one: *Khirurgiya*. And again, if I remember, it was all just on paper and only because we, the residents, demanded it.

A newcomer to the department was František (Fany) Dittrich. A pleasant, honest man and a true intellectual, I liked him a lot. I felt bad later, when I was assistant director and it fell to me to tell him that he was not suited for pediatric surgery. He had deep theoretical knowledge, but surgery is also a craft, and it was felt that Fany was simply not equipped to handle the practical side of our profession. He then devoted most of his time to anesthesia.

The main event of that period – I am talking about the second half of the 1950's – was the arrival of a man who became my mentor in pediatric surgery, and the knowledge he imparted to me is with me till this very day. I kept learning and deepening my proficiency and know-how during the following forty years but the basics that he imbued in me, those basics form the pillars of my expertise throughout my career. I dare say, it was not just pediatric surgery – his influence and effect on my development in a much wider sense was invaluable. His name was Václav Holub and I feel it my duty to dedicate a chapter to him.

33 Pavilion B4

As I said before, the situation in building G2 which housed our patient ward, was truly unbearable. To reach the out-patient department, pavilion V, one had to walk a distance of 300 meters across parkland. Trying to reach the operating theater, Mr. Tůma had to carry stretchers with kids on them to pavilion K. The theater in that building was bare bones only, with no post-op facilities. Right after surgery, the child, still anesthetized, was carried back to the patient ward by Mr. Tůma. Naturally, we had no access to an intensive care unit. And that is how it continued in all seasons, in the rain, the snow and the scorching sun, day and night, weekdays and holidays. I can see it before my eyes now: the elderly Mr. Josef Tůma pushing a cart with one hand, the other hand clutching a tiny human, swaddled in hospital blankets. Mr. Tůma was probably praying for the child not to wake up prematurely and roll down the asphalt into a puddle or snowbank.

What saved our ward was the retreat of tuberculosis. In those days this was a deadly disease and was treated in various buildings within the complex. With its retreat, these buildings subsequently became available for other use. B4 was the home of surgery specializing in tuberculosis. Streptomycin, PAS and Nicotibin were already widely available at the time and so large thorax procedures and bone tuberculosis were almost diseases of the past. So now, with pavilion B4 vacant, three birds were killed with one stone, and a few baby birds too. Pediatric surgery got one half of the second floor; urology got the other half. The whole first floor would be occupied by general (adult) surgery and the ground floor would be home to out-patient clinics for all three departments, X-ray labs and, mainly, operating theaters. Those were the baby birds.

The big move also occasioned personnel changes that affected everyone. Václav Holub from my department became the assistant chief of the general surgery. Holub's departure meant that I became assistant to the Chief Physician. That was 1959. I had finished my surgical board certification (first degree) two year prior and was beginning preparations for board certification exams which I took in 1962. The pediatric surgery team was slowly coming together. Us "old ones", Fany Dittrich and I, were joined several doctors of whom Helena Hájková, the future head of the department and senior lecturer, comes to my mind. That was the team at the time of my departure.

34 Václav Holub, MD

I need to return to pavilion G2 where my pediatric surgery career began. As I said, this was not thanks to the efforts of the Chief. I will take it upon me to declare that Dr. Štol did not teach anybody anything – not in theory and not in practice. The surgeries were performed exclusively by him. We held the hooks, administered anesthesia and counted ourselves really lucky if he let one of his assistants "close up". To be even more precise, I do not remember being present for any of the "bigger" operations. In the field of pediatric surgery, we dealt mostly with inguinal and umbilical hernias – the former ones usually in older kids, not in toddlers or newborns (which fact I only learned after leaving Czechoslovakia). Similarly, after my departure I learned that in most cases it is useless to operate on umbilical hernias. We also did undescended testicle.

So, keep in mind – our work conditions would have been completely unthinkable in the West, even back then...but of course we could not know that! We surgeons were basically craftsmen, handymen. The most important things, pre-op preparation and post-op care, were treated as if they had nothing to do with us. And let me tell you: God knows I felt this once I left Czechoslovakia and was attempting to restart my career in pediatric surgery. As you can see, all the doctors on the ward had the roles of extras or, in a best-case scenario, hook holders. The concept of an "assistant" in pediatric surgery was not applicable. I am not even talking about run-of-the-mill stuff like a seminar, a discussion about a diagnosis, bedside manner, the surgery itself and post-op treatment of difficult operations, discussing what professional literature had to say about this or that congenital defect – none of that took place. Congenital malformations are especially exciting for surgeons, and I do not recall any of those. The problems that were my daily bread in the next 27 years of my career, had never even surfaced back during my twelve years in Krč. If it were not for my theoretical knowledge from my student years and from cramming my board certification exams textbooks, I would probably not even be aware of these malformations. Was all of pediatric surgery just hernias, appendicitis and fractures? It was probably enough for Štol – yet all the good stuff, the stuff that makes pediatric surgery the most beautiful medical discipline in the world, all that was done at the other two pediatric surgery wards in Prague.

I still feel that Chief Physician Štol was not really all that interested in pediatric surgery. Orthopedics was his hobby horse and so the bulk of our operations were hip joint dislocations, equinovarus deformities, Achilles tendon lengthening and after-effects of polio, prior to compulsory inoculation against this insidious disease. In our hospital, in pavilion G3, there was still a polio rehab ward. One reason I knew this activity was closer to his heart than regular pediatric surgery was this: after board certification exams were introduced in the 50's I had to decide in which direction I would continue. I selected pediatric surgery over orthopedics against his will and recommendation. He was quite disappointed and demonstrated it by his obvious dislike, while allowing me to assist with his orthopedic work. I was under no illusion that Štol would see the light and suddenly smack his head and say, "I must teach these people, or they will shame the department on their board certification exams". Nothing changed, and both pediatric surgery and orthopedics continued as before.

Still, a change did occur in 1956, after Štol left as a member of a commission to assist rebuilding North Korea, decimated in the recent war. Apparently, this mission was organized by Dr. Olga Štolová and that was why the Chief Physician flew over there as a doctor. Luckily for us, it was for a longer period. Even though I was the oldest, having graduated three years earlier, the list of my operations comprised of just two. I had to admit I had not grown into the function of deputy chief and no one, including myself, wanted me nominated. A new man came to our ward: an experienced surgeon who was a colleague of Professor Kafka at his pediatric surgery clinic. This man was Václav Holub, MD.

One day a skinny, long stick of a man appeared in G2, thin pale face and long straight hair masking a bald spot. Perhaps Holub most resembled some bohemian, a musician or a tragic hero on a theater stage, an artist, a painter or a sculptor. He was a man of few words but when he did say a sentence or two, he always ended it with "that's right, isn't it"? But what a surgeon he was! In his hand, the scalpel moved like a bow in the hands of a violin virtuoso. He held tweezers and scissors in his hand with the lightness and elegance of an artist. Whether he was sitting, standing, operating, or examining a sick child – always with the same panache. And let me say – a teacher! From the very first day, under the patient guidance of Dr. Holub, all surgery was performed by us, the residents. I was his first choice since I was the oldest in that young crowd but also because he took a liking to me. Not to be immodest about it, he recognized my potential to become a pediatric surgeon in the future.

I keep saying "Dr. Holub". Our usual way of address was using first names or calling each other "colleague" (except for the chief) – but he did not play that game. Holub was always "Dr. Holub" for everyone and conversely, he also used the proper title with all of us. Only later, when we became close friends, we used last names with each other, without the title. He was folksy, friendly and without affectations, as evidenced by the fact that he spent his free moments with us, ward doctors, and not in his office of Chief Physician. He would spend some of his on-call evenings in the Krafts' apartment, still in pavilion G2, even after Irena Kraftová had left the ward. We would discuss the issues of the day over a glass of wine, we would discuss articles we had read in professional periodicals And because he maintained relations with Kafka's clinic, he was able to open doors to real pediatric surgery. I realized later that when it came to quality of work, the clinic did not need to suffer an inferiority complex even when compared with the best and most famous surgical institutions in Sheffield, Liverpool, Chicago, and Los Angeles which I visited and worked at later in life.

It was Dr. Holub who enabled me to get closer to Professor Václav Kafka (not related to the more famous Franz!) and his wife Emilia. There came a point during "Holub's time" when at domestic conferences – which we had begun to attend (and after I had left Czechoslovakia at international meetings) – Kafka would introduce me as "my younger friend".

As time went on, my relationship with Holub grew and we were no longer just teacher and pupil. He became head of the pediatric surgery department after Chief Physician Štol retired. Unfortunately, Holub died in 1976.

ČESKÁ
PEDIATRICKO-CHIRURGICKÁ
SPOLEČNOST

Kafkova medaile je nejvyšší vyznamenání ČPCHS, kterou jsou odměňováni lékaři, kteří se významně podíleli na rozvoji ČPCHS. Zahraničním lékařům je udílena v případě dlouhodobých kontaktů a významné pomoci českým dětským chirurgům.

- 1998 - John J. Corkery, MB,FRCS – Velká Británie
- 1998 - MUDr. Antonín Moťovič - Izrael
- 1998 - prof. MUDr. Josef Koutecký, DrSc.

In 1998 I received the Kafka Medal, the highest decoration of the Czech Society for Pediatric Surgery, given to physicians who made significant contribution to advancing this field of surgery.

35 Helena Hájková, MD

I have left Helena for the end of my Krč chapter mainly because she represents a little bit of continuity between me and pediatric surgery at the Krč hospital. And here is why: she was there when I left and when I came back twenty-five years later, she was a senior lecturer and the director of "my" ward. Sadly, she passed away in 2001, by then she was a professor of pediatric surgery.

In 1963 I was the assistant Chief Physician when she first appeared on the ward, having spent some time in gynecology following her graduation. She was young, intelligent, pretty, and obviously well trained and prepared for a successful career in pediatric surgery. Štol was the king of the ward at the time. I will say it once more: still unchanged...no matter what he did, he was everything but a teacher. Nevertheless, at that time, Holub's influence was already deeply felt, I had been there a whole decade and due to Holub's impact I was no longer reliant on Štol, nor were the new and young doctors any longer vulnerable to the Chief's whims. Perhaps it is not unseemly to say that I was already able to share my not negligible knowledge and expertise with others. And Helena was the hardest working, best educated, with a high degree of dexterity, as well as being the most pleasant. All of these were reasons for making her my favorite co-worker and I tried to impart some of my experience and know-how to her. It was not long, perhaps a year or two, before I knew my hunch was correct. She was trustworthy. Before leaving for my "vacation" at the beginning of August 1965, I took all the negatives of photographs I kept on the ward, along with a list of all my operations and handed them to her for safekeeping. ("You're not planning to come back, are you", she said, and I pretended not to hear, since her remark could be fraught with danger.) Doing what she did could have had serious repercussions. She told me later that she had given all the negatives and the surgery book to Dutch colleagues visiting Czechoslovakia, for them to send to me when they got back home to Holland. Unfortunately, they were searched at the border and the negatives were found but they somehow managed to salvage them, get them safely to Holland and send them to me. I never got the surgery book. Imagine what would have happened if the Dutch doctors had divulged who had given them those dangerous espionage documents and who they were intended for...

Once in the 70's, during a celebratory dinner at the annual conference of the British Pediatric Surgeons Association, I found myself at a table with a group of Dutch surgeons. We proceeded to introduce each other, looking at our lapel name tags – nothing out of the ordinary about it. The only thing is, when someone is from Israel, there is always the inevitable follow-up question of "where are you originally from?" I would always reply proudly "From Czechoslovakia". In those years, the response was usually something like "Ah, Dubček!" This time it was different. One guy's eyes lit up: "I was in Prague last week. I travel there often. I have good friends there – maybe you know them...the lady is also a pediatric surgeon." I interrupted him and said instinctively: "Her name is Dr. Hájková" "Yes!" he answered, and the rest of the night we talked of nothing but Prague and Hájková. And so, I learned that Hájková had guested at his clinic during her preparation for board exams. They had become good friends and he traveled to Prague frequently and would be there again the following month. I scribbled a few words on a napkin for him to give to Helena and told the Dutchman about the photo negatives and the surgery book. You know the rest...

36 I betrayed my Homeland that I Loved

I was a person who had betrayed his socialist homeland. In the judicial language of the district court for Prague 10, on January 28, 1966: *"The accused, Dr. Antonín Moťovič and Alice Moťovičová have been found guilty of dwelling abroad without permission of Czechoslovak authorities since August 31, 1965. To this aim, they misused vacation travel to Bulgaria and have remained abroad without an appropriate permit. Their act therefore constitutes the criminal act of illegally leaving the Republic and they are hereby sentenced to imprisonment. The accused Dr. Antonín Moťovič for a duration of 12 months and the accused Alice Moťovičová for a duration of 8 months. Under paragraph...the court orders confiscation of all their property..."* I never knew whether I should have been happy, bitter or sad that *"both shall serve their sentence in a correctional institution, level one..."*

That was reason enough not to even try to get a visa to visit our homeland and mainly Prague, for which my longing was almost pathological. And my sin was even more enormous. I had brought my family to Israel, a country that my old homeland boycotted. Diplomatic relations were cut in 1967 even though in Israel, a whole generation of the 1940's had nothing but supreme praise for the military aid Czechoslovakia had given to the Jewish state after it was attacked by all the Arab countries. Its creation was based on a 1947 UN resolution that divided Palestine into two parts: one for the Jews, one for the Arabs. The Arabs rejected the resolution, attacked the newly created state which emerged victorious thanks to armaments obtained from Czechoslovakia. The Palestinian refugee problem was a consequence of this war. I still do not understand why Czechoslovakia became the country most hostile to Israel, more so even than the Soviet Union. The fact is that all the socialist countries cut their diplomatic relations with Israel after its Six Day War victory over its neighbors Egypt, Syria and Jordan – all countries armed by the Soviet Union and to a large degree by Czechoslovakia as well. The *casus bel'i* for the war was the Egyptian blockade and expulsion of UN troops that were tasked with maintaining the ceasefire between Israel and its neighbors. The occupied territories problem dates back to that time. I still do not quite get why it was only Czechoslovakia that was hermetically closed to any Israeli passport holder. That was not the case with the USSR and the other socialist countries. There were a few exceptions: functionaries of both Communist parties (yes, Israel had two such parties, both represented in the Parliament) were welcome in Prague where they traveled to study Marxist wisdom. Or they went to luxuriate and recuperate in the spa of Karlovy Vary after their demanding political work. Many of the visitors were Arab students (they were not yet called Palestinians in those days). The students were sent out by the local Communist Party to study at various universities there. (Who financed all of that? What do I care?!) However, scientists or artists from Israel could not travel to Czechoslovakia unless they traveled on a third country passport but those were few and far between.

As an example, let me mention my daughter Ivana. When she was a university student, she moonlighted as a flight attendant for the Israeli airline, El Al. The crew would sometimes spend the night in Vienna and occasionally, when time permitted, they would rent a car and drive around the beautiful Austrian countryside. On one such trip they found themselves not far from the Czechoslovakian border, a hop and a skip from Bratislava. The more experienced members of the crew knew that one could spend a pleasant, inexpensive night there with good food and excellent wine. Ivana's blood ran cold when she saw the signage of her country of birth, but she soon woke up from the dream that almost became reality. A dour looking guard told them to get out of their van and barked: "Papers and passports on top of the vehicle" (no "please"). The uptight guard overheard Ivana translating his words to the others, demonstrating the meaning of the poet Mayakovski's verses *"The Poem of the Soviet passport"*. He stepped up to Ivana: "You speak Slovak?" he roared and literally yanked her passport from her hand. Oh boy! He held the passport, glanced at it, and saw she had been born in Prague. His arm began circling as if he were holding a red-hot iron, his mouth foaming. He started screaming that she could not enter the Czechoslovak Socialist Republic with that passport, ordered an about face and told them to beat it and return to Austria. He then calmed down a bit and looked at all the other passports. One was American, one British and one South African. Those folks were told they could enter the country but since Ivana and two others were Israeli passport holders, they all said thank you very much and gladly turned around and drove back to Vienna.

For years, I was obsessed with the thought of returning. I am sure I was the object of ridicule for many people, and maybe there were some who had me pegged as an agent of the communist regime because I constantly talked about Prague. My apartment was saturated with everything Czech: records, photographs, pictures, books, calendars – everything that found its way into our place was Czech. It affected my little daughters. Here is a small example: I happened to find a small hammer in a hardware store. The hammer had a "Made in Czechoslovakia" sticker on it. I am not sure

I needed a hammer, but the sticker was enough for me to buy it. I brought it home and one of my daughters, not sure if it were Ivana or Zuzana, asked quite seriously whether it would go into the "art objects" display cabinet which contained all manner of bric-a-brac. In short, at home and outside of the home, we never stopped speaking Czech with ex-pat friends, we ate and lived Czech and we dreamed in Czech. And of course, I collared anyone I could to tell them everything I could, and there was no shortage of listeners at that time. Mostly those who had left the Czechoslovakia during the first wave at the end of the 1930's, and the second wave who came directly from liberated concentration camps in 1945 or between 1948–1949.

No difference was made between someone born in the Czech lands, in Moravia, Slovakia or Subcarpathian Ruthenia. And there were many people whose eyes misted up when they heard the word Czechoslovakia. Those were the folks who were sucked into the vortex of combat immediately after arriving in Israel. They may have come legally or illegally but as soon as the new state was declared they had to defend their country with their bare hands against the attacking Arab hordes who had refused the UN partition. Their hands were bare...until weapons from Czechoslovakia arrived! *Haganah* units (a military organization, predecessor to the Israel Defense Force) had been trained in Czechoslovakia, as were pilots. Airplanes were supplied by Czechoslovakia to the newly created state as well. There was no child and no adult who would have forgotten, that if it had not been for the assistance and the supply of armaments from Czechoslovakia, Israel would have been swiftly decimated by the vastly more numerous Arab armies. All politicians and public figures reiterated this fact at every opportunity, starting with Ben Gurion through to Ezer Weizmann (a retired air force general and president of Israel when I wrote these lines): the Israeli Air Force was formed in Czechoslovakia back in 1948. When my daughter Ivana started her compulsory military service in 1972, she was issued, like all the other recruits a rifle marked ČS – Made in Czechoslovakia.

There were plenty of willing listeners to my stories about Czechoslovakia and Prague, and the storyteller himself was enthusiastic and often uncritical. After the Czechoslovak "Velvet Revolution", the country opened to everybody, including Israeli tourists. It started slowly but the stream became stronger and more powerful, and today (the year 2000) it is almost impossible to run into anyone who has not been to Prague. It is almost a daily occurrence: parents come into my office with their child and gawk at the large black and white photographs of Prague on my walls. Then they exclaim: "Look, Prague!" and proceed to tell me it is the most beautiful city they have ever seen, though I am sad to hear their experience was spoiled by the rudeness of salespeople, waiters, and taxi drivers. I usually say nothing, but I know the truth is on their side. But I did not want to write about that. I wanted to write about the folks who had to listen to me for years rhapsodize about Prague and for whom I became a guide/instructor prior to their first trip there. I would spread out a map and advise them where to visit, what to see, what to take in and what to avoid. They would leave with precise hand-drawn maps (if I had no access to printed ones), detailed walking tour routes and an initiation into the culture, art, architecture and transportation (the metro!). These folk could then concentrate on all these things instead of the waiters, taxi drivers and salespeople.

37 Fast Forward a Quarter of a Century

Almost a quarter of a century had elapsed from the moment I left the country till the summer of 1989 when I appeared there again, in a quasi-illegal manner. Anyone who knew me had to realize that I surely would not be able to depart this mortal coil without seeing Prague once again.

And so, it happened that one day a travel agency reached out to me to tell me that they were organizing a tour to Czechoslovakia after a thirty-year hiatus. I told them that both my wife and I had been sentenced in absentia to a one-year jail term for our illegal departure and so did not see a tour as a realistic proposal. The agency said that my wife and I would be the perfect foil to find out whether the Czech authorities were in fact serious when they claimed they would grant visas to everybody on the agency's list. These would not be individual visas in each person's passport but rather a group visa for everyone on the list, as was the custom then. We were also told that the other people in the group did not know about a contract that the travel agencies on both sides were party to: if anyone on the list got crossed out, the whole tour would be canceled.

A few days later we were notified we had not been crossed out – the tour was on! It would be futile to try and describe our happiness and excitement: our dream was about to become a reality. We were dead set on going, despite the objections of our daughters, pressure from friends and silly jokes like "we'll send you packages to prison". Some people advised consulting the Israeli Ministry of Foreign Affairs or the security apparatus, but I had no connection to either. And so, I came up with the idea of informing our hospital security guy. He probably did not even have an idea where Czechoslovakia was on the map, much less about its political situation or the status of a convicted fugitive. But he promised me he would inform people in "certain places" about the matter. Not long afterwards, perhaps a week, the nice man called me with some very confused information. No one could restrain me from travelling to any country I wished, other than countries officially deemed hostile by the government (in our case, the Arab countries). There was no law impeding my travel to Eastern Europe but if I did, it would be at my own risk. Since the incident of the body of an employee of JOINT (Jewish relief organization based in New York, established after World War II to help repatriate concentration camp survivors) having been pulled out of the Vltava River, Czechoslovakia was not considered a safe country for Israeli citizens. The Party and the government, the press, radio, television were explicitly hostile, diplomatic relations had been severed 22 years previously (in 1967) and there was no one in any official capacity who would help you out in a crisis. There had been some signs of a thaw, mostly in the sports arena – the Davis cup had been played in Hradec

Králové, soccer players from the Sparta Prague played a game in Israel ("my" Sparta: they came for dinner in our house when they were in Israel). The game was a part of the Intertoto Cup competition and only happened after international pressure by various sports organizations had been brought to bear. To sum up, the hospital security guy said, if you go – you are on your own!

Things kept moving forward. After a while, the travel agency informed us that although the Czech authorities had not crossed anyone off the list, final decisions would only be made in Vienna. That is where we were supposed to pick up our group visas. In other words, we were going to Vienna not having seen a single Czechoslovak document. The "everyone or no-one rule" still applied and the other members of the group had gotten wind of my wife and I being the potential spoilers who could cause the whole trip to end in Vienna. They concluded it would have been our fault if folks in their seventies and eighties, who had been waiting for perhaps fifty years to visit the homeland for perhaps the last and only time, would have their trip called off! Most of them had left the country in the late 1930's, to save their lives.

From the moment our plane took off from Tel Aviv on its way to Vienna, the tension was palpable. It was two-fold: some were tense at the thought of the dreamed-of return to their distant, happy and tragic past, but some were tense because they feared that dream could vanish into thin air within hours. I did not know any of the people on the plane but looking at their faces, overhearing snippets of their conversation with their seatmates (some knew each other, some did not) affected me greatly. I began thinking about whether I had the moral, or any other right to ruin the dream that was now an imminent reality. None of them made the journey to search for property or for money. They wanted to see the place of their birth and where they went to school, to see whether the school was still there, to see their childhood home. That is where their brothers and sisters were born. That is where uncles and aunties – and even more importantly, grandmas and grandpas – had come to visit, bearing sweets and pastries and gifts. Maybe they would still find an old classmate, a boyfriend, a girlfriend. Maybe they would be able to find a tombstone in the Strašnice cemetery – a tombstone of one of their grandparents or great grandparents, who did not end up like so many others – without a tangible sign they had ever even lived.

As a result of these thoughts, I concluded that we, who were younger than the others and perhaps had more time to wait for real changes in Czechoslovakia, should not be the cause of these folks' bitter disappointment. (Who in the world could have possibly known that real, incredible change – the Velvet Revolution – was around the corner and would come about in a mere three months?) Shortly before landing in Vienna, I went up to the guide and explained my thoughts to him. The plane landed and we agreed to be patient. In about an hour we would be in our hotel where we were to meet representatives of *Slovturist* (the Slovak state travel company) and all would become clear. We had mixed feelings, fear, and hope, as we watched our guide negotiating in the hotel lobby. As they shook hands, it turned out that the man speaking with our guide was actually the organizer of the whole tour...not directly (after all we were from Israel) but through an Austrian intermediary. A large, thick envelope changed hands. Our guide took it to a side table, opened it, pored over the list, stamps, letters, documents, and inspected the travel plans. He glanced at the group standing by the reception desk, getting our room keys and gave us a conspiratorial wink. Done deal! We celebrated in hushed voices, but my wife and I still had some doubt left in our hearts. We were still not at the actual border crossing. The border guard in his green uniform had not yet looked at the list. He had not yet checked his list of persons convicted of illegal departure.

38 In Prague Again

I write terribly slowly. We are now in the year 2001, it is August, we are in Prague again. I have bought myself a computer and I am writing these lines here, not in faraway Israel. This is how I have imagined it for all those years: I would like to talk about my first return to Prague after twenty-five years (as well as my first arrival in Prague in 1945), WHILE ACTUALLY IN PRAGUE. It had been possible – and will be possible – to write the about other events far away from here.

Our tour in the summer of 1989 started with three days in Vienna. The days were spent doing all the normal tourist stuff, running from one tourist spot to another, whether we had seen the sight before or whether it was the first visit to the Austrian capital. We took part in only a few excursions. For one thing, Alizka had left Israel with a cold which she was still nursing but also because in our thoughts we were already on the way to Prague and in Prague itself. And still uncertain. We left a friend's phone number with our daughters back home, "just in case", but let's face it: what friends? There was only one. The one and only Sťopka (plenty more about him later). In our hand luggage we carried a photocopy of the verdict which contained an important sentence that might help in a hairy situation. The sentence said that we left the country illegally not because of a "hostile attitude to our socialist homeland" but due to our desire to reunite with our family in Israel. The verdict also mentions that we had sought official permission to emigrate which had been denied. Another important document we carried was our amnesty certificate. The amnesty was conferred on us during the Dubček era, and no one had ever told us if it was still valid after that era had ended. Be we took it with us.

We sailed from Vienna to Bratislava on a steamboat which was a good thing because as we sailed along, I had no idea whether we were already in Czechoslovak territory, and so my pulse remained within the normal range. It quickened a little when I saw the steamship port and above it a sign in large letters: BRATISLAVA. I would be fabricating if I tried to describe my feelings at that moment. My mind was somewhat dull. Everything seemed fast and unreal, it all took just a few minutes and we got through passport control without any inquiries or questions. In a matter of minutes we stood on the sidewalk outside the main harbor building and we got onto a waiting bus. Everything was going smoothly and only my quickened heartbeat and fleeting sideways glances were proof that something important had just happened. And it was not a dream. This was reality. We were back in Czechoslovakia and after a day's stay, we would head to Prague, the main, the most important, the only destination of our long-dreamed-of journey.

39 The Journey from Bratislava to Prague

Our one day and one night in Bratislava passed relatively quietly. The tension was almost gone – we would now reach Prague come what may. If we went to prison, we could comfort ourselves with the thought that we were in Prague and I would see the city, even if just through the tiny windows of a green paddy wagon or through the bars of my jail cell…Forgive me, not jail, "correctional institution". Was I exaggerating? Who knew? I had no idea what the situation on the ground was. Something must have changed during those twenty-five years – for the better? Or for the worse? I believed – because I wanted to believe – that the country and mostly the city that I lovingly carried in my heart all those years, would not punish its insubordinate stepson.

Those were the thoughts that were running through my head in the first moments after getting on the bus. From that point on, I had no time for anything: my eyes were fixed on the country we were passing through, the fields, the well-known names of towns and villages. I did not want to miss a single centimeter and so I sat in the front seat of the bus to peer through the large wind shield. Each sign with the name of each town and, more importantly, each road sign telling us how many more kilometers separated us from our dream destination… I needed to take a photograph of everything! The way I acted was contagious: the driver would slow down before every decent size town and when necessary, he would even stop the bus. And so it happened that when we were about to enter the city of Prague, he pulled over to the shoulder of the road, stopped, and let me get off and photograph the most important sign, the one that said:

THE CAPITAL CITY OF PRAGUE

And now, standing in front of this magic sign, I cast my mind back 44 years. I return to the day in the autumn of 1945, when I left you, dear reader, outside of the Masaryk railway station... I was standing there, with my small military rucksack on my back, containing all my worldly possessions and one piece of information about the number 14 streetcar route that ran from the train station to Pankrác, to my gymnasium and boarding school. It was late in the evening, I left the poorly lit arrivals hall and found myself in an even worse lit square in front of the station (let us remember the war had just recently ended). Not a soul in the streets, a cold autumn night and in those first moments I had no idea how and where to go. I assumed that, at that hour, the streetcars would arrive after long intervals, if at all, not to mention I did not have money for the fare anyway. I saw the tracks, the safety dividers – called islands – for alighting the tram, and I decided to just walk along the tracks...but in which direction? The streets were empty. Now and again a car would zoom by and a few garbage trucks, like the ones I had seen in Teplice. No one noticed the scrawny young man standing on the streetcar safety island. Why would they? There must have been hundreds like me in right after the war!

I started to explore my surroundings and noticed that at the end of each safety island there was an iron post, painted faded yellow and red. On top of the post there was a light bulb emitting a weak light. Directly under the bulb there were a few round plates, one of them bearing the number "14" in blue. There were about six such plates in two vertical rows and each of the rows had an arrow attached to it. The row that contained the number "14" had an arrow pointed to the right. There were tracks on Hybernská Street, where I stood but the streetcars did not make a turn into it from Masaryk Station. I had noticed that when I left the station. Even in the gloom I was able to read a sentence or two and my innate intelligence told me those were the names of stops: Václavské náměstí (Wenceslas Square), Myslíkova, Karlovo náměstí (Charles Square), Moran and a few others...and then I saw the word "Pankrác" (there was another word, maybe "square" or "court"). That was my direction and I started walking.

I walked about 200 meters and suddenly saw the tracks splitting, veering both right and left. I remembered the arrow that pointed to the right under the number "14" and so I relied on instinct and marched alongside some tower (later I learned its name: Jindřišská), I walked past what I thought was another safety island. I saw no signage, on my right-hand side there was a well-lit imposing building – the main post office – and about fifty meters further a stop with a plate that said: Václavské náměstí...I looked at the other names and realized I was walking in the right direction. I had heard about Wenceslas Square; I knew it was a famous spot and bingo! Right on the corner I saw a red and white street sign "Jindřišská ulice" and on the other corner "Václavske náměstí". And there I was! The tracks kept running straight, I saw a sign for "Vodičkova ulice" and I kept walking for about 15 minutes more, then stopped, uncertain how to continue. On the left I saw a splendid looking grand building, obviously a court edifice. The street opposite was Myslíkova. On the left, something like a square and, indeed, the sign said Karlovo náměstí (*Charles square*). But which way would route 14 go? Would it turn right into Myslíkova or continue straight onto Charles Square? Once again, I remembered the iron post and the round plates and arrows, and I continued straight ahead with some certainty. At the next streetcar stop I double checked the plates and the arrows and numbers and they confirmed I was walking in the right direction – straight ahead, not left into Ječná street (though of course at the time I did not know the names of all the streets or where they led). It was a short walk to reach Moran Station but I did not find a plate or a number there. I made my first error. I followed the tracks to the right and walked for 10 minutes (more tracks intertwining!) – now there were tracks leading in all directions but no round plate with the number "14" in sight. What a strange twist of fate!

Not far from this bridge, called Palacký bridge, though on the other side of the river, I had an apartment a few years later, where I lived with my family, on Janaček Quay. This time I had no choice: I had to turn back and when I reached Moran, I made a right turn. I walked through the whole Nusle valley without further complications. I made one more mistake later and instead of heading to Pankrác, I started marching toward Michle at an intersection that led to Vršovice. On my way, I met the first person I had seen all night. He seemed a little inebriated but was able to tell me that the direction I was going was not going to take me to Pankrác. He instructed me to turn around, walk about a hundred meters and continue straight following a gentle turn in the road. There would be a large courthouse on my left-hand side. I would continue uphill where I would reach the tram stop "Na Paloučku". I did as he said and soon I saw Courthouse Square, with the majestic building of the Supreme Court on my left. A well-lit streetcar was passing the building, followed by two others in quick succession and one of them had a large sign on its side: "*Vozovna Pankrác*" (Pankrác Depot). That is what I was looking for! A uniformed man got on to the leading tram and sat in the driver's seat. Three other guys in identical uniforms and carrying satchels got on the remaining trams. In a day or two I knew they were the guys who sold, checked, and punched your tickets: the conductors.

As the tram bell sounded and the man with the satchel hopped on the slowly departing streetcar, I managed to ask where May 5th Street was. That was my final destination. His outstretched arm and pointed finger showed me the way. A few more minutes walking in the dark and I saw the street sign. At that point I must have fainted. Or perhaps I took a little nap on a park bench. I awoke to the sounds of passing streetcars, their squealing brakes. My bench was about 50 meters away from a large square; figures emerged from the dark and hurried past me to the tram stop and an older lady who was in no hurry showed me the rest of the way. It took about seventy or eighty more meters of walking and I stood in front of a large schoolhouse. Atop its wide entrance – still locked – there was an old sign in Czech and Russian: "Russian Gymnasium". It took me a second to see a newer sign to the right of the entrance. It bore the state emblem of the Soviet Union and it said in both languages again: "Soviet High School in Prague". It is hard to describe how awkward and confused I felt seeing this sign. But after the past few weeks and the unforgettable night spent walking, I just did not care. I just wanted to be able to sit down, lay my head down somewhere and get some liquid into my mouth and if the liquid were to be hot, it would most definitely be paradise on earth.

Around the corner from the schoolhouse, I saw the new name of the street: November 1st Street! A few steps away there was another entrance to a building somewhat lower than the school itself but evidently a part of it. The sign above it said, "Boarding School". Dawn began to break, and a new day was beginning. One chapter of my life was closing and a new one was about to open. I was eighteen-and-a-half, and this was surely a milestone in my life. The decisive chapter was about to unfold there, at that point, at that moment.

40 Nikolaj Nikolayevich Dreyer

Much as I would love to, today, after more than half a century, I am not able to describe the events of my first day in Prague. I did not know what time it was (how could I? I had no watch!) when I stood in front of the glass doors that led into the school and into warmth. I thought it was too early to enter, or maybe it was just a lack of confidence, the feeling of being lost, maybe I had lost my nerve... Whatever it was, I decided to wait a bit longer. Like I had on the bench previously, here too, I collapsed from hunger and exhaustion right on the concrete steps. I had emptied my bag of broken or sharp-edged items such as my plastic shaver, my toothpaste and toothbrush and I put the bag under my butt to temper the feeling of cold concrete. It did not help much. The cold was unbearable and so I stood up and put all my worldly goods back into my little bag (it was a knapsack I got somewhere after my liberation from the camp) and I began pacing, walking around the whole complex until I felt the boarding school was starting to come to life.

My index finger touched the bell and hesitatingly, with a pounding heart, I pressed it. I heard the short and muffled ring echoing through the hall inside and soon I saw someone behind the glass door. They put their key in the lock, opened the door and the sweet warm air from the inside almost caused me to pass out. The man introduced himself as Mr.

Petrunčík. He and his wife were the janitors, cleaners, maintenance people and cooks. Very nice people! Their ground floor apartment became a refuge – not just for a friendly chat with good people, but also a place where one could circumvent various rules, regulations and prohibitions the school put in place. One could take a puff on a cigarette or have a splash of wine. A key or two to the boarding school entrance could be found there for those sneaky late-night arrivals. The Petrunčíks, possibly with the quiet assent of the principal, concluded that we were not children. After all, many of us had gone through concentration camps, the Red Army or Svoboda's Army – in general, young people who had lost a lot of time during the war and some of us were somewhat old for the grade we were in. In addition: the after-war period was simply laxer.

My Teplice Gymnasium professor had done his homework and had prepared the ground for me, so I did not need to explain too much. Still, just one look at me, gaunt and at the brink of exhaustion after the previous night and Mr. Petrunčík clasped his hands, took my knapsack, and held my arm gently. For a moment I thought he was going to lift me up. He took me to an airy dining hall with a few rows of long tables and simple chairs. He sat me down close to a large opening in the wall through which you could see the kitchen. The warm air in the dining hall and the hot, beautiful, sweet tea and the freshly baked cheese pastry...bliss! Never before and never since have I tasted anything so divine.

While I was eating, Mr. Petrunčík sat across from me. Mrs. Petrunčíkova managed to emerge from the kitchen during those few minutes and kept offering "One more pastry, perhaps? A little more tea?" And every time she came out, she would put down baskets full of fresh rolls and slices of bread, as well as small cubes of butter and margarine on the kitchen window counter. She also brought out steaming glass jugs from which wafted the delicious smell of chicory. Voices were heard throughout the building, bearing witness to the school waking up to the new day. Two girls and two boys showed up in the dining hall and started distributing the jugs and plates to all the tables. They were students on dining hall duty that day. When I finally raised my head from the empty plate and cup, I saw a thin man standing beside me and I felt his hand on my shoulder. He did not say a word, but Mr. Petrunčík spoke and introduced the gentleman who stood next to me. I stood up to meet the boarding schoolboys' schoolmaster. The girls had their own schoolmistress. Right after his first sentence it was clear that I had been expected and they already had some information about me. The dining hall started filling up and the master asked me to follow him to his office. He sat me down on a modest, comfortable sofa and began asking questions in a fatherly tone, trying to ascertain things that the Teplice Gymnasium had not been able to tell him. He sketched out the schedule for the day but at seven thirty I first had to have my all-important interview with the principal. That is all the master said. But whilst I had been eating Mr. Petrunčik had told me a little more about the new female principal who had just been hired a few days prior and apparently was nothing like the mild and empathetic Mr. Dreyer... "well, you'll see...I wish you good luck!"

There was no direct hallway connecting the boarding school with the schoolhouse, so I had to exit the building and enter the school from the outside. I was accompanied by Nikolaj Nikolayevich. He handed me over to the secretary. At exactly seven thirty, the principal's door opened and there appeared in the doorframe a plump, middle-aged *baryshnya* (a Russian matron of a certain age and weight), tidily and elegantly dressed but with a look so unpleasant and piercingly cold, it made me feel nauseous. I guess I was not much to look at, either. I was tired, sleepy and had had no time to even wash my face. When she asked me to step in, I felt like doing an about-face and galloping away from that cold, unpleasant spot. She sat down behind a large, luxurious looking desk and immersed herself in reading my file – a single hand-written page. I was standing there, watching her expressions and at a certain point I saw a grimace and a movement, as if she was struck by lightning. She lay the paper down. I saw her lips move but could not hear a word coming out of her mouth (was she even speaking at all? Or were her lips just twitching?). Her cold eyes were fixed somewhere in the middle distance, certainly not on me, and the words came out of her mouth: "So you were born in Subcarpathian Ukraine?" Without thinking and without realizing the impact of my words I answered: "I was born in Khust, Subcarpathian Ruthenia which, at the time of my birth, was Czechoslovakia."

To this day I see her fuming face, intermittently pale and red, and to this day I can hear the awkward silence in that large, beautiful room. She left without saying a word and while I heard muffled words from next door where the secretary was sitting, I realized what I had done and cursed myself – you idiot, you nitwit, you blockhead, proud of being born in Czechoslovakia but in her eyes, you fool, in the eyes of that patriotic woman you are a traitor, an emigrant who had fled and never returned in 1945 to what was now the Soviet Union. That was not the kind of paradise you wanted to live in. I heard the receiver being set down and the principal, Miss Nyekludovskaya returned to the office. Without looking directly at me, her narrow, vicious eyes stared at some undetermined spot again and she asked me, in a somewhat calmer voice: "What is your citizenship, your parents' citizenship and where do your parents live?" "I don't have a father. He perished at the age of 45 in a concentration camp. My mother lives in Teplice with her sister, whose husband is a soldier in the Czechoslovak Army, and he has fought in Svoboda's Army. My father was a Czechoslovak citizen, as is my mother and myself." A moment of silence. Another departure from the room to the adjoining office, a lengthy discussion and after her return she graced me with another question – actually, a statement: "You were a student in the seventh grade at the Teplice Gymnasium, in other words you had one more year to graduation. Here, you will start the ninth grade, which is the penultimate year in our school. The tenth grade here is the last one." (I learned much later that the school was not permitted to turn down any Czechoslovak citizen who was qualified to study in Czech schools. It was 1945, Czechoslovakia was again a democracy, it was still two and a half years prior to the "Victorious February"). In order not to have to write any more about this nasty person, let me just say that for the next two years, all the way to my graduation, she never looked me in the eye directly. I had the impression when I saw her in the hallways, that she tried to avoid me at all costs – she made sure I was not able to even say "Hello", so she would not be forced to greet me back. I never saw her smile at anyone else either.

41 St'opka

A dream, a challenge – my stubbornness, my purposefulness? I was not aware of any of that as I left the principal's office accepted as a ninth-grade student (*septima* equivalent). From that moment on I only had one goal in my mind and that was to leave the school after two years with a gymnasium (high school) diploma in my pocket. That was my one and only goal – despite the Germans' plans from a short time ago. If those plans had succeeded, I would not be alive!

First, I had to see to my extracurricular duties, let us call them the red tape procedures. I was informed of this by Mr. Dreyer, who was waiting for me outside the secretary's office. A great man! He really wanted me to be accepted and he was pacing the hall outside while I was sweating bullets on the inside. He wanted to hear the good news immediately. His only question was – had I also been accepted into the boarding school? I told him I did not know because I never asked about it, but my answers "in there" made it clear that I had no other home. He nodded his head and his kind, fatherly smile signaled "everything will be alright". But as we walked back to the boarding school, I learned it was not all that simple. For everything "to be alright", there were several tasks to be taken care of. Police registration was the first thing – but to get that, one needed a de-registration from one's last domicile and I did not know whether I had ever been registered in Teplice. Indeed, where had I been registered in the last few years? I had documents clearly indicating that my most recent domiciles had been Auschwitz, Mauthausen and Ebensee and we all know that one typical German characteristic is, as the Good Soldier Švejk says "there must be order!" And so there was registration, but it would have no validity here because we were nameless, our only registration being a number. My next task: food stamps. You could not get those if you did not have a police registration certificate, plus they wanted to know for how long my food stamps were valid. I also needed medical clearance. I cannot remember what else was required but the most crucial demand was naming the person who would be financially responsible for my stay at the boarding school. I could find a way to solve all the other problems, but I had no idea how to tackle the financial question. This was the first time in my life that I had to deal with it. I could not even answer where I would be living during school holidays while the boarding school was not operating. The other students considered this weird and funny. They did not have to worry about such humdrum problems like a warm winter coat, proper clothing – I had none of that and winter was around the corner. They had parents and homes. I was alone. Completely alone in a city and in circumstances that found me completely unprepared – inexperienced in basic life questions.

I cannot remember how long it took me to start living like any other student. However, I remember where the first help came from. The memory has often been refreshed by long reminiscences – recalling and reconstructing events that began unfolding from my first day at the boarding school, from the moment Nikolaj Nikolayevich showed me my bed in the dorm and my spot in the study hall. One spot to lay my tired bones to rest at night, one spot to do my homework and, "if God willed it", where I would be getting ready for my final exams the following year. In both spots, my neighbor would be a blue-eyed blond boy – a nice-looking lad my age. What he said about me is that "one day, there appeared next to him this emaciated, silent, 90-pound *muselmann* (a skeletal camp survivor)". Both of us swear, even today, after more than five decades, that the chemical reaction was immediate. Right from the start, there was some kind of glue that bonded us from the fall of 1945 till this very day in 2001. Separate fates, different regimes, separate continents – nothing could divide us physically or spiritually, despite the fact we only saw each other twice between 1965 and 1989 – once in Switzerland and once in Hungary. We never stopped corresponding, even though it occasionally became more sporadic. Our letters' journeys were often twisting and tortuous – through Yugoslavia, France and who knows where? Every year on New Year's Eve we could hear each other's voice, starting in the 1970's when it became possible to direct-dial from Israel. We assumed that bugging these direct lines by "interested parties" was a bit more complicated, but mostly we knew these said parties would be more inclined to celebrate the New Year than try to stop two old friends talking and sending each other good wishes. Maybe even this cautiousness was not needed. HE always mentioned in all his "political vetting questionnaires" the friend abroad with whom he kept up correspondence

That man answered to the name ŠŤOPKA. His full name was Vyacheslav Stepanov. He was half a year younger than me, born in Kosoř and his home was in Radotín, a village near Prague. He lived with his parents – his mother a Czech, his father a Russian émigré, a Don Cossack. Šťopka was the only kid. From the day I met him and for years to come, his family became my family, and his home became my home. More so, because shortly after my departure for Prague, my family literally married my mother off to a man who was anything but a fitting replacement for my father! And Šťopka? He became my brother, and he remains one till this day.

I have mentioned all the steps I needed to take, to be accepted into the boarding school. Well, now I had a brother by my side, someone well versed in the workings of local bureaucracy. He immediately sensed my confusion and helplessness, and, without a word, he began traipsing around various offices with me: police registration, food stamps. He helped me get my city travel card; he came with me to the State Office for War Victims (I think that was the approximate name of that office) and the financing of my boarding school got arranged fairly smoothly through that very office. He helped me draft telegrams to Teplice to obtain my police de-registration from that city; he helped me get my citizenship certificate and a certificate of membership in the Prague Jewish community. That was important, as it had been pointed out to me that I would be eligible for financial aid through it. (I am ashamed to say that they proved much more difficult and their bureaucracy harder to navigate than the other government institutions I mentioned. It was the Jewish community that demanded the strictest proof of my internment in concentration camps and my status as an orphan. Had I not had a letter of confirmation from Teplice, I guess I would have had to drop my pants before those arrogant self-important matrons and nabobs, to prove I was a co-religionist!) I was able to organize a grant from JOINT and was given some used clothing as well. The very best thing I got was a brand-new green American army blanket, and I was able to greet the upcoming cold season in a warm winter coat, made out of it by a dexterous Prague tailor. And so, the extracurricular stuff was all taken care of, and I could sit behind my desk and begin my path to graduation. My finances were relatively good, I had a warm, friendly and carefree home, which significantly helped me to come to terms with the past years; but not to forget them. All that remained was to study and to begin my new, normal life.

With Stopka in 1947.

42 Catching Up

Well, it is easy to write "begin my new, normal life". The following days showed me immediately that yes, it would be fairly easy from the point of view of study. My educational foundation was solid and I didn't feel too acutely the academic interruption I was forced to endure. From the beginning I felt I would do well, and this gave me a good feeling. It transpired early on that Subcarpathian Ruthenia and mainly my town of Khust were equal to the challenges of basic school education. There simply was not enough time for me to complete it, what with all the historical events and abrupt changes in daily life. Let us remember for twelve years I lived in Czechoslovakia, two years in Hungary, followed by four years of deportation, which included a spell back "home", and then concentration camps till the age of eighteen. And the Hungarian education system attempted to squeeze all the knowledge gained up until 1939 out of my brain and replace it with new material. Growing persecution, *numerus clausus*, a Babylon of languages, many classes and courses not available to me. And just because I was a Jew. Being branded as different was not just the ill-will of an individual or two – it was official policy, encoded in laws and regulations. My point is – all of that was reflected in my education. Up until 1939, till the age of twelve, I could read whatever I wanted but not everything was always available. The Czech colony had its own books, as did the Hungarians, as well as the Ruthenians and the Jews. Compulsory school reading began as I started the Gymnasium in September 1938 as a freshman (a student of the *prima* – the first grade under the old high school system) but half a year later the regime had changed.

I need to complete the picture by describing my extracurricular education in Khust. There was no radio at home – almost no one had one. Newspapers were read with a week's delay. I read *A-Zet* (a magazine) frequently, but I have no idea who I got it from. Some people had record players, old gramophones, though our family did not. We would visit the luckier friends whose families did own this miraculous invention but the only music available for listening were the overplayed hits of the day.

There was one place where you could occasionally catch snippets of other types of music: folk tunes, movie hits as well as instrumental and operatic music. That was from the open windows inside the Czech colony, not far from the Gymnasium building where I sometimes strayed.

And so, when I reached Prague in 1945, I knew of the existence of Bedřich Smetana, whose *Bartered Bride* had emanated from an open window in my childhood; I had also heard his arias and other pieces from the speakers installed in Czech owned shops (such as Baťa's shoe shop). The main source for learning both classical and popular music were the exercise grounds of the Khust *Sokol*. As a small kid, I used to stand around there and observe the goings on as the *Sokols* practiced athletics and warm-ups, getting ready for their upcoming *Sokol* rally. In the winter, the exercise grounds turned to natural ice and those silly Czechs ran around with a bent stick, chasing a little black disc known as a *puck*, trying with all their might to shoot it into a small goal, manned by a bent over little man whose task it was to prevent it! My love for hockey dates back to that time. Later on, even my bosses knew that I simply had to be at Štvanice (a hockey arena in Prague) no matter whether it was an inter-league game or an international one, not to mention the World Championship. On those days I was nowhere near an operating room.

Let us return to music. I must definitely have heard *Má vlast* ("My Homeland", Smetana's famous instrumental piece) – and, as mentioned, all or maybe just the arias from *The Bartered Bride*. The name Smetana was familiar to me. Similarly, the names Dvořák and *Rusalka* (his best-known opera) were there in my subconscious, although I may just be imagining it. At any rate, I knew nothing of the existence of Fibich, Janáček, Martinů and others. I loved music, mostly the opera and symphonies, something I only realized then, in 1945, in Prague. I began gobbling it up and getting to know it through Sťopka who was a great lover of and expert in music. He was my shadow (or I, his?) and still is to this day. In my childhood I never had the time or the chance to get to know about Beethoven, Mozart, Mahler or Wagner. We knew, perhaps, a tiny bit about Tchaikovsky, Borodin, and Rimski-Korsakov. We knew a bit more about Bartók, Liszt, and Kodály during the Hungarian rule.

I was almost nineteen when I arrived in Prague. People in my age group had already absorbed basic knowledge and knew their way around literature and art, as well as sport. I was the definition of *tabula rasa*, I felt an indescribable urge to catch up and be on equal footing with my classmates and my social circle, and from there commenced a battle with time: I wanted to absorb everything in the least amount of time possible. The only way to do this was at the expense of studying. It was not easy: a language gap (fluency in Czech improved with the years!), empty pockets and a limited possibility to navigate the complex, crowded, churning city of Prague after the war. Navigating the geography of the city was easy – I could rely on Sťopka for that; navigating life in general (intellectually, socially and otherwise) was much harder.

43 Life around me Has Many Faces

It all started with what was simple and, in those day, the closest to my heart: sporting activity. I began a morning ritual: before breakfast, I would walk over to a kiosk that was in one of the corners of the boarding school and I would buy the daily *Československý sport* (Czechoslovak Sport). After the first period I was already informed about all the sporting events of the previous day – assuming my newspaper was not confiscated by my math professor. Once, he caught me not paying attention to equations with two unknowns (or some other such subject), as I was absorbed in my paper. He immediately snatched it from me and continued his lecture. Following this incident, he would begin his class every day by walking over to my desk and confiscating my newspaper. In the end, let it be said in his defense, he returned the whole lot during our graduation party. They were a nicely folded, untouched, solid bundle, for sure. It was clear that the good professor had not taken them to enlighten himself in all things sport but rather for reasons of discipline. He was certain he was doing the right thing but was ruining me financially: I had to spend an extra 30 *hellers* (Czech small change, one *koruna* – crown – is 100 hellers) on a new copy of *Sport*. That is how it went when math was the first period. If it were later in the day, I would have the time to read it cover to cover and the disciplinary efforts of the good prof were for naught.

Aside from being a regular reader of Czechoslovak sport, I was mainly interested in Josef Laufer's reporting on current and past sporting events and sports personalities. Every boy at that time grew up with Plánička in his heart and mind (František Plánička – a legendary Czech goalkeeper) and it was no different with a boy from Subcarpathian Ruthenia, who was forcibly torn away from his dreams and fancies in 1939, when he was barely twelve years old. In Prague I found there were other famous names, aside from Plánička's. The list is long and partly forgotten.

But soccer was not the only thing in life. Just as I spent hours watching my favorite club Sparta Prague play at the Letná stadium, I spent hundreds of hours sitting or standing watching ice hockey at Štvanice (an island in the river Vltava). Hockey was not new to me. Back in Khust I watched the Czech colony players chase each other on natural ice.

After soccer and hockey, my third favorite sport was athletics. In that field, I had to start learning from scratch. I knew nothing about athletics. I was lucky though because precisely at that time, the brightest star in the Czech athletics firmament made his appearance: Emil Zátopek.

And what about other sports and sports figures during that time when I thirsted and searched for knowledge? I was a frequent visitor at Štvanice, not just for ice hockey but also for figure skating. There was also a tennis facility on the island. Here I could watch Jaroslav Drobný, a later Wimbledon champion, who split his talent between ice hockey and tennis. Moreover, at the time of my metamorphosis, the gymnast Eva Bosáková (long before Věra Čáslavská) and the cyclist Jan Veselý were two more sports figures I admired.

I agree, there is more to life than sport. To achieve my goal of being an equal among equals, I also needed to fill the gaps in my knowledge of culture and arts. I have spoken of music already. Despite having no formal musical instruction, other than the basic scales, notes and time signatures taught at school, I had always liked music and it was close to my heart. It did not take much effort to make giant strides in my education. The width, if not the depth of my knowledge became substantial. The source of getting to know the magic of music were performances: daytime shows (less frequently nighttime), plays (less), opera (more) and as time went on, more frequently concert halls. I took advantage of cheap gallery or standing room only tickets, or I would sit on the theater steps. Occasionally I would have a free ticket, sometimes given to me by a good person whose husband or wife did not show up. A favorite was to sneak in and mingle with a group of kids or adults. This way I got to know the conductor Rafael Kubelík and I was enchanted by the tenors Beno Blachut and Ivo Žídek. It did not take long for me to start singing – or mumbling – the most famous arias from domestic and foreign operas, mostly the domestic ones. I only got to the foreign ones later, as an "adult".

It would be wrong to categorize me as a snob. It was not just classical and operatic music that enchanted me. My body began to twitch as soon as the theme song of Karel Vlach's orchestra came on the radio. His band played all the popular domestic and foreign tunes composed before and during the war. Folk songs also spoke to my soul, mainly Slovak ones, and I loved folk music choirs and folk-dance troupes. Suddenly I was able to take part in all our parties, dancing and singing. At the time, all manner of Russian music was popular with the youth as well: variety show tunes, war songs, folk songs and *chastushkas* (traditional Russian songs played at high tempos). I also liked – and still do – brass bands and army bands. They all enriched my life. I liked listening to choirs, both classical and modern, except when they were singing odes of praise for one current luminary or another.

I was less attracted to dramatic plays. Perhaps that was because my Czech was not quite yet what it ought to have been. Nevertheless, I still wanted to know the actors on the scene. Doing it through movies proved to be the easiest way. And there was a plethora of gorgeous old pre-war films. I was lucky enough to see Jan Werich and Jiří Voskovec work together, prior to Voskovec leaving the country for good. (Werich and Voskovec were the founders and the actors in the most popular musical theater in Czechoslovakia – "The Liberated Theater". Their songs, composed by Jaroslav Ježek, with their lyrics, have become a part of the national lore. Voskovec had a second acting career in the USA, where he changed his first name to George.)

I must mention one thing: I really liked the movies that were produced during the war. They were light, obviously non-political, possessed of a good dose of healthy Czech folk wisdom and sarcasm – as necessitated by the times. Mind you, I am talking about a period that was still very recent, close to my wartime travails and suffering, and so I would often leave the movie theater with mixed feelings. Judging by my own experiences, I had assumed that life as we knew it had come to a grinding halt everywhere. And yet...films were being produced, the soccer and ice hockey leagues still competed, all sports continued apace, and life went on. This is not a reproach or a criticism, the two experiences cannot be compared. Perhaps I was jealous, but I am glad that others were able to live while I could not – it had nothing to do with what I had to endure. This paragraph may not be relevant: I wrote it as an aside to my main narrative.

I should at least touch upon literature. My connection with it was dictated by the regime and events in my life. Pre 1939, when the lessons I attended were mainly in Czech, I remember *The Grandmother*, the classic novel of Božena Němcová. I reconnected to Czechoslovak culture six and a half years later when I reached the gymnasium in Prague. A whole new world of Czech literature opened to me. Some of it belonged to the pre-war period. For example, the brothers Karel and Josef Čapek or Jaroslav Hašek and his *Good Soldier Švejk*. Jaroslav Seifert belongs to both periods. (I got to know him better after he got his Nobel prize but until 1989 knowledge of his work was superficial. None of his works were available and only recently have I been able to lay my hands on his slim volume *All the Beauty of the World*, with the subtitle – *Stories and Memories*. What a nice read! What a repository of information about legendary poets, authors, artists, and sculptors! What poetic language in prose format!) In 1965, when we escaped to Israel, the Iron Curtain separated us. But I was not cut off from the exiled Czech writers like Milan Kundera or Josef Škvorecký. The opening up of Czechoslovakia with the Velvet Revolution of 1989 renewed my connections.

And so, we are left with a short paragraph about visual art and sculpture. I have never become an expert. The quarter of a century spent outside my native land and lifestyle, in a country that the Czechoslovak regime totally ignored (hated would be a better word), and thus unable to directly access the information I wanted, has certainly not helped improve my understanding of the arts and culture in the old country. And so, I have not reached new heights, and my education in this field has remained mainly superficial and general. Still, I am not a total ignoramus and have been enraptured by the works of Czech artists such as Jiří Trnka, Josef Lada, Antonín Mánes, Alfons Mucha and Max Švabinský.

I cannot precisely determine the length of time it took to gain my knowledge of the Arts. It was all still superficial and got progressively more sophisticated with time (sadly, once again interrupted in 1965 but, luckily, 1989 came along and with it a chance to reconnect with the past). If I should determine the time frame for the process of my transformation after all, I would do it indirectly. There was a period of five years when my head was everywhere except focused on my studies. It started prior to my high school graduation, continued through my theoretical studies of medicine up until I began my clinical studies, when the lecture halls were replaced by hospital wards. And my results showed it. My high school graduation grades were decent enough; the theoretical subjects in my medical studies...not so good: I was a poor student and had to be re-tested a number of times.

Those five years were the time of sport, theatre, movie houses, but most of all endless strolls through Prague, through every nook and cranny, not just the historic part... I did my walks with Sťopka, as well as by myself. I got to know the city inside and out, and when I returned after 25 years, I needed no guide despite the changes that had occurred during my absence – the completed Metro and the alterations necessary for the new stations. The Nusle bridge and new roads leading to major highways – those were a pleasant surprise. When, during the last decade of the 20th century, the borders opened for tourists, even to residents of Israel, I became the main source of information – a guide and an unabashed exponent of Czechoslovakia, and especially of Prague, to all our friends and anyone who asked. Before I was able to obtain maps of Prague, I would draw them by hand, pointing out the best routes to see Prague's historical monuments and sights. I did it with pride because Prague was so close to my heart. I felt at home there and I have never had a home that felt so true. I am not ashamed to admit that if it were not for my family, mostly my grandchildren, Prague would become my permanent home. (Incidentally, it is now September 2003 and I am in Prague, though once again only for three-four months.)

During the time after the war, during my metamorphosis, my Czech, only rudimentary up until then, improved, became my main language and remains so. That, too, was a factor in my feeling equal to those born and raised in Prague. I was proud of it then and I am proud of it now.

In this chapter thus far I have described my personal metamorphosis and growth. Another aspect of my maturing, a more outward going one, was my integration into post World War II society in Czechoslovakia, alongside the "Victorious February" revolution of 1948. It was more than graduating from high school and studying medicine. It formed my life (or, more precisely, Alizka's and my life) and eventually led to the events of 1965. But, dear reader, let me not jump ahead…

My diligence and perseverance, along with Stopka's assistance, would not have been enough for the gradual switch in my life, which made me into a new man. In the case of a "normal" kid and a normal young man, the change is put in motion by the family. I did not have one. Therefore, school had a tremendous influence on me – I found myself in the right place at the right time! The atmosphere in the city and the school that had just changed its name from "Russian Gymnasium" to "Soviet High School in Prague" – all that played a key role in my transformation. To start with, unlike many others in a similar situation, I was free of mundane, everyday concerns. I had a roof over my head, and it was a good roof. I was not hungry, I was not cold, and I had a warm, clean bed.

Later, it came to light that the Soviets had intended for the school to become a model high school, to be imitated and followed by others. They brought in first class instructors from the Soviet Union and left a part of the old Russian émigré faculty in place. It is well known that during those immediate post war years, before the "Victorious February", Soviet ideology had begun infiltrating into hitherto democratic Czechoslovakia. This was done via a national coalition that was dominated by the strongest party, the Communist Party. The ideological creep had begun, thanks to Klement Gottwald, Zdeněk Fierlinger and others who spent the war years in Moscow.

I guess our school, too, was on the leading edge of the coming fateful changes in the country, mainly in education. We felt it at school mostly during history and geography lessons. Everything was tied to the Soviet homeland, to the class struggle, to the struggle of workers and peasants against the ruling class and the Tsars. There was almost nothing else taught about the rest of the world, other than the struggle of workers against factory owners and exploiters of all sorts. As for thinkers – they were Marx and Engels in the main. Tolstoy could not be ignored, but no words were wasted on Dostoyevsky. Gorky was tolerated but Mayakovsky was the writer to top all writers, mainly due to his pride in his Soviet passport. The rest of the world did not come into view. That is how our studies were set up, but already back then we knew how to filter things and we learned a thing or two from classmates who had survived the war in the Soviet Union. I have also mentioned elsewhere Red Army officers who would sometimes speak freely. Then there was the world outside of school that had not yet fallen victim to insidious propaganda. Back in 1939, some of my classmates and I had already experienced a re-evaluation – a revision of the past and a force-feeding of a new view of the world and of everything a new regime demanded.

But, I do not think the school had a fundamental influence on my burgeoning worldview. That had begun forming without any connection to the school. The ground had been laid to accept a socialist, truly socialist (or should I say social?) view of things and events. Let me remind you, and not for the first time, that I belonged to a group of people, Jewish people, who had gone through the hell of the recent years and like many of my contemporaries I came to believe in the regime's clever propaganda. This propaganda, disseminated at every step, claimed that there was only one ideology capable of correcting all wrongdoing and ensuring that such misdeeds and wrongs would never be repeated. It did not take long to see this was a colossal illusion.

In the meantime, I lived a carefree life, unburdened by too much ideology. I was able to put the past aside and spent a pleasant two years studying. I graduated in 1947 from a high standard school. I gained knowledge and friends, I got to know the world outside of the school walls. I was gradually absorbed by the environment and the turbulent life of those years. I was not too concerned about my grade average and my most immediate goal was to graduate without an idea what I would do with my graduation certificate and how I would continue. Life was light, like a pleasant waltz and cheap wine helped in elevating the mood and the morale. Student loves were also a part of it all.

Additionally, I was on the high school soccer team which I was proud of. Our team made it to the all-country high school finals in Prague in 1946/1947. We lost but the event culminated in a public commendation for our selfless play in front of the class (read: the girls) in the dining hall: Sťopka as goalkeeper and me as right mid-fielder. Naturally, we were not looking at the speaker. We were busy observing the girls' reactions. They reacted to our full satisfaction which was shown later that night during our regular dance party in the dining hall. The party happened every Saturday and there was no shortage of dance partners. There was one record: one side contained the song *Prague is Beautiful as the Day Dawns over the Vltava* and the flip side had *You Beautiful Gypsy Girl*. The record kept spinning over and over, long after the Witch (the girls' schoolmistress) had repeatedly declared the evening over. It ended up with her grabbing the record player and marching upstairs to the girls' dorm. The boys' schoolmaster just kept sitting there, evidently having a good time. We caught up with the schoolmistress, literally snatched the record player out of her hands and the dance went on. During one such altercation she rolled down the stairs and broke her leg. Somehow, we survived it!

The line-up for high school football final in 1946/47.

To conclude, let me write a few words about the environment of the school from the students' perspective. We were an organic – and not so organic – mix of the children of post-revolution (white) emigrants and a rather large group of Ruthenians from eastern Slovakia. Both groups dated back to the period prior to, and during the German occupation. (Interestingly, they would come there from the Slovak State of 1939–1945.) An additional faction was comprised of kids from the Soviet diplomatic corps. Apparently, in anticipation of future needs, this faction was over-represented, headed by the two daughters of the infamous Ambassador Valerian Zorin. Another rather numerous group comprised the offspring of Soviet citizens, about whose activity nothing was known. After my graduation, and especially following the events of 1948 (more about it below), when I had already been away from the school for some time, I discovered the names of former classmates – evidently their fathers' names – among the various experts, instructors and advisors. I cannot claim this with certainty since after my graduation I did not have any contact with kids from the school, apart from St'opka. Lastly, there was a small contingent of Czechs, mostly kids who lived in the neighborhood and, if I recall, there was one other boy from Subcarpathian Ruthenia, aside from myself. At that point, the region was no longer a part of Czechoslovakia; it belonged to the "great" Soviet Union. That partition happened quite voluntarily, naturally...why bother with a decision of a democratically elected parliament that would have been the only body authorized to give up the territory of the Czechoslovak Republic!

A word about the Babylon that was the student body. I cannot say that any visible tension existed among the various groups. But now, when time has elapsed, I do recall...not exactly an animus but a certain coolness between the factions. You could feel a distance in the air between the boarding school kids and the others. Not to mention the isolation of the kids from the embassy from the others. I still do not feel I was discriminated against, but I do have a sneaky feeling that the "old Russian" group, the kids of emigrants, behaved coolly toward me, with an air of indifference and reserve. I did not care and did not try to find motives. I had my best friend St'opka, and the east Slovak kids were good friends as well – plus I had sport, theaters, concerts and my strolls through the city. When it came to the attitude of the principal though, it was obvious that she felt nothing but an open dislike and undisguised hostility towards me. Miss Ivanovna Nyekliudovskaya, who had not even noticed me throughout my two years, would not look me in the eye and would not reply to my greeting. I was simply a traitor in her eyes because I was supposed to be living in the Soviet Union. She had no idea that my presence at the school was no coincidence, that I had gotten away in the nick of time. I told myself more than once she could go to hell as far as I was concerned! I lived where I wanted to live, I was a Czechoslovak citizen. Legally, she had to accept me as a student and, anyway, this was before the Communist takeover, and she was not yet free to do as she pleased in Czechoslovakia.

And now it was the autumn of 1947, and there I was, my high school diploma in my pocket. It was the end of childish games and hijinks, the end of coming back to the boarding school late at night, climbing up the lightning rod and sneaking in through the window. The light coming on suddenly in the hallway, us with a skeleton key in hand, and the tall figure of Nikolay Nikolayevich towering over us, then serving us a cup of hot tea instead of a reprimand or a call to our "beloved" principal. I was "out of the incubator" and had to decide which steps to take and how to start my life. I was a little stressed out about the night guard in the cherry orchard below Vyšehrad finding out who I was and where I came from...Víťa Minko had been caught by him as he jumped down from a tree and in order to free himself, he shed his jacket and beat it out of there. Maybe there was a paper in one of the pockets that would reveal our identity. And how about the managers of the Nusle Soccer Club when they found out their blue and white flags had disappeared? They would have had no idea that Mrs. Petrunčíková used them to sew us new shorts! Some got white ones, some got blue ones. There is no one left to apologize to. The soccer field is no longer there, replaced by the Hotel Forum. Is the hotel directly where the field was? I am not sure. At any rate – it is a pity. We played our final on that field. But I have already written about that. I guess the biggest prank happened during the final exams when only we, the graduating class, stayed behind at the boarding school. Instead of the kitchen staff cooking for us, we were given coupons for lunches and dinners at Rubeš, a restaurant across the street. We used those coupons for wine. I do not remember – whether we attended our exams with our stomachs filled with cheap wine instead of food.

And so, I stepped into real life out of a carefree existence, out of soft cotton wool, quite unprepared. I was still in my learning, studying and catching-up stages, I still needed to delve into the secrets of that vastly different life that went on around me. There was one thing I decided, and the decision was mine, solely mine, and no one else had any say in it: I decided to study medicine. I will talk about that later. After having been almost completely sheltered, I began to grasp the outside environment and I noticed that new winds had begun to blow – cold winds from the east. The government was composed of a national coalition – communists, social democrats, national socialists, and the People's Party, along with so called community organizations, but the situation was boiling under the surface. The press was still free, and I could read that key positions in government, the police and the armed forces were being filled with people who would remain obedient in the future. They were replacing competent people of a democratic bent. The new cadres were compliant and destined to strangle democracy for forty years, to wreck agriculture and to warp and corrupt the character of two decent peoples.

44 The Events of 1947/48: A Small Political Extempore

Here I interrupt my personal narrative with some thoughts about two political events which occurred during the tumultuous end of 1947 and the beginning of 1948. These were the UN vote of November 29, 1947, which partitioned Palestine between Jews and Arabs, and the overthrow of the democratic government in Czechoslovakia in February 1948, a.k.a. the 'Victorious February'.

I followed these events via the radio and the democratic press, but I cannot evaluate them as a proper historian would do. However, as one who experienced them, I can claim with certainty that a large proportion of middle-aged and young people today (I write this in 2003!) either know nothing of this period or, if they do, they do not care one way or another. But those who personally experienced these events or were told the facts about them, mainly those living in Israel, almost stand to attention at the mere mention of the word "Czechoslovakia". They feel they need to pay their respects to a country that made a huge contribution to the creation of the State of Israel through arms shipments during a time when the whole world turned its back on the new State. And prior to these shipments, the Czechoslovak delegation at the United Nations led by Jan Masaryk (as well as the Soviet delegation) voted for the creation of Israel at the UN and were among the most eager and steadfast supporters and advocates for the establishment of the 'Jewish state'.

What did I explain to people about the events of 1948 in Czechoslovakia? I explained that the Communist Party, led by Gottwald, had gained power by democratic means, following the end of World War 2 and an agreement with the exiled governments in London and Moscow. Later, during the only free post-war elections in 1946, the Communists got the largest number of votes, followed by the national socialists, social democrats, and the People's Party. They called it "a national front government" but the Communists, along with the social democrats, had formed a coalition whose clear aim was to eliminate the other two partners. The social democrats, headed by Fierlinger, merged with the Communists, who prior to the merger had forced President Eduard Beneš to accept the resignation of all democratically inclined ministers. They resigned for the reasons I have spoken about: the willful and undemocratic swap of police and army leaders for people subservient to the Communist Party. A question presents itself: was this, or was it not, a coup d'état? President Beneš accepted the resignations and endorsed the new government. How and why he did it...common people do not know and did not know then either. Who or what persuaded him to take that fateful decision? The fact remains that that single decision facilitated forty-one years of one-party rule. A party that was everything but democratic. It cared much less about the well-being of the people than it did about the well-being of the party faithful. No need to waste words about personal freedom, justice, or prosperity.

I was then twenty years old, with a fresh high school diploma and a harrowing personal life...I was a nobody. The times were historic – and hysterical – and they certainly affected my future life. Those days, at the end of 1947 and in the beginning of 1948, engendered four crucial events that reverberate in my life still today. (It has been 55 years since then...the years pass quickly, it is 2003 now, almost 2004. As I keep writing, I will endeavor to give these events the regard and attention they deserve.)

On the personal level, it was the beginning of my joint life with Alizka and the beginning of my medical studies at Charles University in Prague. The UN vote of November 29, 1947, partitioned Palestine between Jews, who accepted the partition, and Arabs. (Please note that the partition was not between Jews and Palestinians!) However, the Arabs did not accept the partition and incited all the Arab states near and far into a war with Israel. Statehood was proclaimed on May 15, 1948. And in Czechoslovakia on February 25, 1948 the Communist Party grabbed the power from the democratically elected government.

The first country to enthusiastically support and recognize the Jewish state was the Soviet Union. Under its guidance, shipments of weapons began streaming into the newly created country from Czechoslovakia. If not for those shipments, the State of Israel would not exist today. The attitude of Jan Masaryk, the Minister of Foreign Affairs at the time, was clear but what explains the zeal of the Soviet Union? The Jews had fought the British Mandate in Palestine. The mandate was acquired by the United Kingdom, a superpower at the time, after World War I. And because America was not exactly thrilled by the creation of the new state, it stood to reason that Israel would become, without a doubt, an ally of the Soviet Union in its struggle against capitalism and imperialism. We are talking about a strategically very important part of the Middle East! Let us not forget that the person who wrote the statehood proclamation and who is considered Israel's founding father, was none other than labor union leader, David Ben-Gurion. The Labor Party was the ruling party, the Kibbutz Movement was based on socialist principles and kibbutz residents, along with many Israeli citizens, often Russian immigrants, had warm feelings towards their former homeland. They considered the Soviet Union the savior of at least some of their families that had been left behind in Europe. Despite many objections to the Soviet Union, many, having returned from armies, from exile and from concentration camps, believed that their future and their existence as equals among equals could only be secured by the proletariat.

The Israeli government and later its democratically elected Knesset (parliament) were of a different view. They believed Israel's future should be tied with the United States and Western Europe. The reversal was quick and dramatic. For the following forty years the young democratic country became the hated arch-enemy, first of the Soviet Union and then, after the "Victorious February", also of Czechoslovakia. It was not just a diplomatic freeze and later, after the Six Day War in 1967, came the complete cutting off diplomatic, economic and cultural relations. It became open hostility: at the UN, stopping the emigration wave to Israel, show trials against Israeli citizens and openly anti-Semitic campaigns against everything that was Israeli or Jewish. In Prague, there was the trial against the "treasonous conspiracy cell lead by Rudolf Slánský" where the media and the authorities never neglected to mention the former, non-Czech sounding names and the Jewish origins of the accused. Around the same time there were similar show trials going on in Moscow, aimed at Jewish doctors who were accused of trying to poison Stalin. But even Moscow did not manage the level of brutal anti-Semitic venom then extant in Prague. Later, massive Czechoslovak weapon shipments started flowing to all "progressive" feudal lords and dictators the world over. Shipments to countries whose declared aim it was to annihilate the Zionist state and to drive the inhabitants into the Mediterranean Sea. I am sure the Czech apparatchiks were perfectly aware that one lost war meant the end of Israel. Which is unprecedented in our world where a country can continue to exist despite losing several conflicts.

As I have already written, I never personally experienced antisemitism. I still do not understand how it could be that in Czechoslovak People's Army, the army of the post "Victorious February" era, on the military ID cards of soldiers and officers in reserve there could appear a rubric stating their origin: Jewish. It was politely explained to the naïve ones that they were not being asked for their class origin. And I tell them this: your origin was never an issue when you were called to fight, irrespective of whether this was the army of Svoboda in the east or in the Western armies. (Those who were not told I can recommend Erich Kulka's book *Jews in the Czechoslovak Army of Svoboda*, Naše vojsko, Prague 1990, as well as *Jews in the Czechoslovak Forces in the West*, Naše vojsko, Prague, 1992. There was a rumor at one time that a registry of all citizens of Jewish descent was being prepared (perhaps even using the registry taken from Nazi archives). I will try to outline later how these and other events practically and chronologically impacted the second half of my life. To be able to do that, I need to go far back.

45 The Faculty of Medicine, Charles University Prague

The most logical thing is for me to go back in the autumn of 1947, when the graduation euphoria had ebbed, the two carefree years were behind me and life's hard reality became my daily bread. I had not considered my future very seriously up to that point, I was busier suppressing the past. I did know I wanted a university education. Why did I choose medicine? It was not a family tradition. Save for one of my mother's cousins, there were no doctors in my family. It is likely that my wartime experiences, watching those suffering and dying, and specifically my concentration camp experience, played an important role in my career selection. But I cannot swear to it; I do not recall my thoughts wandering in that direction. Perhaps it was subconscious. At one point, not for long,

I harbored the thought of a diplomatic career. I thought I could utilize the fact that at the time I spoke perfect Czech, Russian, German, and Hungarian – and I could not be sold down the river in Yiddish or Ruthenian either. In addition, I could read basic texts and street signs in Polish and Ukrainian and, to be a tad boastful about it, I have added Hebrew and English since then! Most likely it was Alizka's influence. We had begun our inseparable friendship at that time and have now been together more than half a century. She was the main impetus for me to register at the faculty of medicine. I am sure my talks with Sťopka had something to do with it too: he registered the same day and the same hour.

My medical student ID.

46 Out of the Incubator

I could not find a better analogy to my two-year stay at the boarding school than the maturing of a premature baby in an incubator. When a preemie reaches its optimal weight and its vital functions have normalized, it is removed from the incubator and driven home by its jubilant parents. Well, the boarding school was my incubator, and my diploma were the proof of my maturity. But I had nowhere to go. During the previous two years, my mother had gone through her grieving period for my dad, and the family had literally driven her into the arms of a man whom I never saw as a substitute for my father. To compare him to my father would have been an unforgivable sin and so I could never hope to gain a new home through the union of those disastrously different people. My mother's home now was in Ústí nad Labem (a city in northern Bohemia). I had no idea how to find a roof over my head. I was told about students' lodgings, dormitories, but they would not be open until October and it was not easy to be accepted into one. I had to leave the boarding school immediately after graduation and I spent a few nights with Sťopka's parents in Radotín.

I finally gathered the fortitude to travel to mother in Ústí and to meet my stepfather. After about ten days I found a job helping a local farmer. He was also a nature keeper in the borderlands. I found myself in some summer camp, organized by who knows whom, for Jewish youth. I then registered for my medical studies and once I was registered, I could start looking for lodgings. I was turned down for the dorm but got word that the Jewish community of Prague ran a youth home. The house for men was at 13 Krakovská Street and the one for women was at 57 Lublaňská Street– the house where Alizka lived.

But getting into the home was not easy either. After 55 years it is hard to fathom why I needed to fight for it. At first glance, I fit all the needed criteria: I had a high school diploma, I was registered to begin my studies and, after all, the home had been set up for cases like mine in the first place: people who had gone through concentration camps and had lost parents. I vaguely remember the gentlemen who were to decide my case, a Mr. Frishman and a Mr. Goldstein. Those men determined who would be accepted and who would be turned down. I guess I was not likeable enough, or enough of an orphan. They were not enthused about helping me get into Krakovská Street. It is significant, though, that they treated Alizka very rudely too – I will describe it later. In the end, I did manage to get in and the above-mentioned gents became frequent guests at our weekly soirees. Those consisted of Sťopka playing his guitar and me singing. Our repertoire included popular Russian war songs, though the war had begun receding in people's minds. We also sang well-liked Czech and Slovak folk songs, and it did not take long for us to become a hit among the residents. It was a mixed bag of folks that lived there: university students, liberated camp prisoners and orphans whose parents had not lived to see the liberation. There were also members of Svoboda's Army and a mix of nationalities: Czechs, Slovaks, Poles, Bulgarians, Russians and possibly others.

Once again, I got lucky and did not need to worry about my daily needs. I had my bed, breakfast, and dinner (lunch in the student cafeteria), all covered, no out-of-pocket expense for me. In addition to a government grant, I also had financial support in the form of a grant from JOINT, through the Jewish community. But the brightest light in the Krakovská Street house were the Hostovskýs, a married couple who were the building superintendents.

47 Auntie Bílá-Hostovská, Uncle Hostovský

I immediately struck up a friendship with this special, kind couple. Alizka had known them for some time through our common friend Nataša Kieslerová, Mrs. Hostovsky's (nee Kieslerová) niece. That is why she was called "Auntie". We all loved this kind older couple (older from our youthful point of view). Prior to the occupation they were each married to "Aryans" who had divorced them. After this they shared an almost identical fate with me, despite coming from a different background. They were deported to Terezín (a concentration camp near Prague, usually a way station to deportation to Auschwitz). Uncle Jindřich Hostovský, a relative to famous writer Egon Hostovský, had a rather reserved personality and never revealed many details about himself. We know more about Auntie, mainly because she found herself in Israel following the Dubček regime of 1968. Uncle was not with her – he died soon after we had left the country. Auntie has now been gone for some years as well, but we kept in contact for a while and so her "resumé" is better known.

She was born in Rachov, in Subcarpathian Ruthenia and she was one of many Jewish girls who tied her fate to a Czech, a government official who worked in that easternmost region of pre-Munich Czechoslovakia. Unfortunately, things were not simple in that *Golet in the Valley* (a reference to another well-known work by Czech author Ivan Olbracht). Jewish traditions here were rooted very deep. A marriage outside the faith was a tragedy, not just for the family but for the whole Jewish community. Even a loving family was forced to disown the daughter, cast her out and spend seven days in mourning, sitting "shiva" as if for a dead person. The tradition was strict and unforgiving. Auntie's family was not pious, but her fate was marked forever. As if that was not enough, when she reached Prague with her husband, she was faced with a new cruel twist of fate. The anti-Jewish laws gave Mr. Bílý, her husband, a choice: be doomed with your wife or get a divorce. Mr. Bílý chose the latter. Uncle, similarly, was married to a Czech, an Aryan, and she too chose divorce. The Hostovskýs survived both Terezín and Auschwitz. They came back and found their former partners married with children and so they joined forces and lived together happily for at least two decades. In Israel Auntie dropped anchor in Haifa, she lived mostly on welfare and from a bit of support from us and from Nataša, who worked as a secretary at Tel Aviv University. Auntie soon left us – she is buried at a Haifa cemetery on Mount Carmel.

From time to time I have mentioned things I tried to avoid mentioning whilst in Prague, such as the tragic fate of this woman, who without parents, without her family which had cast her out, was later left with no one to whom she could speak about the unspeakable past. No one, not one single person from her family had come back from Hell. We are glad that towards the end of her life we could provide a little support.

48 The Impending Storm

The autumn of 1947 was generally calm. The first semester of my medical studies and my relaxed life on Krakovská Street seemed to be passing by me. Mostly because I had no intention of sitting in stuffy lecture rooms. I was still seeking out and catching up on my extracurricular knowledge. I was taking in the surrounding world in large gulps – not in lecture halls but in stadiums, mostly Sparta, as well as cinemas, theaters, and libraries. And fairly often with a glass of wine or beer in hand, and Sťopka for company. When money was needed for these pursuits, the kitchen at the "Czech Heart" restaurant on Spálená Street came in handy. Sťopka told the owner about my pitiful existence as a concentration camp orphan and I described him as a pathetic pauper, and the nice lady gave us coupons, so that whenever we found ourselves on Spálená Street we knew we could pop into the "Czech Heart" for a free, rib-sticking lunch! Smiles from the kitchen staff were a bonus.

Everything seemed beautiful and fine on the surface. Democracy had been revived, one could get a passport practically on the spot, the movie theaters played Hollywood wartime flicks, books from all over the world were being published with no censorship whatever. "Awesome", as kids would say today. But under the surface, things were at boiling point. I have already written about that – no need to repeat it. People in the know claimed that a storm was approaching, and it was not far. The autumn passed and winter was not yet over, and the storm suddenly arrived – and with it an earthquake: *Victorious February*!

First year medical student, 1948.

49 Alizka

I knew from the radio and from the press what had preceded the events of that February. Mostly the resignation of all the democratic ministers and the reasons that had led to their decision. But during those fateful days, my head and heart were somewhere else. Precisely as Gottwald was addressing the enthusiastic crowd from the balcony of Kinský Palace, announcing that President Beneš had accepted the resignation of the democratic ministers, I was experiencing the pinnacle of all the happiest moments that two young people in love can experience. We did not choose Prague for the act. I am not sure why – perhaps my lack of experience and confidence and doing it in secret...I felt everyone would be able to tell just by looking at me. Certainly, that would have been the case in Krakovská or Lublaňská Street, not to mention it would have been forbidden there anyway. We chose a little hotel close to the Kralupy train station. I had noticed it and had begun dreaming and scheming about it in the preceding weeks when my train stopped at the station. It was *en route* to Ústí nad Labem, where I would sporadically visit my sister Šarlota and mom. I made the trip for my sister, whom I missed very much.

Kralupy was the start of our joint journey through life, a journey that has lasted till this day (as I have said before, I write slowly and with long pauses: it is now June 2004 and we are in Prague again). Our journey together has now lasted 56 years and I am never sorry – quite the opposite! I celebrate each and every day. The main event took place in Kralupy but I had known Alizka from long before, from the time when Alex Treiber (the one from the church clock episode) and I cycled over to Buštino. It was the village where Alizka was born and where she lived (her two sisters were born in Velké Kapušany and Rožňava respectively, in Slovakia, the latter was their mother's birthplace). Buštino was about 20 kilometers south-east from Khust. Alex was the one visiting Alizka and I was there to visit some other young lass. This was in the beginning of the 1940's and the two of us snot-nosed kids were about thirteen. That is how long I have known Alizka. We had no idea what fate had in store for us in the years to come. Alex and I survived. Alizka's mother and oldest sister who was twenty-two, both died in Alizka's arms after the liberation of Bergen Belsen. In the same camp she managed to save her middle sister, who was twenty. (Through a cruel twist of fate, in 2004 we learned that this sister was losing her drawn-out battle with cancer. She underwent two operations and was in a critical condition in a hospital in Haifa, where she lived. We returned home from Prague two months earlier than planned. Alizka sat at the bedside of her dying sister who was fully conscious. Fate had no mercy: the last living member of Alizka's family died a week later in her arms but at least in her own bed – a dignified death. I write this while I am in Israel.)

After the war Alizka found herself in Prague when she was seventeen years old, along with her sick sister and after a long search she was able to find her father, who was even sicker, in a state-run sanatorium (it later became the Institute for the Care of Mother and Child in Prague-Podolí). She spent nights in a shelter for repatriated persons (possibly the YMCA), still wearing the ill-fitting clothes that she was able to snag after the liberation of Bergen Belsen. She would walk to the Podolí sanatorium daily. She did not have money for a tram ticket and because her repatriation certificate was her only ID, she did not have a home address. That meant she could not register with the police, which in turn meant she could not get food stamps. And so, she would arrive at the Podolí sanatorium at all hours of the day, usually hungry. She was not able to buy her usual two rolls and a bag of plums every day. That would have been about as much as she could afford from the tiny stipend she received from a Jewish charity. The nice concierge at the sanatorium welcomed her with a smile but he was not able to allow her in, outside of visiting hours, so she would sit in his small office, sheltered from the vagaries of the weather. More than once, the kind man shared his lunch with her.

She remembers the kind old man very well and with true gratitude. That happens when, after a long period of apparently forgetting her sad past, memories come flooding back – a common experience for many of us. This phenomenon is being studied by psychologists here and some even see a connection between our present dangerous situation (Second Intifada) and the one we found ourselves in sixty years ago. I do not know if there is anything to that theory, but the fact remains that even the second and the third generation of survivors' descendants takes an active interest in their parents' and grandparents' past – even people who used to appear indifferent to the subject. Be that as it may, it is a boom time for psychologists.

I had to write these few words to emphasize how selective our brains are – and I mean that as a positive thing. Alizka does not remember the details of those few months around her sanatorium visits. At the time, we were beginning our life together and the memories became joint memories for the two of us. From the available medical records, we can glean that the staff was doing good work. Many people like Alizka's dad were able to get better – others returned chronically ill with more serious diseases. It was revealed that her father's lung had been infected by Koch's bacterium and he was transferred to the former Masaryk Homes in Krč while suffering active tuberculosis. They served as a hospital for repatriated persons. And because the course of our lives is inscrutable, my friend Alex was hospitalized in the same hospital, possibly in the same ward. Alex was Alizka's close friend prior to being deported to the camps, as well as after his return. Another twist of fate: Alizka was visiting her father, and Alex and I were going there to visit the very same Alex. Naturally, we knew each other but it was destined that our journey together began back then. Soon, the journey will celebrate its sixtieth anniversary. That was also the spot where my medical career began in 1953, as I have already written. The only difference was the name of the locality – it changed from the Masaryk Homes to Thomayer Hospital.

Alizka, October 1948.

50 Alizka's Difficult Beginnings

None of us had it easy and smooth when we started our new lives after the war, after our concentration camp experiences. Most of us, young, inexperienced, mentally and physically wounded people, without the opportunity to seek advice from parents or older members of the family – we began fumbling and searching. Searching for a way forward and literally searching in surrounding countries as well as our own, to see if a miracle might have happened after all, and your father, mother, a sibling, an aunt or uncle had survived. Hundreds of repatriated persons made their way daily to the offices of the Red Cross or some other organization in the hope of "finding someone". Others shuttled between Prague and Budapest or Prague and Bucharest, cities where they could find offices of American charities that might be able to offer material help in addition to information. I was already a student in Prague at the time and so I was cut off from those tens of thousands of people who tried to begin a new life in the Sudetenland border regions, in towns emptied out after the Germans departed. The region was settled by demobilized members of Svoboda's Army, former residents of Subcarpathian Ruthenia, and they were happy to offer shelter to those coming back from the camps without their families. A not negligible number of them lived in Prague, though. Just so that we are clear, I am speaking about *Czechoslovaks of the Jewish faith*, whose homeland, until 1945, was Subcarpathian Ruthenia. Those folks returned from the camps to find their homeland had been taken away from them and given to another country. No one asked them, no one consulted them, they had no say in the matter. They all felt they were Czechoslovaks, but the pre-communist politicians did not share their feelings. It seems that politician's view was that the right of residency was only to be given to former Subcarpathian Ruthenia citizens with pure Czech blood in their veins. Masaryk's democracy had been corrupted and twisted – some citizens were more equal than others. News reached me in Prague that the recently persecuted were being persecuted again. If you cannot prove you are a "real Czech", you have no right to reside in a country that until recently had been your country, your birthplace. And as is often the case in these situations, terrifying news spread like wildfire. For instance, there were rumors that in towns with a larger number of former Subcarpathian Ruthenia citizens, Soviet *NKVD* (the later *KGB*) units had made an appearance, and they were planning raids to catch people and send them back to the Soviet Union, to be tried as "traitors to the motherland" and immediately shipped to Siberia. I do not know a single such actual case. I do know that anyone who made an official request and was able to produce a note from a former teacher from a Czech school confirming the applicant had been a student there, was able to obtain his/her citizenship eventually. Some solved it by wandering over to Hungary. Hungary had previously deported them but now considered them Hungarian citizens. (As an aside: in the Soviet Union after the war, there was a large group of former Subcarpathian Ruthenia residents, mostly young ones, who had sought refuge there from the Hungarians. For some reason they were unable to join Svoboda's Army. They wanted to return to Czechoslovakia but the Czech authorities, namely the embassy in Moscow, showed no interest in helping them. There may have been various reasons, but it is clear that they probably did not want to anger the regime with which they would shortly be "marching together till eternity"! The Hungarians were happy to have them and repatriated the lot to Hungary). Others solved the problem in 1948 – 1949 by leaving for Israel *en masse*: either directly or through the *Haganah* (precursor of the Israel Defense Force) training camps in Czechoslovakia. Till this day they all consider themselves Czechoslovaks.

These were the problems that weighed down seventeen-year-old Alizka. Additionally, there was her gravely ill father. She did not have much time to think about herself. And there was no one to think about her. Her sister, three years older than her, lived a normal life. With a girlfriend she had a place in the Homes for Women in Smíchov. She worked at the Ministry of Social Security not far from Palacký Bridge. For reasons unknown the burden of caring for their father was placed on Alizka's shoulders (the sister is no longer here to explain).

During those post-war and post-camp years the wise saying "life must go on" was everywhere in evidence in all of us survivors and naturally in Alizka as well. The repatriation offices only took care of people for a short time. Everything and everybody were focused on three institutions: the Jewish community of Prague, JOINT, and the Palestine office. Alizka did not know that there existed schools and high schools for kids who had been forced to interrupt their studies – no one had told her about it. It is ironic we were only told about it decades later from Czech friends in Israel. I guess they had two different measuring sticks in those three institutions: one for local kids and one for those who did not only lose their whole families but their homes, too. They did find work for the second group...but what work! Alizka, who was not yet seventeen, was sent to work as a maid for a large family that had come back from America. She had to perform all the tough, dirty jobs almost twenty-four hours a day. Till this day she cannot forget the toughest job: cleaning the unbelievably filthy bathtub after the whole family had taken a bath. But at least she had a roof over her head, food (she ate in some corner, separate from the family), and a few crowns to buy some clothes and a tram ticket whenever her employer gave her leave to travel to Podolí, to visit her father.

It must have been in the summer of 1945, two or three months after the war and after the camps. We wanted to live, somehow to reconnect with a time that would never come back. Living with a heartless family was not exactly the right environment for returning to normal life. And so, as far as Alizka can remember, her next job was in a lab on Václavské náměstí (Wenceslas Square), The name of the company was Borochema and her main job was to wash out and polish test tubes. I remember waiting for her outside Borochema from time to time. This was still before February 1948 (before **our** February, not the historic February though the dates are identical). Her next job was far more dignified. She became assistant to Professor Berthold Epstein, a well-known pediatrician whose reputation had been known far and wide since before the occupation. He had a private practice in Smíchov. Alizka likes remembering this period because the professor treated her with kindness. Unlike the way he treated the mothers of some of his patients, to whom he was too strict and authoritarian. Sometimes it fell to Alizka to mediate and reconcile the two sides.

This period did not last very long. The Podolí sanatorium doctors were able to get her father well enough to be discharged. He was not sent home but rather to a sanatorium in Nový Smokovec in the Tatra mountains with intermittent periods in a convalescent home in Kostelec nad Černými lesy near Prague. Alizka was no longer compelled to reside in Prague and she left for Liberec where a few war-ravaged, decimated families had gathered around one surviving uncle. He ran a tight ship with unbending rules and regulations, he was a veritable dictator. When Alizka registered with the local high school in an effort to complete her studies and get a diploma, the good uncle declared that with a sick, widowed father one was not permitted to study because there was no one to finance it. This, despite the fact that he knew full well the government gave grants to kids like Alizka and, when necessary, even a boarding school spot (I was the best example of that). Evidently, his main aim was for another pair of hands to bring in a few crowns to that ghetto family of his. And so Alizka was left with no choice but to abandon her studies and to never obtain her high school diploma. Her desire for education was more powerful than her uncle's despotism. Along with her job in a nursery school, where she eventually became the manager, she completed her studies at a textile college and got a diploma in the English language. Still, when I compare her with many friends in our old homeland, as well as the new one, I must state that she was one of the most intelligent people, with a deep general knowledge without ever formally finishing high school. But I get ahead of myself: we exchanged our vows in November 1952 at the Old City Hall in Prague and celebrated with a few good friends in a lecture hall of the May 5th College in Žižkov (a Prague district). Together, we moved into our apartment on Janáček Quay prior my graduation from medical school in November 1953. The apartment was given to us, as Alizka's father had been officially recognized as disabled due to his concentration camp internment. My new wife confirmed that which we all knew: her knowledge and intelligence. Prior to, and following the birth of our daughters (Ivana in 1954 and Zuzana in 1960), she was employed as a respected copy editor in the State publishing house for technical literature and later as a tourist guide for *Čedok* (state travel agency). She shuttled between Czechoslovakia, Poland, Hungary, and East Germany, guiding groups of Czech tourists. She probably had the wrong "political profile" for contact or travel to other countries – despite her fluency in German and English (a language in which she had official certification). Getting ahead of myself one more time: Her work for *Čedok* was most useful later when we decided to leave Czechoslovakia.

Newlyweds on Wenceslas Square in 1953.

51 Trains from Prague to Liberec and back

We are now at the end of 1948, start of 1949. The intervals between Alizka's dad's hospitalizations became longer and it became necessary for father and daughter to live under one roof. The natural pull was to live with family in Liberec. What that meant for Alizka and me was spending almost every weekend, or a part thereof, in uncomfortable post war trains, shuttling between Prague and Liberec – in both directions. But trifles such as an uncomfortable train, wooden benches, freezing cold in the winter, stifling heat in the summer – none of that could deter young lovers who knew that hours of indescribable happiness awaited at the end of each journey. At the college dorm it was simple: my roommate Honza Mach would leave for the weekend to visit his parents in Benešov, near Prague (he always came back laden with delicacies that lasted us the whole week). Alizka and I had the room to ourselves. It was more complicated in Liberec when her father was at home and not in one of his convalescent homes. But young people were no less resourceful then than they are now. And since this whole chronicle is about memories, I can say without exaggeration that this was the most beautiful and the happiest period of my life. This was the time for the beginning of our joint dreams, and I can say that I cannot find a single dream that has gone unfulfilled. I talk about dreams one could call realistic. It would be too simple, too untruthful, too improbable for every person's each and every rosy dream to come true. The first fulfilled dream was getting married and then, exactly a year later, following my graduation from medical school, the start of my career in medicine. This period has now lasted fifty-two or fifty-three years (to my regret, I write very slowly...it is now 2005 and I will be 79 in a few months). But many very important things have occurred in the interim, and so let me put the gearbox in reverse and let us return to 1948/49.

52 You Want to Live in the Dormitory? Sign this!

The new regime did not remain idle for long. All aspects of life began to be impacted immediately after the Victorious February. Keeping a close watch over everyone and everything that could have indirect connections to imperialist-Zionist agents was at the top of its list. JOINT was adjudged to be such an agent, since they financed housing for Jewish youths left homeless or orphaned after the war. In my first year after high school graduation, and already in my first year of medical school, I lived in just such a house in Krakovská Street. In the fall of 1948, whispered rumors were circulating...and then the voices got louder: the days of JOINT financed homes were numbered. For one thing, religious organizations had no right to provide housing and corrupt our youth with their unprogressive policies. Also, our people's democracy did not need the dirty dollars that came from sources of foreign espionage, which JOINT undoubtedly was involved in! (Incidentally, if memory serves, Mr. Charles Jordan, a representative of this organization, was found dead in the Vltava river in 1967). Clearly it made sense to find lodgings for the beginning of the 1948/49 school year. In my case, the only possible solution would have been a college dorm. One could pick up the application forms at the Dean's office on Kateřinská Street, then submit the filled-out forms and a personal letter to the University Students' Union in Opletalová Street. It took less than a week and I got a letter telling me to show up for my interview to discuss my application for dormitory accommodation.

I was met by the smiling faces of two female students, called by the now current form address as "comrades". They were evidently somewhat older, in the later years of medical studies, as it turned out. They were seated comfortably in armchairs around a small coffee table. I was shown a third armchair, a box of Partizán cigarettes and two steaming, delicious cups of coffee were on the table. (Partizán cigarettes was the cheapest brand smoked by students and laborers. Only one or two other brands were available.) A third cup of coffee appeared in front of me and the Partizáns were pushed towards me with a friendly: "Light up, dear colleague" (how did they know I smoked this brand? I smoked them not because of their quality but because of their bottom basement price, the only smokes I could afford). One of the young women produced a thick file out of her briefcase (let me comment here that I saw these girls later at the university and I know their names...there is no need to mention them here, it is completely irrelevant). I noticed my application form, my application letter and a sheet of paper filled with dense writing, each sentence followed by either a question mark or an exclamation point – or both. I did not read it and did not try to read it despite the distance between me and the nonchalantly laid down paper being only the width of the small coffee table. It was easy to see the question marks and exclamations, as they were written in red ink. I saw the same punctuation in red when one of the girls leafed through the thick file.

I had anticipated and was ready for the interview. I was ready to improvise and change some answers on the fly when I found out who my interviewers were – my only goal was to get a roof over my head. Aside from a few perfunctory questions which checked off a few items off their list – and probably had no effect on my being accepted into the dorm – the whole exercise became a monologue of the two young women who took on the roles of comrades. The monologue came intermittently from the mouths of one or the other female comrade, usually trying to butter me up and convince me of the wonderful future stretching out before us. The monologues were full of cliched phrases, treacly sweet or pompous but always examining my expression and not waiting for a reply. I began suspecting something, it all pointed in one direction, and I began planning my responses. This is how it went approximately (I will not use quotation marks, it has been fifty-seven years, the year now being 2005 and so I cannot quote directly): We have carefully studied your application, dear colleague, and despite the fact that your CV is short, one could say almost telegraphic, it has left a deep impression. We would like to hear details from you directly, about you, about your family, about your reasons for leaving Subcarpathian Ruthenia, about the impact of your high school studies and your opinion – you are Jewish, if we are not mistaken – about the newly created state of Israel.

I took a Partizán cigarette after politely asking for permission, I took a sip of the now cold black coffee, and I began. In the spirit of the times and also because of the desired effect, I spoke sentences full of wooden phrases and lofty language, making it all sound good to their ears. That way of speaking is foreign to me and when I remember my speech, I blush, just like I did throughout the interview itself. Call it opportunism, the one and only time I have been guilty of it. My desperate need to get a room in the dorm, since I had no other home, was so pressing that I forgive myself this one-time transgression. It would be impossible to judge for anyone who was not there and so it is useless trying to apologize or explain to anybody.

My comrade colleagues made themselves comfortable as I was puffing on my Partizán and sipping my coffee that made a gurgling sound as it flowed down my gullet. I began my short but mostly sad curriculum vitae from birth till the fall of 1948. (I declare that what I said was the whole truth and it remains the whole truth, though today I distance myself from the pathetically cliché-filled way in which I expressed it.) Perhaps I said things I did not need to say, did not want to say, did not have to say. I will repeat my CV here so that the following chapters get written.

53 Curriculum Vitae

I started this book by focusing on my hometown, Khust. Now let me turn to my family and me.

I have already revealed elsewhere that my date of birth is January 17th, 1927. I was born in Khust, Subcarpathian Ruthenia, a part of Czechoslovakia at the time. In 1945 the region was magnanimously gifted to the Soviet Union and from its demise in the early 1990's it has been a part of Ukraine. (This is the reason that my Czech passport and other documents show I was born in Ukraine even though my place of birth was

Czechoslovakia. I have never lived in Ukraine, yet when, after the Velvet Revolution of 1989, crossing into the Czech Republic I have had to explain I was not a foreign laborer and did not need a residence permit. Also, Alizka and I arose suspicion when crossing into Slovakia, mainly when coming back from Hungary as well as when crossing the border between the Czech Republic and Slovakia. The friends we travelled with, whose places of birth were beyond suspicion, were left alone while we were cross-examined from all angles.) The place of my birth was remote and provincial as we used to say, "where foxes bid each other good night". But it was the county seat and for one historic day, March 15, 1939, it was the capital of a single day independent state of Subcarpathian Ruthenia The following day we were occupied by Hungary. Like the Slovak State this too, was the last nail in the coffin of the First Czechoslovak Republic.

I was born as the second son, two years younger than the first one and two years older than my little sister who completed our five-member family. We were so poor than only a church mouse could claim to be poorer. I have written elsewhere that my most remote memory goes back to the September day in 1937 when our home room teacher made the announcement that our Liberator President, our Old Father, President Masaryk, had passed away.

I remember that my father worked as a stock keeper for a corn wholesaler. The company was owned by Mr. Wolf. Father's job was to carry full sacks of corn on his back from the trucks and spill it on the clean warehouse floor, only to fill more sacks with it during the next few days for the customers – usually peasants from the surrounding villages –, then carry the sacks to the waiting horse-drawn carriages. The corn served as feed for pigs, chickens and geese. I would bring him his lunches to work and part of his salary was the privilege of filling up pots with corn which mother could use to feed geese. She could sell the geese to well-to-do farmers' wives who would pre-order them. In other words, corn played an important part in feeding our five-member family. That system held until the new regime, the Hungarians, had taken away the right for Jews to run wholesale businesses. An Aryan supplanted Mr. Wolf and no Jewish laborers were wanted.

As an aside: the Wolf family became my sort of patron. When I started high school they gave me a gift – an old, rectangular wristwatch that was in perfect working order and served me well until a Hungarian gendarme became its new owner before we were dragged away to a concentration camp: "You soon won't be needing it anyway!" I always showed the Wolfs each new report card, they praised my excellent results – nothing but A's – and a coin would appear in my palm for my "educational needs".

After the Aryan takeover of the corn warehouse my father was not able to find another job until the Hungarian authorities began mercilessly cutting down the surrounding forests. The wood was loaded on trucks, brought to the Khust railway station, loaded onto rail cars, and taken to Hungary. They were not capable of transporting everything in a timely fashion and so large quantities of wood were lying around the station, and the treasure needed to be guarded. And so, my dad became a night guardsman and stayed one for a long time. I remember that very well because he slept on a sofa (our kitchen was a shabby add-on that could only be used when the temperature stayed above freezing).

When I come to think of it, the whole apartment was an add-on to the long side of my paternal grandparents' house, but I do not know when it was added on. To enter their house, people had to pass from room to room to room. As I mentioned earlier, my grandfather was the only member of my family who found a place of eternal peace in the Jewish cemetery of Khust...

54 Our One Room Home

Let us return to our one room "residence". One look from the outside was enough to see that no architect, no blueprint, no expert was ever involved in building it. And most definitely, no permit was ever received from city authorities (if they even existed) to build additional rooms. The front wall was an artificial continuation of the main building but at first glance its tin roof, painted brown, looked quite surrealistic. It was deeply concave in the middle and you felt like it was going to cave in any minute. In the winter, there could be fifty centimeters of snow on it, and the snow's weight would be greatly increased if it was wet. Every time as we walked home, our eyes darted upwards to see if the roof had bent inwards some more. Naturally, we felt obliged to shovel the frequent snow off, to ward off the danger to its stability. Our roof was clearly crippled! Also, with the help of a ladder, we often visited the attic through a door on the side of the roof. That way we could gauge the state of the roof from the inside. Let me calm you, dear reader – assuming people in the future read this – nothing happened to the roof until the "final solution" of the Jewish question: when my grandmother and my family were forcibly dragged from our home, and yet the house remained standing. Years later I was told it had been demolished, or maybe had collapsed, which would have certainly been symbolic: there was no one left who could or wanted to return.

We have not visited our one room apartment. Enter along with me, through the ill-fitting door (construction quality!) and you will immediately bump into a large kitchen cabinet since there is no mud room or entry room. The cabinet ran almost along the whole length of the wall. The drawers were used for cutlery, plates, and all manner of kitchen utensils. Nothing sophisticated in there, everything was done by hand. The top of the cabinet was used to put down anything and everything you could not hold at the moment. The whole piece was made of used wood, no locks, no keys, just simple wooden drawer handles. Next to the cabinet, there was a table which served as a dining table, work desk and writing desk, meaning we ate at it, did our homework on it and whatever other work needed to be done. There were six simple wooden chairs arranged around the table. Two and two on each side, one at the head of the table, one facing the head. The one facing the head was just there for the look. There was not enough room to pull it out without shoving it into the cabinet. When the family sat together, father sat at the head of the table, with mother and my sister on his right-hand side. That side was roomier, and mom needed space to maneuver between the stove and the table. My brother and I sat opposite, literally flush with the wall. When one of us needed to get up or sit down, the other had to stand, get out and let the first one in or out. Through many years of experience, we had a system worked out before we ever sat down, so these problems only occurred very seldom. The family was not together often during the work week. The mood was brighter on Saturdays and holidays and so we each took our spot without grumbling or shoving.

Since I write about our dining table, this "girl Friday", this "Jack of all trades", I would like to write a few words about the menu and describe the dishes that made the most frequent appearances on our table – then I will continue the tour of our family nest. The basic dish was – what else – the potato! Not as a side but rather as main course. In my mother's skilled hands, the potato received so many different treatments that we could have a different meal every day, for two or three weeks without repeating the same dish. Her palette was truly wide. From boiled potatoes, spread with one teaspoon of Ceres margarine, or half a cup of sour cream on the potatoes or served on the side. Potatoes could be sliced and fried in sunflower oil (we called them *roshayben*, the Hungarian equivalent of chips). Potato latkes were a delicacy – made either from raw or cooked potatoes (mostly around Christmas time when they were served in chicken or beef soup). In the summer, the favorite dish was a so-called cold white soup...mildly sour but tasting delicious. With a piece of fresh bread, it was a real delicacy, and you could stuff yourself like a lumberjack. When they were in season, fresh green beans could be added to the soup – that was a real special day! I do not remember potato salad from my childhood. What I do recall are potatoes roasted upon the glowing embers left when the wood in our primitive iron stove burned out (primitive as seen by today's eyes). And the very best, the prize meal? That would have been the festive Shabbat meal. From grandmother's fragrant village oven out came the *cholent* – redolent for miles. The cholent was accompanied by potato pie, called a *kugl*, baked in a stone dish. Both dishes would have been in the earthen oven since Friday. The oven was blazing hot and tamped down by mounds of clay. Who knows what other magic dishes mom's nifty hands and inventive mind could conjure up? All I know is that remembering those feasts, I am slobbering like Pavlov's dogs. Even though the ingredients for all our meals were exceedingly simple, only things our family income could afford, the dishes were heavenly. We still serve some of those meals today, though the main ingredient of our white soup is now cream and the cholent does not only consist of beans or other legumes Today's version includes large chunks of meat – beef, smoked duck, or goose. In mother's variant the most you would find would have been chicken giblets to add some fragrance and taste. (All of this is not to demean the culinary artistry of Alizka, who is famous in our family as well as all our friends here and abroad. A wizard without competition!)

But a poor, penniless person does not live by potatoes alone. The second spot on our menu were beans and sauerkraut that was pickled in the fall to last through the winter. And there was corn, mostly corn flour. What dishes can one create from corn flour and use as a solid meal? Corn bread, corn pancakes, porridge (called *tokány* locally, *mamaliga* by the Romanians). You could pour some milk over it and voila – dinner! And then the real delicacy: you put some sheep cheese (*bryndza*) on the pancake, corn paste on top, more *bryndza*, more paste. You put the whole thing in the oven...words are not enough to describe the divine taste of this ambrosia. I would need to be endowed with poetic talent. Homemade pastries and again, not as a side, but served as main course. Occasionally a herring, bought in the store, scooped out of a large barrel, and wrapped up in a newspaper (I had reading material for a while). Vegetables, only rarely – in the summer, of course. They were not bought. Mother grew them on a little scrap of land left to her by a cousin who used to live in Khust. Occasionally, I would accompany my mother to help her work and harvest those two or three rows. My God, the memories this brings up!

I could probably recall some other kitchen smells if I would continue in this direction, but I believe that is sufficient. Mostly because I need to talk about one other thing. About the holiday table during Shabbat and holidays. Some classic Jewish traditions were observed by everyone, not just strictly observant families or people who adhered to every edict. This was simply the tradition and every Jewish family kept it. Observing Shabbat and the holidays – despite obvious religious content – was a given, even if you were not particularly religious or a regular attendee of the synagogue. Everyone felt the need to distinguish these days from the mundane, the everyday. Even those who had distanced themselves from the faith would include some meat in their Shabbat and holiday celebrations (in the religious tradition Shabbat is the holiday of holidays!) Usually, it would have been a chicken, and mother's nifty hands and her culinary imagination could magically produce a "meat" holiday dinner for Friday evening using just the wings and giblets. The festive Shabbat mid-day meal would contain the best parts of the chicken in a cholent. This meal would start with chicken soup made from the remaining carcass and homemade noodles, served with radish. If my memory serves, at the end of this royal meal would be a dessert, most frequently fruit when in season – mainly beautiful red, sweet watermelon that had been lowered down into the well on Friday to be served cold.

In the summer, a glass of sour milk in the afternoon was a great delicacy. It was homemade – we put the milk aside the day before and let it go sour. We usually drank it after coming back from some piece of land that served as a soccer field. Naturally, our ball was a few rags stitched together. We usually stole back home quietly, so that mother would not notice that our shoes had also been transformed into rags and the holiday trousers went straight into the laundry so they would be clean and ready to wear next Saturday. Jackets and sweaters stayed clean. The Saturday afternoon soccer match (our team from Žatkovičová Street against some other street or a group of streets) often ended badly and not only because of the sporting component. Sometimes, a large ram from a herd of sheep grazing on a nearby field took it into his head to run as well. Usually, he would not chase the ball; he preferred chasing the ones chasing the ball! He would pick a victim (it was me once), bow his head and sprint straight ahead, aiming for the buttocks of one of the soccer players. The player would tumble down and roll up in a ball and would be saved from bad injury only through the heroic actions of his teammates. When I was the victim of the attack, my shirt and pants were in tatters, and I walked away with painful bruises on my butt and the backs of my thighs. Clear proof that this was a vile, unsportsmanlike attack from behind, as I was fleeing the pitch, not as a striker!

I have lost my original thread – describing our dwelling. We need to complete the tour of our one room apartment. As for the interior, my last description was that of father's chair. Behind his chair, as seen from the doorway, there was a rather small double wardrobe, divided so that the right half could contain hanging clothing and the left all the underwear for the family. There was plenty of room for all of it. The women, mother and my sister, probably had more whites and more clothes but us, men, had one spare suit of clothes – everything we could ever need. Always clean, ironed, tidy. Under the window which looked out to a storage shed in a neighbor's yard, there was a sofa – a narrow piece just about sufficient for one person, in our case, our father's sleeping quarters. The shed outside the window blocked all light and air. In the corner there was the above-mentioned iron stove with a tin chimney that ran through the wall and outside. There were two openings on the top surface of the stove. The openings were covered by circular iron covers that were removed for cooking so that the pot could be in direct contact with the burning wood inside. In the winter, the stove was our source of heat. The third wall was where the headboards of our two beds were. The headboards had a nightstand in between them, and the beds had straw mattresses – burlap stuffed with straw. One bed was shared by my mother and my sister, the other bed was for mine and my brother's place of nightly rest. The second bed was flush with the fourth wall which had two windows. Each window had colorful flowers in it – except in the winter season – a decoration for the inside and the outside and mainly warming up the heart of my mother who loved flowers. The only decoration in the actual room was a large color photograph on the wall between the beds: mother's brother David, resplendent in red jodhpurs and an elegant military tunic, atop a beautiful steed – the pride of the family, a *hussar* (light cavalry soldier) in the Czechoslovak army. He survived but lost his young wife and four little children in the Nazi inferno.

The apartment was modest in the utmost for a family of five. I do not know what would have befallen us three children and what future we would have faced had we stayed there and not been forced to start new lives on three different continents. But for the time being, the family was together.

55 My Parents

My father, a man with a kind personality, amiable and docile and with no formal education, was apparently unable to fight for his place in society. My little sister was the apple of his eye. She was two years younger than me and only fifteen when that good man was torn away from us, but she still remembers his boundless goodness, she still recalls her loving father who coddled her. No one in our whole family has a single photograph of him and his great grandchildren's desire to at least see the face of this lovely man, is in vain. His face, his contours all slowly fade from my memory...I see before me a slim man, almost too thin, with bright blue eyes that radiate goodness and light, copper-red thinning hair, wearing shabby work clothes except on holidays when he put on his tailor made dark grey suit. The suit had probably been purchased in better times. He was a sweet and loving man – but he was not able to support his family.

A part of that responsibility fell to my mother. She was the dominant force in the family: assertive, dynamic, with the command of her family firmly in hand. I do not remember much from that time period, but family old timers say that she started selling shots in a tavern and collecting the money when she was ten years old. She had to stand on a stool to reach the bar and across the bar. On family matters she made all the decisions.

And she was a workhorse. As I have said, she got vegetables for the family, she fed geese for the market and when the going got tough, she took on a job as cleaning lady for the Elek and Wolf pharmacy (which belonged to the son of our father's employer). I was aware of her level of activity as a child, though with the passing years I have forgotten the various tasks and jobs she had labored on.

The household poverty, the daily struggle to keep the family afloat – and later simply alive – did not and could not create conditions for a family life full of love and contentment. There were no loud words, and I am sure there was love, support and compassion below the surface but I do not recall any overt expressions of content family life. Mother did not have a formal education, but she was naturally intelligent, always ready and able to help anyone, anytime. She was sought after as a family counsellor, dispensing advice on a variety of everyday matters to friends and neighbors. Many young girls and women from the village of Zolotarevo (my mother's birthplace) would visit Khust to buy clothes and other fashionable items. My mother was their guide and consultant. I do not recall her having a single enemy or being part of any clash. She took care of the family correspondence, she communicated with the authorities in at least four languages despite not being perfect in some of them.

My mother's indomitable will to survive, no matter how impossibly tough life got, helped her live through the hell of the concentration camps and she was able to save my little sister – both during our 1941 deportation but mainly in the camps during 1944–45. Luckily, they went in together and came back together.

It is sad that not even her old age was easy. Not wanting to be a burden to our relatives, she gave in to their pressure and married a man who ensured her material survival but nothing else. Having two granddaughters in the 1950's was a small balm for her pain, but fate was unjust to her: she was unable to see her other two grandchildren: my brother's sons. He and his family lived in Israel and the old, retired lady presented such danger to the regime of the day, they would not let her visit – traveling to the enemy state of Israel was taboo.

But she visited my brother for the first time in almost twenty years and saw her grandchildren, who had by then grown into young adults. The visit, like everything else she did, was the result of her strong will, determination, and perseverance. She only lost those qualities when she was quite old.

One day, I think the year was 1963 and she would have been close to seventy, she decided the time had come to see her son and his family before she left this world. Her grandchildren were the main impetus. Her application for a passport and exit visa was denied. She was told the rejection had come from the highest possible authority. She decided that the highest authority was the Central Committee of the Communist Party. She walked from Karlín (the Prague district where she lived) to the bank of the river nearby, and she found the appropriate building. She told the doorman very simply that she wanted to see "the highest possible comrade, the comrade who decided who could travel to visit family". She sat down in the doorman's booth and proclaimed she would not budge until she saw the person she had come to see. Phones began ringing off the hook, chance (or not so chance) office personnel came to take their measure of this weird old lady. And wonder of wonders...mother found herself in a luxurious office and quickly addressed the comrade, who sat behind his luxurious desk and did not think to get up to offer the old lady a chair: "Comrade, do you have a son?" The comrade replied in the affirmative. "And do you have grandchildren?" That, too, was not denied by the comrade. "And comrade, when was the last time you saw them?" she asked. "This past weekend, at the cottage", the stalwart comrade replied, not understanding what this was about. "See?", my mother said. "I am a pensioner, almost seventy years old, a widow whose husband died in a Nazi concentration camp. I do not want any foreign currency from you" (a shortage of foreign currency was the usual official refusal to issue an exit visa). "So what, even if I do not come back? It will be no loss to the state, I am not going to be building socialism at my age and, what is more, you could keep my pension. Do I not have a right to see my son who has survived the camps and has also survived two wars since then? And my grandchildren! What grandmother would not want to see her grandchildren?"

The comrade understood that the lady in front of him might not have been formally educated but she was certainly very bright, toughened by life and very determined. He began to show certain signs of understanding and kindness. "Let me have a look at your application and I will see what I can do", he said in a friendly tone. "Now go home, comrade, we will advise you of our decision as soon as possible"

It took less than two weeks and mother got a short letter, informing her that her application for travel to Israel had been approved. She got her passport, her exit visa and ten British pounds and she flew to Israel via Switzerland. She spent about a month there and had the pleasure of spending time not just with her son and grandsons. My little sister flew in from America and so, after about fifteen years, mother was able to see her son, her daughter, and grandchildren. My family and I waited for her return to Prague with bated breath, wanting to hear first-hand news of the family whom the current Czechoslovakian regime had decreed unfit to live and rejoice together. I have written these paragraphs to illustrate my mother's character.

It is possible that our family circumstances as well as the terrible situation in the 1940's, a time I clearly remember, caused us kids to mature before our time. We never rebelled, and we did not realize that our obedient behavior would not make a bad situation worse. We were kids who made no extravagant demands, good kids who respected their parents. No one would have known whether we were sated or hungry (not that I remember ever being hungry – our home always had the necessary staples). None of us kids would have been seen outside the house, at school, in public places, on visits to friends and relatives, unclean, untidy, or unkempt. This, even though our whole wardrobe consisted of one change of clothes. I remember getting my first tailor made suit when I was in the fifth grade of the gymnasium (the equivalent of about tenth grade). And what a dandy three piece it was! We selected the material ourselves in our local tailor shop. I chose a blue stripe, my brother preferred dark grey. We later said good-bye to our suits in Auschwitz.

To end this chapter, I must write a cliché – one that every writer uses in similar cases. Outside of the home, wherever and whenever, in public or at school – aside from the closest family, no one had an idea of the effort and work it took to always appear clean, polite, cheerful, and always ready and willing to help others and never ask anything of anyone. If we could give – we would. It might be a bit of an exaggeration to claim this for the time in question, especially about us kids. We were minors and it was a time of persecution. I am talking about later years when we were older and independent. Our childhood had a positive influence on all of us.

I struggle to recollect details about our childhood together. It has been a long time, more than sixty years since circumstances tossed us into the wind and scattered us on three different continents. My brother and sister had an easier time of it. They lived in a world where writing to each other was not a sin and if they had the resources, they could see each other too. Neither my brother in Israel, nor my sister in America had the means to travel in those first years after the war. And me? For about twenty years a meet-up was only a dream and correspondence was a personal risk, even if one wrote only about family matters and nothing else. And so, the gap grew wider. We parted when we were still almost children and we met when half our lives were behind us – it was during that time that we were able to reconstruct certain events and experiences. And so, I apologize in advance for planning to write a few more sentences about myself. Just what I remember – more or less.

56 My Brother and Sister

There will not be much about my brother. Till the age of six, till the age of compulsory school attendance, he had been raised by mother's parents in the village of Zolotarevo. My brother called one of mother's sisters, Lea, "mom" long after he had come back home. This was my mother's family's way of helping my parents. I remember more about my brother from his time in elementary school and later when he was an apprentice auto mechanic in Krajník's auto repair shop. He made a bit of money there and was able to help the family out a little bit. We said good-bye to each other on the Auschwitz *Appelplatz* (roll call) after an SS guard ordered everyone with a specialized trade, including mechanics, to step out of the line.

My brother survived but we did not get a chance to meet after the war, because he immediately left for Palestine via Romania and Italy. That was before the creation of the state of Israel. Like many others, he was apprehended by the British and interned in Cyprus. When he reached Israel, he started working right away in the technical department of the General Health Insurance Agency, which covered all healthcare before and after statehood. Those days physicians who worked in distant settlements and kibbutzim were provided with an unusual mode of transportation − a donkey. Cars came later. My brother oversaw maintaining the cars his whole working life until he retired. Even now, in 2005, at the age of 80, he is still being asked to help. Why not? He is good at what he does, has been doing it for 59 years and now as a volunteer. Those who remember say that he resembles my father in his character. You would be hard pressed to find a nicer, more devoted man in this world. He even served in the reserves till the age of 60 instead of the usual 45 because his vehicle maintenance expertise was so crucial during training and war time. That is what the commanders thought but it was possibly because he was never able to say no to anyone. But mostly because he was an expert and a totally reliable worker.

I am glad he is still healthy. He is an incredibly quiet, good man whom I love and whom my sister adores. If you talk to anyone from Rehovot, the town he settled in when he arrived and where he still lives, you will blush when you hear the praise heaped upon this simple, modest man.

A single black and white photograph of my four-year-old sister remains in the family since childhood. One look suffices to bring up the deepest, oldest memories of my slim, graceful, beautiful little sister. I remember taking her to kindergarten, there was always a ribbon in her beautiful chestnut-colored hair. I remember her smiling little blue eyes. She was the darling of the family, loved by all. She returned the love and kindness in equal measure. She loved our father and still remembers him with tenderness. Sometimes it seems to me that those six decades since he was torn from his family have only deepened her love and admiration.

But the saddest memory is still with me. It fell to me to tell this frail little girl, who was barely alive, who seemed like the wind could just blow her away any second, it fell to me to tell her the painful news that she would never again see her beloved and most loving father. I will never forget her sad eyes and I cannot shake the feeling her profound sorrow has never left those eyes. She has told me several times that my father's love was the only parental love she truly felt. I suppose every mother loves her child and vice versa. We only have one mother, and we cling to her, as children we need her, she feeds us, clothes us, heals us when we are sick. As children, the most we can do in return is "be good". (I do not think mother played favorites, though rumor had it that I was the favorite child – I excelled in my studies.)

I remember a pretty, slim, elegantly dressed adolescent after the war, between the ages of sixteen and eighteen and how she enjoyed my visits "home" in Ústí nad Labem. Her fate was like that of many girls of her age who had managed to survive: not finishing high school and then, after liberation, due to family circumstances, the inability to further their education. She completed a sewing course, sponsored by the international Jewish orphan charity ORT and got married. While waiting with her husband for their American visa, the Iron Curtain fell. This meant they had to leave Czechoslovakia illegally. I accompanied them to Bratislava (more about that later) and there I waited for word that they had safely reached Austria. Their immigration papers came after they had stayed in Austria for several months, and they were finally able to reach the land of boundless opportunity. Back-breaking labor in a clothing factory in New York followed, and then a move to California, where they were able to strike roots and prosper. My brother-in-law became a clothing manufacturer and my sister assisted him. I had precious little information about them until 1965. Her correspondence with our mother was my source of intermittent information (do young people today even know that contact with a sister residing in a "hostile country" was a crime then?). They visited us in Israel after we emigrated. A twenty-year separation – and suddenly adults with their own families, still subconsciously living in the memories of sixteen and seventeen-year-olds.

My little sister was not able to escape her sad fate in later life either, when she lived in peace and quiet and comparative affluence in faraway California. Her husband died around the age of forty, following a pernicious disease, and she has remained on her own, with an adopted daughter. Her frequent visits to Israel were but a weak substitute for close personal contact. I was able to visit her in her Beverly Hills home in California when I attended various pediatric surgery conferences, as well as during the four four-month sabbaticals I spent in the U.S. – mostly in the Chicago area. In recent years the visits have dwindled almost to zero. As she ages, my sister finds the almost twenty-hour flight progressively more grueling and, being retired, I can no longer attend conferences, not to mention go on sabbaticals. A get-together in Prague five years ago was the most amazing of all our meetings. Truly an unforgettable time.

We both love Prague. Our frequent and long transatlantic phone conversations make up for the lack of contact only to a small degree.

57 Earning a Living

The picture of my family and of myself would be incomplete if I did not describe the situation of a poor boy studying at the gymnasium and speak about the expenses related to his studies. Food and basic, decent clothing were taken care of by my parents. But let me use the old cliché and say *man does not live by bread alone.* It was not possible to borrow every book from friends or from the library. Since my student days till today I remain a devourer of books. There were ways to see a soccer match but if you wanted to see a movie, you needed to buy a ticket. The situation

My sister Šarlota and brother Natan (right) and I in 1985 at Zuzana's wedding.

did not change when I was accepted at the gymnasium. I started my first grade, the *prima*, (equivalent of sixth grade in grammar school) before World War II, while we were still a part of Czechoslovakia. Tuition was free but books, study aids, gym clothes, better clothes, school excursions, attendance of compulsory shows and other cultural events and who knows what else – for all that you had to pay. I know one thing: it disrupted the family budget in a much more impactful way than was seen from the outside.

The bearable situation did not last long. Six and a half months after the beginning of the school year, a bit longer than the first semester and the

Czechoslovak State Gymnasium became the Hungarian Royal Gymnasium, along with everything the change brought with it.

The worst hardship was having to pay tuition. And it was a pretty hefty sum – not something that just anyone could afford. My parents most certainly could not. Despite all that, there was some promise in the beginning. Students with an excellent grade average were exempt from paying tuition. Unfortunately, that only meant one year in my case. When it came to the curtailing of Jewish rights, the regime worked quickly and efficiently. One of the first measures was the cancelation of the excellence exemption for "students of the Israelite faith". You could be the best student to the power of ten…you would not be exempt if you were Jewish. The sliding scale, previously in effect for people with low incomes, also did not apply. Everyone had to pay the same tuition, without exception. I say "everyone". Well, how many were there? One of the first racist enactments was an immediate *numerus clausus*.

I was about twelve years old when I understood a life's little secret: I realized that if I wanted to continue with my studies – and I wanted that more than anything else then – I had no choice but to get cracking and find work. I can say without hyperbole that since that time I have always been able to be financially self-sufficient and make enough to support myself and later my family, then with Alizka's help. The exception to this was a period of two years right after the war, when I had some support from various Jewish repatriation charities and foundations in the form of a stipend while at high school. I have never had any other financial support or an inheritance.

It was clear to me, then, that although I was only twelve, I needed to make enough to see me through my gymnasium studies. That is when I first heard the word "tutoring". There were plenty of students who needed it. Mostly kids from well-to-do families whom the parents had already marked for a career in law, medicine, or banking. I started offering my services for free and when the parents saw the improvement in their youngsters' grades, they began demanding more hours and started paying me. It did not take long, and our family budget was at least partly freed from the necessity to pay for my studies. More and more tutoring clients came my way, and I was able to focus on my goal: a gymnasium diploma. That was still far in the future and not even the greatest pessimist could have foretold the obstacles I needed to overcome to reach that goal.

My tutoring did not bring in enough to cover all my study expenses. My income from it was meagre and it made great demands on my time; time that perhaps should have been spent studying and preparing. But I was somehow able to do it all and not only that – I continued to increase my earnings by adding other sources of income during vacation and holidays. I remember making caramel out of sugar at home, sometimes adding nuts or sunflower seeds, and I would sell my product to folks we shared our yard with: all the aunties and uncles and cousins. The older ones might have had boyfriends or girlfriends and I would sell to them too. In fact, they were my best buyers as they wanted to impress their girl (or boy). Another source of income was collecting financial contributions from well-to-do families and distributing them to the needy, mostly before holidays. The collector would be given a tip. What was ironic was the fact that I was a collector, but my family was never on the list of the needy. Parents' pride!

The good results my tutoring clients were achieving did not escape the attention of the parents of my Jewish classmate, Alexander Pikkel. His family had recently moved to Khust from Hungary. The father was from Subcarpathian Ruthenia, the mother from Hungary's inland. I do not know what their source of income was, but they certainly led the life of rich people – at least the way I saw it then. Alex was an only child, raised in a Hungarian speaking household, quite capable but obviously spoiled. His studies did not progress as well as the parents would have wished. They offered me a job: not just to tutor Alex but take him under my wing and turn him into a solid, tenacious student. In other words, not just the occasional tutoring session but steady, daily work. We were to do our homework together, prepare for exams together, even read the compulsory works of literature together and go on trips together. The reward was highly tempting: my school tuition paid in full, plus pocket money.

Additionally, I would be given a great snack along with Alex, certainly much better than anything I could have brought from home. I let all my other tutoring work go – I would have had no time for it anyway – and I did all my schoolwork at Alex's place with him. This went on for two full school years: the fifth and the sixth gymnasium grade (approximately equivalent to ninth and tenth grades in today's high school).

I was sixteen, seventeen years old and I know I made my parents' life substantially easier, but it still was not enough money for the common expenses of a maturing student because there was so much that needed to be purchased, such as study aids and books, plus there were other miscellaneous expenses. This was the time I really started noticing girls and to make an impression, you had to dress better, go to the cinema and other, often modest and primitive, "cultural" events. And the books! The huge need for books! I did not have money to buy them and not all the ones I needed were to be found in the school library whose one great advantage was that there was no charge. The public city library did demand a small fee. And there were many things around me that were simply inaccessible. No two ways about it: you had to hear the clink of silver in your pocket.

As student of the higher gymnasium grades in a small town I became somewhat of a celebrity. It was well known that I could handle a pen, a pencil and paper, could write and work out numbers quickly and that I had excellent penmanship. It was also known that for a small fee I was ready and willing to help. And so, I found it fairly easy to get work with local offices or small merchants. Writing letters – longhand! – to offices, banks, clients, going over accounts or tidying up paperwork. I must reveal a basic, maybe even sad, reality here: Very often there was a language problem, a language barrier. In places that were a veritable Babylon of languages, there were some business owners who could speak a few languages fluently but had difficulty writing.

As for the long summer vacation, I usually had a full-time job for the whole two months (the notion of "vacation" and "rest" was the privilege of the well-to-do).

As I have mentioned, after finishing school my brother apprenticed in the car repair shop of Mr. Krajník and later became an auto mechanic. The shop he worked at serviced and repaired mainly trucks that hauled in wood from the surrounding forests, near and far. In those days the forests were plundered mercilessly. Occasionally, a passenger car would stray into the shop (there were very few back then). Mr. Krajník would often complain about the various issues and problems in the administrative part of his business, and my brother remarked (probably just mumbled quietly since an apprentice did not speak to the boss unless spoken to directly) that he knew someone who could do this type of work, someone who did similar jobs for others, a student who made a few extra pennies that way. It just so happens, my brother said, that he is my younger brother. "Bring him over in the morning, let him show me what he can do!"

And so, the next morning, bright and early at six o'clock, I stood in front of Mr. Krajník, who looked me up and down and said: "Very well, go sit in the office and wait for their excellencies, my staff, to get here at eight o'clock. They'll show you what a car repair shop job is all about". Around eight o'clock (actually even later), "their excellencies" arrived. There were about four of them. It took me a while to get my bearings (what the heck did I know about trucks?). But it really was not too complicated: which truck came in, what problem was diagnosed, was it there for service or a repair, who worked on it and for how many hours, what parts were needed at what cost, which and how many tires were changed, was the truck and the cab cleaned inside and out? The main thing was the cost of parts and other materials and the cost of labor. Basically, the amount of the full bill and how much was outstanding. We had to order new parts and new material, and calculate the workers' salaries, depending on whether they worked on an hourly, daily, or weekly basis. Once a month we made sure to deduct the proper sum for health insurance, social insurance and, of course, never forget the tax man! (I hope I did not forget anything; it has been more than sixty years...yes, that is how slowly I write, it is December 2006. On that day, it all seemed pretty simple to me. I knew I could manage it and just waited for the owner's decision.) To my surprise, around noontime, his just-washed, wet hand slapped my shoulder and said: "Start working". I did not even go home that day and worked a full shift. And that is how it went right through the summer vacation and, if needed, sometimes even during the school year.

Another curious money-making venture came up when the countries changed hands: signs and shingles for storefronts and workshops needed to be replaced. My youngest uncle (Dad's youngest brother, only about four years older than me) took the initiative and dragged me into it as well, to make use of my beautiful handwriting, and we began making signs to order. I must say, they came out no worse than the ones previously done by professionals. This work was long-term, and no one protested that we amateurs were moonlighting. And some more silver came in.

58 Events I Will Not Write About

All those events happened prior to, as well as following our Ukrainian exile – till the spring of 1944, when all things pointed to the fact that since I had the necessary talent and all the necessary conditions were in place, I would soon reach my first desired goal, a gymnasium diploma. When the thundering of cannons was heard during quiet nights and the liberating armies were approaching, it was clear the end of the war was near. But the Hungarian-German alliance found it necessary to complete the business at hand and make Europe *Judenfrei*, despite the obvious need to employ all available means and personnel on the collapsing eastern front. The goal of Jew-free Europe took precedence over everything. We may have been winning, we may have been losing but *Ordnung muss sein* ("there must be order" in German). The Wannsee conference resolution (January 1942) must be carried out to the letter!

As I have said, I will not write about what followed. I do not want to, and I cannot. Others have written about it plenty and if in the future thousands more books are written, no one can ever describe the incredible horror. I do not believe it is possible to describe it.

The previous pages are a significantly expanded version of the statement I gave to two female comrades sitting opposite me at the interview for a place in the student dormitory. I have a sneaky feeling – it has been almost sixty years after all – that my narration was somewhat bombastic and cliché-ridden, probably formulated to play on the emotions of the two young women. For one thing, people tended to talk like that in those days. For another thing, I wanted to make sure I got through to them in a way they would understand, and I would surely get what I went there for. I was desperate to find my own warm place, with a bed and a roof over my head. Let me remind you: I had no home – the Jewish youth home in Krakovská Street had been closed by the "authorities" in accordance with the demands of the prevailing ideology. I had no money for rent, even if I could find a place.

There was a short silence, then one of the lady comrades pulled out a sheet of paper and put it down in front of me. I had suspected something was up during the interview. Nevertheless, the heading on the page took me by surprise: "The Communist Party of Czechoslovakia". Before I had a chance to utter a word, one of the comrades took the floor and said in a jubilant voice: "*The Party needs people like you! A young intelligent man who is receiving a state scholarship, from working class origins, a man who has survived concentration camps and lost his father and countless relatives there, a man educated in a progressive high school and with the potential to take him far – but only with the Party's assistance. We call on you and we recommend that you sign an application to become a member of the Party. We will sponsor your application and at the same time we will facilitate your request to get a room at the dormitory.*" At that moment I grasped the meaning of the saying "the end justifies the means". I was young but my life experience definitely also played a role in my decision to sign. I saw a gleam of satisfaction in both comrades' eyes and understood that I had signed up for more than just the thing I had come for. I felt a measure of guilt that I had – for the first and last time in my life – acted opportunistically. It was opportunistic in the sense that I needed a spot in the dorm, not party opportunism – I had absolutely no desire for a political career. By way of explanation, not an excuse, let me say that the events I have thus far described and the upheavals I had gone through dictated that I look for ways never to experience anything like it again. It turned out that this method did not work either – more about that later.

I did get my spot at the dorm, but I had no idea what was expected of me as a party member, what my rights and my duties would be. I did not know, and no one had told me that I must register not just in the school cell of the party but also the larger local cell. I did not set-in motion any initiative in that direction. I do not remember the exact course of events that followed but I do recall all sorts of party and study-related screenings. I will mention the study screenings later. The party screenings did not go well. I got reprimanded due to my "passivity" and was put on a two-year waiting list as a candidate. Incidentally, this turned out to be no punishment at all: everyone who signed up to become a member of the party after the "Victorious February" was put on a two-year waiting list.

Something else did happen at that point, though. The political screenings took place during a time when the wave of emigration to the recently created State of Israel was at its peak. This emigration was done with the full knowledge and support of the ruling Communist Party. The Party was hoping that a country with a socialist, nearly communist system of collective farms (*kibbutzim*) which played first fiddle in the political and economic life of Israel, a country lead by a Labor party headed by the leftist politician Ben Gurion, a country which had absorbed thousands of survivors of Nazi camps who, in the main, believed the propaganda emanating from the East about the supposed total equality of all races and nationalities in Israel, was ripe to become the first socialist country in the Middle East. What it meant in practice was arranging a massive supply of armaments to the imperiled country and thereby preventing a military chokehold on the new state. The state was barely breathing but Czechoslovakia seemed proud to be helping. The thought of lifting anchor and following the thousands who had left for Israel, was definitely on my mind. I was about to start a course that was helping establish the Israeli Air Force on Czechoslovakian soil. (At that time I met Ezer Weizmann, the future general and Israeli Air Force commander, and later still the President of Israel. His son served in the vicinity of the Suez Canal where the Israeli army was stationed following the Six Day War. Weizmann's son was shot in the head by an Egyptian sniper. He recovered but his injury caused him to be impulsive and lose control easily. Later, he was badly injured, this time while driving his car. Once again, he received serious injuries. He was brought to my hospital where his father was a frequent visitor. We renewed our acquaintance and we reminisced about Hotel Flora in the Prague district of Vinohrady – a hotel where Israeli arms buyers and organizers of various military courses used to be billeted.)

59 Serious and Fateful Decisions

Around that time I finished my first and second semester with a pretty weak grade average, partly because I could not decide whether to follow the thousands who had emigrated to Israel. I had begun contemplating enrolling in a course organized by the *Haganah* under the auspices of the Czechoslovak army. I had interrupted my studies for a year, though I had not given up on my plan to become a doctor in the future. My exchange of letters with my brother in Israel and the sister of my wife to be, Maňka, both of whom having already settled in Israel was clear: continuing my medical studies in Israel was an unrealistic dream. First of all, as soon as I disembarked, I would be drafted into the armed services, and even after peace was achieved, I would only have had the slimmest of chances to enroll in the only small faculty of medicine at the Hebrew University in Jerusalem. Moreover, medical studies were extremely expensive – who would finance such a luxury? Taking my decision was a slow process, there were a lot of points for and a lot against. Why run away now when life in Prague had begun to unfold quite nicely and I had even found my life partner? I already had my Alizka and was head over heels in love. To leave would have meant leaving her alone with her sick father, who was receiving the medical care he could not have received anywhere else in the world.

And as I was slowly deciding and going back and forth in my mind, forces beyond my control made the decision for me – almost overnight. Israel's political direction began leaning further west towards America and western liberal democracy in general. The cold war had begun and the hope that Israel would become a member of the "progressive peace camp" seemed more and more distant. The East European Communist Parties had been hoping for more from the people who had recently been fighting British imperialism and whose new state had all the prerequisites to continue as a member of the "peace camp", as it was called. What is more, Israel turned out to be a most ungrateful country. During the long and intense UN debates about the fate of Palestine after the dissolution of the British mandate, it was Jan Masaryk who used his prestige and amiable personality to advocate for a Jewish homeland. The head of the Soviet delegation, Andrey Gromyko, later a USSR foreign minister, gave Zionist speeches unmatched by any other delegate. And it was the USSR and the other socialist countries who recognized Israel instantly, right after Ben Gurion's Independence Proclamation in May 1948 in Tel Aviv. When the USSR and socialist countries realized that Israel was irreversibly turning to the West, they had to retaliate for this perfidy. Consequently, they instantly stopped all emigration and put in place an immediate embargo on arms supplies and military training. And that was not enough: forthwith, Czechoslovakia began arming and training the Egyptians and the other countries neighboring Israel (save for Jordan). They made no secret of the weapons and training being squarely aimed at Israel.

This sudden ban on travel caught many people by surprise. No personal travel, no family or friends' visits. Emigrating was now completely out of the question and made the reunification of families, the remnants of families impossible. Families only recently completely decimated, families that had only found each other four years prior, families scattered throughout the world who had barely escaped with their lives. The travel ban was mainly, we can say exclusively, meant for Israel, a country that was suddenly not "kosher". Some families had been able to get away but those who stayed behind were stuck without a chance of appeal.

I was indecisive; perhaps I was just flirting with the idea of emigrating. My main goal was to study and to stay with Alizka, who could not and did not want to leave her sick father. On the other hand, my sister had just gotten married, and her husband had been promised "papers", supposedly to be sent to him by an uncle in America. They preferred America to Israel.

There was a buzzword going around among those caught in the turmoil. The word was *Brikha*, Hebrew for "flight", more precisely "escape". I am not sure what the source of the word was and who led the eponymous organization, but it had already been known during the war, when it helped Jews escape occupied Europe. They gathered people and transported them to safety and to Palestine. Palestine was a British mandate, and the Brits did their best to block immigration. Those that made it illegally, sailing across the sea, were often caught by British police or army forces, and immediately transferred to Cyprus (also under British rule), where they were interned in camps. That was my brother's fate. After the creation of Israel this chapter of Jewish history ended, and he could immigrate to Israel legally. Legally, yes, but under fierce attack of all the Arab armies, who assaulted Israel after her declaration of independence. And so, a new field of activity was born. There was a need to save Jews in peril and help them escape to Israel.

My sister and brother-in-law had found out that *Brikha* was active in Slovakia – illegally, naturally – and they were helping folks escape to Austria, where they ran refugee camps with the intention to later transport people to Israel. Such camps also existed in other countries, mainly in Italy and France. It must be stated that these camps were illegal prior to the establishment of Israel because British politicians blocked all immigration to Palestine and so European countries outlawed such camps. No one stopped to think that the people being persecuted were all recent survivors, liberated from other camps, the camps of Nazi horror!

One day, in the first half of 1949, matters advanced, so my sister and her husband, a small suitcase in hand, bought tickets for a Bratislava bound train. After a short deliberation, Alizka and I joined them, and we reached Bratislava with the intention that I get out of the country. Alizka and I promised each other to make every effort and use all means necessary for her to join me once her father's health improved. We stayed in a small hotel and waited, to be told that only my sister and her husband would be able to continue, and I would have to return to Prague with Alizka: the guys of the *Brikha* could not take me. That was another attempted escape – an unsuccessful one. I was not really sorry. I was able to stay with Alizka. Today, I am filled with horror when I realize how little we knew then about the regime's ability to punish those who betray it. Most likely she would never have been able to get out.

I returned to my medical studies in the winter semester of 1949/50, completed them in 1953, and became a pediatric surgeon. Alizka and I married in 1952 and we had two beautiful daughters. I allowed Prague to worm its way into my heart. Therefore, Israel had to wait for us for another sixteen years. No one ever found out that I had in fact committed a criminal act: at that time, in that country my act would have been labeled "an attempt to illegally flee the republic".

During the ensuing sixteen years, as a part of continuous political profiling, I had to fill out various human resources forms and questionnaires, which all included the same crafty question: "Do you have a parent, a sibling, a relative or a friend living abroad", followed by "if you answered in the affirmative, state where they live and their profession" and, finally, "do you maintain correspondence or another form of contact with them". I answered some of those questions truthfully and some things I kept to myself. For example, I answered truthfully, yes, I did have a brother in Israel, and I added a comment that he had left immediately after his liberation from the concentration camp and that he worked as an auto mechanic of the General Health Insurance Company. I concealed my sister's flight from the country but did say she was a housewife, which was true. What I mostly concealed was the fact that my mother's sister and brother, as well as four cousins lived in the USA. Mother's brother and his wife also lived in Israel – he was childless, having lost his wife and four children in that place that will not be named. And my father, who perished in the camp, had three siblings and their seven children living in America. I did tell the truth when I stated that I had no direct contact with my brother and sister, but I knew about their lives through their correspondence with my mother. Who would believe today that I was not permitted to have contact with my rather large extended family abroad? Perhaps not a completely accurate statement: at the end of the 1950's and the beginning of the 1960's (I am writing this in 2007) it was not that big a sin to correspond with someone in America. But in Israel? Nothing could have been a blacker stain on my resumé than that – nothing at all! I will describe later what impact my decision to leave the country had, whether it was legal or illegal. I have written this section as clarification of the reasoning that led me to leave. The dice had been cast.

60 The Court's verdict

As the years passed, I was able to wrap my mind around certain things and understand them differently to the way they were presented to the public on a daily basis. I had laid the groundwork for a successful life – I had finished my studies and gained a profession. I had begun to resent the fact that having siblings and relatives abroad meant hardship for me. God forbid that I should have publicly stated something positive about Israel. Anti-Semitism was fostered by the Communist Party and state authorities. Unlike in Poland, Hungary, even Slovakia, where that vile tradition sprouted from the masses, in Czechoslovakia, it spread shamelessly from above, from the authorities. I observed a change in my character – a I refused to accept that someone would constantly tell me or order me what I could or could not do, what I could or could not say and whom I could or could not be in touch with. I do not speak about flaunting the law. In my daily life and while contemplating my future professional career I foolishly assumed that I must "behave properly", while hoping that my most terrible sin, i.e. siblings living in "enemy countries", would be forgiven. It turned out that Big Brother's vigilance was omnipresent and "behaving properly" would not help my case. I was branded as unfit for a "leading role in healthcare". Who cared that I was a good, conscientious worker, that I had never asked for or accepted a bribe, not a single cent, and that I was a law-abiding man who took exemplary care of his wife and two children?

I do not know why but I feel that I should begin at the end. That way I can show how the authorities and the court saw the matter of our escape and, later, I can describe the circumstances and our reasons for leaving. I have the court's verdict in front of me. It is a one-sheet document, densely typewritten on both sides and it states that my wife and I...*"as Czechoslovak citizens have remained abroad without permission of the authorities. Their act therefore constitutes the criminal act of forsaking the republic and they are hereby sentenced to the denial of freedom. The accused Dr. Antonín Moťovič for a duration of 12 months imprisonment, and the accused Alice Moťovičová for a duration of 8 months imprisonment. Under paragraph (such and such) the court orders complete confiscation of all property"*.

The reverse side is more interesting – the reasoning behind the verdict. First of all, it is interesting because it does not contain descriptions so frequently used by the former regime, such as "traitor, spy, imperialist and Zionist minion, war monger" – those were the denunciations then in common use. Secondly, as I read the document now, half a century later, I am quite surprised at its matter of fact, even acceptable tone. Was it because the time of Dubček was approaching? I will try to explain later why I consider the document important. Here it is, verbatim: *"Both accused left on August 9, 1965, in their own car, together with their daughters Ivana and Zuzana, on a trip to Bulgaria, whence they departed for Israel in a manner thus far undetermined. They remain in Israel and have no intention of returning to the ČSSR. It has been determined that they do not plan to return which is clear from their correspondence with relatives in the ČSSR. They had both intended to emigrate to Israel in December of 1964. Authorization for this was refused. The activity of both accused constitutes the criminal act of abandoning the republic according to paragraph 109/2 of the criminal statutes, as they have been dwelling abroad without proper authorization.*

"Both accused were penalized according to paragraph 109/1,2 of the criminal statutes but the court weighed the relative societal menace of the accused as compared with their personal standing. It has been found that neither accused has a criminal record. The accused Moťovič worked as a physician. He was the assistant director of the pediatric surgery department of the Thomayer hospital in Prague. He is valued as a very good worker, with a good attitude to his patients and co-workers. He is similarly characterized at his place of residence. The accused Moťovičová was a housewife, likewise, receiving positive reviews. They both took care to raise their children well. They both have relatives abroad, especially in Israel, which no doubt motivated their criminal activity. Both are sentenced to imprisonment. The court finds that the accused Moťovič bears a larger part of the legal responsibility, as he is a qualified worker who has completed his qualifications in the ČSSR. The court has also decided to confiscate the property of both the accused, according to paragraph 39/1,2 of the criminal statutes. Both accused are to serve their sentence in a correctional institution, first grade..."

I thought it necessary to quote the judge's words so as not to have to give myself a review. Reading the reasoning, it seems I should have been satisfied: just get more professional experience and my career progress would have been guaranteed. The 1950's and 1960's taught me that the future was not necessarily going to be rosy. The disappointment we felt in the prevailing atmosphere grew by the week. I needed to think about the future of my family, about raising my little girls, and as the years passed, my mind became more and more feverish trying to find a solution. As time went on, our relationship with our closest relatives changed as well. My wife's father passed away in 1958 and her only relative, a sister in Israel, was unreachable. That only increased her longing. And that which had been latent in me for the longest time – missing my brother and my sister – was becoming more and more intense. Let us not forget: the very fact they were alive was a miracle and that made it all the more difficult to live so far away from them.

Another facet of the fifties was the intensifying racist monster of anti-Semitism. Not among the people, I had never felt it there, but official anti-Semitism. How else to explain the fact that the whole nation heard about Slánský being not just an agent of imperialism but also a Zionist agent from a Jewish family, whose original name was Salzmann? All this from the mouth of the state attorney and the print media, which followed the government line slavishly. It was the same with all the others accused of Jewish origins in the "Trial of the conspiracy center headed by Rudolf Slánský". And it was the same in the official saber dance around the Jewish doctors accused of conspiracy of to assassinate Stalin and other leaders. And the amount of bootlicking! During the same time, the chief urologist of Bulovka hospital, Dr. Braun, was indicted for allegedly dealing in foreign currency, but my hunch is that his indictment stemmed from the fact he had done it at the Old-New Synagogue with American tourists. Jewish tourists – naturally.

61 Meeting the man from State Security

At that time the StB ("state security" – Czech secret police) attempted to recruit me as an informer. The agent's name was Daněk – or something similar, obviously fake. He was not looking for me to be an informer on my ward or at the hospital, or to inform on my wife or the neighbors: he wanted to recruit me as an informer at the Old-New Synagogue. This is how it went down: one day I got a phone call at work. A man introduced himself by the above-mentioned name, told me straight out he worked for state security and said he needed to speak to me about something important. He said he was calling from downstairs, and would I come down so we can sit down on a bench in front of the building and talk? It is clear what I felt and thought at the moment. Obviously, a request from such an important person amounted to an order. I had no choice but to acquiesce.

There was a young man sitting on the bench who obviously knew me by sight which he revealed by asking: "So, did you enjoy the Sparta match yesterday?" I was evidently being followed – I had indeed been to a Sparta match the day before. I was so surprised I did not even answer him. He did not seem to care and did not really expect a reply. His script was well prepared. He started by asking what my father-in-law was doing at the Israeli embassy, which he would visit about once a month. My answer was that although my father-in-law lived with us, we did not make it a habit to ask each other where we were going or who we were visiting. And I most definitely would not have asked him for his reasons of visiting anyone, anywhere. I do not know how I got the nerve, but I told the agent that maybe he could tell me because he clearly knew, and I did not. Of course, I was lying. It was no coincidence that approximately once a month there suddenly appeared Israeli newspapers and magazines in Yiddish or Hungarian and during Jewish holidays a few extra pennies materialized in the family. Later, when I lived in Israel, I found out through a former emissary at the Prague Israeli embassy that banned American Jewish organizations, such as JOINT, distributed holiday gifts to the needy through the embassy.

Daněk, or Dušek, or whatever his name was, did not get anywhere asking about my father-in-law, which was just a light ice breaking opening gambit anyway, so he tried a direct hit: "Look here, Comrade (up until then I had usually been addressed as Mr. or Doctor), we know your co-religionists do not visit the Old-New Synagogue only to pray but they use it as a cover for their anti-state activity. Undercover Western spies posing as tourists meet "unreliable elements" there (read: Jews) and beside dealing in black market dollars, they give dollars to anyone supplying information about the situation in our republic. We need a man such as yourself to keep us informed about the goings on there". My blood froze in my veins. I felt weak, and my confidence evaporated. It probably took a while to recover from my shock, but I told him fairly firmly that if he knew I went to Sparta soccer matches, he must also know that I did not attend synagogue and had no contact with "suspicious elements". My whole life was dedicated to my work and pediatric surgery was my life's only ambition – therefore, I had time for nothing else. And to spy on people – that was not something I was able to do. I could not be a rat, an informer. If for no other reason, then just because of what I had been through. I felt like standing up and getting the heck out of there, leaving him on the bench but I was not quite that brave. It was not necessary. He stood up and with a menacing "We'll see each other again", he left. He was probably in a hurry and snaring me in his net was not his only job that day, but his threat was not idle.

The phone rang again after about two weeks. Interestingly, he called me at work, never at home. A familiar voice said: "Sir, (no longer 'comrade'), let me treat you to a coffee on such and such a day, such and such coffee shop in the Old Town Square". He did not seem like a stupid man, but he was not intelligent enough to realize that unwanted ears could be listening around me. I guess I started stuttering and Mr. Daněk/Dušek understood this was not a good time to call. He wanted to know when he could see me. I was able to sputter: "Give me your phone number and I will call you". My hunch was correct. He did not give me a phone number but said he would call back in an hour and advised that I should be alone. He called back exactly after an hour, and I did manage to be alone – not easy on a busy ward. I had spent the hour feverishly contemplating what to say and avoiding other doctors' glances. They knew something was up because I would hear an ambiguous remark or two. I decided I would tell the agent that it was a surgery day (this was true) and that I was scheduled for night shifts the whole month. And because the regime had taught us we always had to have an explanation for everything and a handy alibi, I had indeed swapped shifts with a colleague while I waiting for the call. That way, my statements were true and could be verified. While I was working on swapping my shifts, some more cryptic words were said by colleagues, only heightening my tension.

To my surprise, my explanation worked. The agent did not seem taken aback and let me know with a good measure of sarcasm, to make sure I understood he was not going to let me bamboozle him, that we could get together a day later. And then, out of the blue, this threat: "Understand that this is an official summons – there is no room for excuses". I went to meet him at the appointed time. I felt he had prepared some new bait for me, some new pressure tactic, some new threat. And I was right. The coffee we had ordered had not arrived yet and he began: "We are aware (yeah, discovering America, I thought) that your wife has recently returned from a visit to Israel. (That was true: they had rejected our application for a family trip. Suspecting we had the wicked intentions of not returning, the authorities had decided to let my wife and kids go and hold me back as ransom). What did she tell you? Whom did she meet? Had anyone inquired about matters that could undermine our republic?" I was not too surprised, and his question did not shock me.

As I had walked to our meeting in the Old Town Square, I had been pondering the question of the Israel trip – how come no one had asked a single question yet? The truth is that around that time, in 1963 or 1964, there was a certain amount of liberalization, a bit of a thaw, and perhaps the atmosphere around foreign visits had lightened up. It turned out there was indeed a liberalization in the matters of emigration and family reunification – more about that later. Perhaps even our fear of officialdom had lessened. And so, I told him, with a good amount of self-confidence and without beating around the bush that he knew as well as I did why my wife had gone to Israel without me. I said that he knew my brother and my wife's sister lived there, with their extended families and children whom we had never seen, and it was obvious that our desire to meet them was great. And as for whom my wife had contacted: well, my wife was her own person, he could speak to her himself. I said I was confident she would divulge anything he wanted to know. However, I said, again, without fear or hesitation, I was sure that was not the reason I had been ordered to meet with him. He told me I was right and asked if I had thought about his previous proposal and what my decision was. My decision is clear, I said. There was no change in my position since the last time and to be specific, I added: "I do not attend synagogue services and have no intention of attending. I have no time and no talent for being a stool pigeon." He went red but did not say a word. "Mainly, I do not want to do it." "Very well", he said, obviously furious and turning beet red. He muttered something through his teeth which I did not understand but the tone was unmistakably threatening. He got up, left the unfinished coffee on the table, and got out of there. I admit I was shaken and scared. I remained seated for a few seconds and then also stood up to leave. Then I realized that we had not paid for our unfinished coffee, and I showed my wallet to the waiter, indicating I wanted to pay. The waiter told me that "the gentleman" had taken care of it prior to my arrival and it was abundantly clear that he was Mr. Daněk's – or Dušek's or whatever his name was – partner.

I was convinced that was not the end of that business. Maybe a miracle would happen, and the agent would cease trying to recruit me. But it seemed more likely to me that I would soon find myself in some dank, dark and stinky basement, and circumstances would compel me to co-operate with the secret police, with humility and enthusiasm and without conditions. One thing I did not believe. I did not believe they would let it slide. I knew they would be looking – or perhaps had already found – some real or trumped-up transgressions, which they would toss in my face at the first opportunity, forcing me to raise my arms in surrender in order to save myself and my family from a catastrophe. I felt I had no right to submit my wife and kids to the ordeal, so maybe I should tell my wife about the whole thing. I had been hoping to spare Alizka by keeping everything to myself, but I finally felt compelled to spill the beans. I felt a great relief since I had been living with the constant tension of being cornered.

It was the right decision. That leech Daněk or Dušek did not take long to call back again but this time he dialed my home number. I am not sure why he had not called home before this. Maybe he thought he would get me in his clutches on the very first try and finalize our conspiracy. It would have all remained between the two of us and my wife would not need to be party to it. His voice sounded official, strict, stern and bossy: "Doctor, I would like to continue our last unfinished conversation from the coffee shop. You will come to a meeting with me on such and such a date and time, in the Interior Ministry building on Letná Square. You know the building. You pass it when you go to your Sparta soccer matches. You tell the officer at the reception that you have an appointment with me. And no excuses please. I have made a few calls and I know you are not on call, and it is not surgery day. And just like I said last time: This is an official summons. You do not have the option of refusal". And he hung up.

Fortunately, Alizka was not at home, so I did not need to worry her, but I felt like a Swiss knife was snapping open in my pocket: I was completely determined to put an end to it, come what may. Aside from everything else, becoming an informer would have meant having to attend Synagogue services and attract attention. Some people there doubtless knew my mother or my father-in-law, since they occasionally visited the temple (I have no doubt this fact has not escaped your vigilant attention; you must have been in a tight spot or needed to prove something to you superiors even at the risk of being unmasked). And here is the main point: I had long lost my faith in the regime and resolved to leave the country by legal or illegal means. Yes, you are right Mr. Daněk or Dušek or whatever the heck your name is! Jews help each other in times of need, whether directly on a personal level, or collectively. Perhaps that is the reason we have survived all our troubles – to use a very mild term – and are still around, even if only a fraction of our original number.

These were the thoughts flooding my mind as I took the long streetcar trip from my hospital in Krč to the "tiled building" in Letná. (The Ministry of the Interior was an infamous building that all Prague residents feared. It featured a white tiled exterior.) My resolve to end this business, to stand my ground, not to give an inch, grew with every stop. That was my mindset as I entered the famous white building. I was greeted by a uniformed officer. He asked whom I had an appointment with and checked my ID. He made a call and within a minute or two "my" agent was by my side.

He, in obviously cheerful spirits and I mentally, perhaps even physically at rock bottom, but all the more stubborn and determined. I found strength in thinking about my exile in Ukraine, which was the first trial by fire in my life. We reached his office on an upper floor – I do not remember if we walked or took the elevator. The office contained a desk, two chairs and a radio box (the original wording is *rozhlas po drátě* which translates as "radio over the wires"). He showed me a chair without saying a word and he left the room. I looked around instinctively and I did not see a camera but I did hear a click in the radio box and then a hum like when you turn on a radio but there is no broadcast. The door flew open and my agent stormed in, grabbing the chair across from me. Without offering me a sip of water or – God forbid – a cup of some stale office coffee, he barked: "Well, what did you decide?" The ringing of the phone saved me from an immediate reply. The agent left again. The radio box started making clicking and hiccupping noises and sounds I cannot even describe.

I do not know where I found the courage to say to him in a steady voice: "What's wrong? Your tape recorder is broken and you cannot record our conversation? It should make no difference to you anyway. My decision stands. I do not mind if you turn the recorder on in here. You do not need to run to the next room to scold the knucklehead who cannot get your gear to work!" He was as silent as a grave and I continued: "I'm asking you very kindly, please stop visiting me at work and phoning me. It is very awkward because the other doctors are getting suspicious. They are not used to me getting mysterious calls or disappearing from the ward. And one more thing. I have told my wife about this. She was in shock, but she fully supports my resolve never to go down this path and become an informer. My final word is NO!"

The agent remained seated. He did not even seem surprised. After a while he stood up, left the room and the hissing and humming of the radio box abruptly stopped. I heard his disappointed voice from the next room: "You can go". I stood up to leave but as he accompanied me downstairs, I could not shake a fear that I would be arrested and thrown into some basement cell. And then my ID was given back to me, and I stood outside in the fresh air on Letná Square, not far from the stadium of my beloved Sparta soccer club.

It could have been fate, an accident, a coincidence but the agent and I saw each other again, far from home, in the Romanian town of Mamaia. That meeting possibly spelled the end of his career. This is how it came about. In the summer of 1963 or 1964 (who could remember the exact dates, it is enough that I remember the events of forty-five years ago... Yes, it is May 2008. This is how slow my writing is, with frequent long interruptions. Plus, keep in mind the writer is now over eighty years old). Anyway, during the time my wife worked as a *Čedok* guide (*Čedok* was the state tourist agency), she got me a stint as a tour physician. It was customary for all the people in positions of responsibility for the tour to have regular meetings: a *Čedok* representative, an airline rep, the tour doctor, and there was usually another person whom I never identified but in whose presence everyone's way of speaking suddenly became stilted, wooden, cliché-heavy, as if sourced directly from Communist Party educational brochures.

During one such meeting the door flew open and what do you know? It was my secret agent! Without thinking, I greeted him with "Long live the working class, Comrade Daněk!" or Dušek or whatever his name was. (The actual greeting in Czech is *Čest práci* which translates verbatim as "honor [the] labor".) The people in the room looked at each other and at the man, but no one looked very surprised. Not so my buddy. All the colors of the rainbow danced on his face, with red being dominant. He leaped towards me, sat down and hissed angrily: "Shut up! That is not my name here!" The others pretended not to hear but the agent stood up and ran out, and I have never seen him or heard from him since. The airline rep who was my friend told me later that he had put him on a flight back to Prague that very night. He never bothered me again.

Others did try, by various methods. As I mentioned, Alizka and the kids were allowed to visit my sister-in-law in Israel in 1963 (they kept me in Prague as security). After her return I had another visitor (again at work) who was very curious to hear about whom my wife had seen in Israel, what she was saying about her visit and what she had been asked about while there. I asked my guest to reach out to my wife, who was perfectly capable of formulating her own responses and did not need me to speak in her name. I also had the nerve to tell him he was not the first one from his office to seek me out and asked him if they were using this method to discredit me at the hospital, or were they still trying to soften me up and scare me into collaborating?

I need to add two remarks here: firstly, I really do not know how I had the guts to speak to him that way and, secondly, it has been a very long time and I do not remember all the details – may the eighty-one-year-old man be forgiven? It is possible that the chronology of events is a bit different. It had conceivably been the first agent to whom I reacted the way I just described, not the second one...but the substance of the matter remains unchanged.

To conclude, and based on my own personal experience, a word to those who were "forced" to sign on as collaborators: In the 1960's those who did not want to...did not sign. Those who did sign must have had a "compelling" reason. They will have to live with their own consciences. How it was before, in the 1950's, I can only guess – I do not know. And I certainly do not know how it was during the "normalization" years (after the Soviet occupation in 1968). I was not there any longer because I had put into action what I had resolved to do at the beginning of the 60's.

62 A Bitter, though not deciding Incident

Before I get to the deciding incident that was the reason for my decision to leave Czechoslovakia at all costs – although I loved the republic and especially Prague, the place where I became what I am now, knowing that under the then current rules of the then regime it could happen that I would never be able to return, and all contact with friends would be forever interrupted – I need to speak about an event that happened in 1951 or 1952. It was the bleakest period of the new regime, a period that would not have been out of place during Nazism.

All reserve soldiers were getting new identity cards. In my dormitory, called the May 5th Dormitory, there lived about five Jewish students (including me) – two who were born in Bohemia, three from Slovakia or Subcarpathian Ruthenia. We were summoned to the army headquarters and questioned about our "origin". I will intentionally use the words "Jewish origin" not just Jews because "origin" was the operative word in the story I am about to relate. The two guys who were born in Bohemia were given their new ID's without questions. We three were questioned as to our "origin". I sat across from an officer who held my ID card and before handing it to me told me somewhat hesitantly, with perhaps a shade of shame in his voice: "I need to fill in the question about your origin". Well, during that time, the meaning of the word "origin" was clearly defined in three categories: working class origin, peasant origin or bourgeois origin – and that was it. Naturally, I told him truthfully: "Working class". I remember how embarrassed he seemed. I still think today that he felt ashamed about having to explain it. I must have looked surprised too because I did not understand what "origin" he was talking about when he said: "Well, Comrade, that's not the origin I have in mind". I was livid and could not believe my ears. I raised my voice: "I am of working-class origin and I do not understand your question!". It seemed that he felt relieved while writing down what I was saying, and he handed me my new ID without looking me in the eye.

Back at the dormitory it transpired that all three of us had the same thing written on the line in question: "Jewish origin". None of us could work out why those two guys born in Bohemia were not asked what their "origin" was. (The explanation came much later, after the Velvet Revolution, the overthrow of communism in 1989. Rumor had it that the secret police was getting its information from lists made by the Gestapo during the war.) Let it be said that after Stalin's death and after the official repudiation of the Slánský trials (the show trials of 1950's), new military IDs were issued without this racist branding.

These things went on in a country founded by Masaryk, in a country with a liberal democratic tradition, not too long after that sort of branding had been inflicted on people denigrated and demeaned and forced to wear a special badge on their clothes. Those who wanted to know, knew this led to doom. As I said, I never felt anti-Semitism either from the people or in the environment around me. I did not think that gas chambers and crematoria were about to be built. But it is quite easy to hoodwink and mislead a nation, and I would be lying and engaging in ostrich behavior if I claimed that the above episode did not leave a dark stain in my heart and on my soul. And it certainly played a role in the events that followed, if not the main one. I am not too sensitive to expressions of anti-Semitism (I do not like the word much, it is often misused). I never did anything in my life that could arouse such expressions in others. Not everyone needs to like me, just as I do not have to like everyone. But I could not stomach the regime then in power in Czechoslovakia because it reminded me of the one I was trying so hard to forget!

63 Alea Iacta Est

Something else was needed, something profoundly serious, for the dice resting deep in my pocket to be pulled out and cast. And the dice was cast unexpectedly one day towards the end of 1964. This was the deciding incident I mentioned earlier: I had begun my stint as the stand-in for the Chief Physician who was abroad (I mentioned elsewhere that his wife, in her job at the pediatric department of the Ministry of Health took good care of her husband, including arranging foreign trips). One day, there was a party following a departmental meeting in the "main building". Glasses were raised but I do not remember what we were celebrating. There was a regular guest at these shindigs, a woman with the official title "administrator for special assignments". This was a euphemism for what was known as a "political vetter", someone tasked with looking into people's class origins. She sidled up to me, quite drunk and in a good mood. She looked at me with her glassy eyes and said, holding nothing back: "*I have been wanting to tell you something for some time because I like you. You are considered to be an excellent and principled pediatric surgeon. You are one of the few that never takes a bribe. But I have to tell you: you'll never make Chief Physician of the ward. Don't ask me how I know*". Before I had time to say anything, she added: "*The nominating committee doesn't mind that your sister lives in America. Your brother in Israel is the problem*". I am not sure of her exact words but that was the gist of what she said. She did not say anything that I had not long suspected anyway...but her words were like an icy shower. The next morning my secretary told me I was to check in with the "special assignment" officer. The officer looked serious and inquired if she had said something to me that she was not supposed to and not allowed to say. "*You know, when I have a bit to drink, I cannot control my tongue.*" I assured her that she had not revealed anything despite being drunk. She tried to keep me there for a longer talk but I said I was needed in the operating theater, I did an about-turn and got out of there without saying good-bye.

I certainly do not want to give an impression of someone immodest, full of himself and with an exaggerated sense of his own accomplishments. Quite the contrary: the thought of becoming Chief in the immediate future had not crossed my mind and was not my burning ambition. Yes, I had passed two board certification exams in general and pediatric surgery, but I was a realistic enough – they called it "self-critical" in those days – to know I still had a lot to learn before I could apply for such a position. Whenever I did think of the progress of my career, I thought of advancing my professional abilities. The Chief Physician was a prime example of what sort of chief I would never want to be. Still, the thought that my future would most likely mean a position of general surgeon in some clinic (no pediatric surgeon positions existed in such clinics), caused me immense sadness and disappointment. I must humbly say – and this was confirmed by colleagues – that I was capable of more than just cutting out bunions, lancing abscesses, removing stitches, dress scrapes and occasionally sewing up a small wound. (Incidentally, this was something I refused later in Israel as well, when given a choice between being a surgeon in a clinic or work in a hospital, but start at the bottom, as a lowly resident. I chose the second option with all that it entailed: working like a slave while my two framed board certification diplomas hung on a wall at home.)

What happened at that party finally made it clear to me that no matter what I did, how hard I work and how good a boy I was, no matter if I became the best surgeon in the country, my brother, my hardworking, honest auto mechanic brother toiling away fixing cars for the General Health Insurance in Israel, would always be the cause of my political unreliability and my inability to become chief of surgery for ever and ever. And in that moment, I told myself *Alea iacta est*. The dice has been cast.

The timing was just right. In 1963 the Party and the government loosened the reins a little and one heard talk about the possibility of foreign travel. Not just idle tongues wagging but even the press started mentioning it and, in cases of family reunification, even emigration was spoken of. I have written about my wife's visit to my brother and her sister in Israel. Her information and observations from the visit confirmed that it might be a good idea to live in the vicinity of family and former friends. It also confirmed what we had subconsciously known: there was a place under the sun where we could find shelter and that place was Israel. There was another alternative – we could have theoretically applied to join my sister in the USA, but we never considered it. What was encouraging and what made the decision easier was the fact that my medical diploma from Charles University and possibly my two board certification diplomas would be recognized in Israel, and no lengthy re-qualification was necessary. There is no need to stress how important the emotional and family aspect was. I have spoken at length about my brother and my emotional ties to the family. Living where he lived, being near him...that had been a dream for a long time.

The following year it was "our turn to travel" – Alizka visited her sister (I mentioned my mother's trip to Israel earlier). My sister-in-law had left the country legally, just like my brother. That was during the time when Czechoslovakia was still on friendly terms with Israel and *Haganah* units were training on Czechoslovak territory. She was a *Haganah* member, and she left her home country as a combatant in a *Haganah* unit. We knew that the regime would not allow the whole family to leave, in fact even applying for passports for everyone was not recommended. I stayed behind as surety. Alizka, along with our two daughters, nine-year-old Ivana and three-year-old Zuzana set out on their journey at the start of their summer vacation, armed with ten dollars per person. The flight had to be paid for in full, from abroad, that was a condition of travel.

My sister-in-law had two boys about the same age as our girls and this was the first time the children would see each other, and my daughters would see their aunt and uncle. Her husband, originally from Vienna, had left Austria with a youth group at the last moment, before the Anschluss. The brother-in-law ended up in a kibbutz, along with the whole Viennese youth group, some of whom were later murdered by Arab terrorists. He left the kibbutz and with the help of his parents (who managed to escape to the USA) became a member of the *Egged* co-operative, *Egged* being the largest bus company in Israel that served intercity as well as city routes. You could buy membership in the co-op and be rewarded by an above the average salary. *Egged* was active in the tourist industry at the time and drivers who could speak a few languages were trained as tour guides. One had to know every nook and cranny of the country, its thousands of years of history, its culture, holy places and its three religions. My brother-in-law became one such guide. Those guides were among the country's elite, with additional bonuses. You can imagine the trips he undertook with my family, starting from their home on the Carmel Mountain range in Haifa. They visited all the historic places all over the country, as well as family from whom we had been cut off for twenty years. Staying in his house, with a view of the Mediterranean, was definitely a pleasant part of the trip.

They spent long hours talking and discussing, trying to find a method for me to be able to come out as well. Various ways and means were devised. Alizka had left Prague with a plan to get a doctor's note just before returning home, stating that one of the girls had taken ill. To make her request look credible, she went to the Czechoslovak embassy in Tel Aviv to ask them to wire the Ministry of the Interior and certify that the child needed to be accompanied by a physician on the way home – which just happened to be her father's profession! To make the whole deal less suspicious, Alizka's brother-in-law, a Vienna native, was to travel with them to the city of his birth he had not seen since the war, and I was supposed to travel from Prague to Vienna to meet them and take the family home. I was informed in a letter that my wife had visited the embassy in Tel Aviv (she asked to have her exit visa extended, which was done on the spot), got a friendly reception but was told that yes, they could wire Prague, but it was inappropriate for them to get in touch with the Interior Ministry. They could only contact the Ministry of Foreign Affairs. "They will know how to proceed". And so, I applied for a one-day exit permit to travel to Vienna. I described the situation in detail, presented the doctor's note, described my wife's visit to the embassy in Israel. I was sent home without the StB (state security police) officer as much as glancing up at me. He did not say a single word while I was there. I left and expected that my impertinent request would be miraculously granted. The family came back, I was interrogated as already described, and about two months after their return I received a letter from the Interior Ministry. The letter contained one sentence: *Your application for travel abroad has been denied.*

64 The Uninformed and Naïve French and their Stupidity

I had not expected humane treatment or humane words, I even admired the cunning of the officials at the Interior Ministry for having seen through my devious plan, but I could not come to terms with the contemptuous attitude. They took me for a complete idiot, having sent their letter of refusal two months after the return of the "sick" child. Their actions added to the reasons for deciding to leave the country. An individual could not defy the regime openly, but I was determined to continue my efforts and see who would come up trumps. My sense of security was helped by the knowledge that we had a place to land and the belief – not certainty – that there were people out there willing to help.

As I have mentioned, the period of the early 60's was one of a gradual thaw. One felt the restraints loosening. Alizka had come back from Israel with certain plans that she and I examined and analyzed in detail. During her visit, one of her cousins, Tibor, who lived in France, was also in Israel. It had been decided that we should try to get to the west somewhere, preferably Austria, or to him in France, or even just to Yugoslavia and he would take care of us from there. I knew nothing about the situation in Yugoslavia but why would I need anyone in Austria? Would the Austrians hand us back to the Czechoslovakian authorities? That was one of the delusions people in the west seemed to have (there were other delusions, about which I will write later).

But there was another idea which was clever: to start by getting my diploma out of the country. He seemed to have a solution for that. A friend of his who worked in textile exporting (as Tibor did, too) was supposed to travel to Prague in the near future. He was going to visit us, introduce himself and we would give him the document. We were assured he was reliable. The plan went off without a hitch. My main document, an official copy of my diploma was out. I got the copy along with my original when I graduated. We were informed the diploma was in Israel. That was really the only country we wanted to go to, despite the possibility of emigrating to the US to join my sister. The Israelis were very careful when it came to official documents, having had a bad experience with forgeries during mass immigration waves in the forties and fifties. To ask Czechoslovak authorities, or the university, for confirmation that I had indeed graduated or for a copy of my diploma later – that was a pipe dream for the next few decades.

I have no idea where, in 1964, we got the *chutzpah* (as every Jew and every American would say) to apply for a travel permit to visit France. Since we did not want to cause the authorities unnecessary headaches, we stated on our application that the kids would stay in Prague with their grandmother. We did not even ask for a foreign currency allotment, as a cousin would take care of us. The incredible happened, wonder of wonders – we got our passports and our exit permits. We bought our round-trip train tickets to Paris with Czech crowns. The cousin picked us up at the beautifully decorated train station (it was Christmas) and drove us to Lille through lovely wintery countryside.

A quick aside: I was never blinded by other people's achievements or possessions. I did not care about how beautiful other cities looked – Prague was and remains my favorite city in the world. But the difference between a communist country and free, capitalist France was so striking we could barely catch our breath. We were hardly aware of our surroundings the whole long trip from the train station to Lille and that is the way it continued for the whole ten days.

One day Tibor told us we were going to Paris. We got there in the afternoon hours and checked into the Napoleon Hotel, close to the *Arc de Triomphe*. He told us during dinner that we would be meeting with a highly positioned official of some bureau or other (he said it in French, so we did not understand). Apparently, this was the most highly specialized office and the only one able to get us out of Czechoslovakia. The next day, we parked our cars at a building complex that had the look of an army barracks. Our documents were checked multiple times by both uniformed personnel and civilians. We were led through a large hall to a smaller room, in which a uniformed officer and a few other military men were sitting behind a desk. I guessed his rank must have been high. The melodious, mellifluous French language echoed through the room as we stood to the side. We understood nothing, but obviously, our fates were being discussed as the approximately five men present kept glancing at us, gesticulating and mentioning the word *Tchécoslovaquie* occasionally. It took a fairly long time – after all these years it is hard to remember how long – but it was finally time to let us in on the secret of what was being debated. I think that those esteemed gentlemen must have thought that they had before them a world-famous pediatric surgeon, some genius that one meets only once in a lifetime and that in the interests of humanity they must yank this savant out of the clutches of the communist regime and deliver him to freedom. It turned out they had absolutely zero idea of the said regime. The cousin took the floor, though it seemed to me that one of the men present, judging by his periodic facial expressions, was quite well versed in the language of Komenský, i.e., Czech. (Jan Amos Komenský was an early 17th century Czech philosopher, educator and leader of the Moravian Brethern.)

If I had not been brought up right and if I had not taken care not to break the somber mood and earnest facial expressions, I would have laughed my head off as soon as the cousin began speaking. What were the solutions to our problem proposed by this august group? I will describe only two; enough to illustrate the stupidity, naivety, lack of information and total ignorance of how a totalitarian regime operated. If it was just that, I would actually have laughed – albeit with tears in my eyes – but to suggest a solution that would endanger the lives of two beautiful little girls, ten and four and a half years old? That really took the cake!

One proposal was for us, the parents, to remain in France and to have the children brought out of the country with the help of the International Red Cross. What could I say? How could I counter this genius brainstorm? Let me just say this. From the start of the communist dictatorship in Czechoslovakia, since 1948, I am certain many children have been left behind in the country. There has never, ever, been a single case where the regime would kindly – accompanied by nice music, perhaps? – ship the children to parents who resided in the west, and decided not to return, even if their departure had been legal. Quite the opposite. The children became hostages of the regime which used them to put pressure on the parents to return. Once they did return, they were indicted, put in front of a judge, and sentenced to many years of imprisonment. Rumor had it that the children were not left in the care of grandparents or other close relatives. They ended up in orphanages or some re-educational institutions and when they grew up, they stood zero chance of getting a higher education or any kind of decent job. I still get flashbacks of panic just thinking about it. To think that my little Ivana, the beautiful ten-year-old excellent, highly praised student who recited poetry about the color red, the color of workers' blood, and who had taken her "Young Pioneer" vow (I don't remember where – I was too busy to be there with her, she was accompanied by her mom). To think that this lovely girl would end up in an institution. And what about the little one, my tiny Zuzana, not even five years old, who had been born premature and had breathing difficulties? Should we leave her there, without her parents' love, alone, at her tender age? Allow me to use a cliché here: when has it ever happened that Jewish parents would abandon their children, and especially parents who had only survived by chance, who survived in the face of an unspeakable evil that had sought to deprive them of a chance to bring beautiful, innocent children into the world?

We said nothing and kept our mouths shut. But we thought their suggestion was stupid and useless – and that was before they came up with another solution about which I can only say one thing: it was a solution that could only have been hatched in a sick brain, a brain that has nothing but contempt for human life. Now we were not just talking about unrealistic stupidity but an outright deadly gamble. The suggestion was for a nice uncle to travel to Prague, load up my daughters into his car, equipped with a double bottom. The girls would lie quietly in their hiding place and once the uncle reached the border, he would turn on his radio really loudly, playing some enchanting melody – how about one of

Strauss' famous waltzes? – and voila! the border is crossed. A few meters later the double bottom is removed, and two happy girls spring out and run into the loving arms of their parents, exactly at the right spot, right day, right time. Obviously planned by someone who had read too many detective novels and was completely divorced from reality. Our lives and our livelihood were not in such mortal peril that we would stoop to endangering the only thing we had: our girls.

We did not speak much with the cousin on the way back. Our stance was clear and firm. I do not know if our ridicule had an effect on those very important "high positioned" gentlemen, but it was obvious we would be on our train, homeward bound, on the planned day. I just asked him to take good care of my diploma. Its turn to be useful would come one day. He promised he would. No further attempt to leave the country without our children was made.

65 Emigrant Passports: Yes, no, yes and no

I am not sure if the winter of 1964/1965 featured any special events. Perhaps just one thing: rumors were rife that the authorities would enable family reunification across international borders. One heard through the grapevine that this would mainly apply to Germans – those who had not been expelled after the war would be permitted to reunite with those living in Germany. It was worth a shot. Perhaps we could apply for emigrant passports (special passports which were essentially one-way documents) for travel to Israel. Another country would not have been a problem. People correctly guessed that the authorities were interested in the apartments and mainly the pensions to which emigrants must surrender any claim. It turned out the rumors were indeed completely correct. And so, we decided to test the veracity of the grapevine on my mother. She was retired and had an apartment in Karlín, a nice district of Prague. Originally, it was a large apartment that was divided for two families – each one a two-bedroom apartment with its own kitchen and bathroom.

My impression was that considering the changing political climate, everything would go quickly and smoothly. It did not take more than a month and mom had her emigration passport and a license to export her furniture. The ostensible reason was her son who lived in Israel, though they must have forgotten in their eternal vigilance that she had another son, who lived a few miles away, a doctor to boot – in other words someone who could have been helpful in her old age.

My mother with Ivana (standing) and Zuzana, Prague, 1960.

We knew that it was not going to be quite as easy with us. We were young, I was a doctor, assistant to the chief surgeon, two children...there was even some trepidation that my application would counteract or nullify my mother's! Nevertheless, we did apply. There followed a protracted dance: Bring us official consent from the military. I went to headquarters, they were genuinely nice to me and spoke soothingly: "Ah, too bad you're planning to leave us, we have just received a recommendation for your promotion to a higher rank. If there is a war, you would be named commander of a surgical unit. Very well, leave your military ID card here and we will notify the passport authorities of our decision". The next document I needed was a court order, allowing me to take our children abroad with us. My wife and I attended court at *Ovocný trh* (Fruit Market) in Prague, where we had to explain to the judge why we intended to take our children and settle abroad. They did not omit to tell us that the state is responsible for the children (I am tempted to say the expression was "the children belong to the state" – but I would be lying). The court did not say anything more than the military did. No decision. They wanted some other authorization which I was able to get. I put everything together and handed it over in Bartolomějská Street (where the headquarters of the StB, the state security police, were located).

We waited for a few weeks and then were notified that our application had been rejected, without a single word of explanation. And so, it did not surprise me when my mother called the same day to tell me her emigration papers had been revoked as well. The reason she was given was that her departure would not constitute true family reunification, as she had a son and his family who lived in Prague. I was more sad than angry. Not for myself, after all, I had expected to be turned down, but for causing mother's emigration to be denied. She was close to seventy then. I am not certain she would have gone by herself. She had gotten very used to Alizka taking care of her and to me following her state of health. She had her pension, an apartment and there was not anything she really lacked. On the other hand, she had not had my brother by her side for twenty years. In other words, I did not understand why the authorities had to punish an old person. I decided to visit Bartolomějská Street and find out why they were playing games with an old retiree. Whatever the reason might have been, in her case it could not possibly have been political, so why toy with a person like that – grant permission, then yank it away?

I did not get to make my speech. A young sergeant, no more than twenty-three or twenty-four years old sat at the front desk and asked if I needed help with something. I said that I needed some information, namely, why had my mother been given an emigration permit, only to have it revoked (I did not tell him I was her son and I do not think he cared). He did not ask my name, did not pick up the phone, did not speak with anyone to find out more: "Comrade" (he quickly corrected himself and said "Sir"), "we are not obliged to explain anything to anybody!" As I wrote before, at that time I seemed to have lost all fear. I was convinced nothing could happen to me and felt I had nothing to lose. My professional career was being stymied and nothing else mattered. My instinct was to yell at that snotty little whippersnapper and ask him why he needed to humiliate people and throw his weight around. But then I realized: the very fact of his youth and inexperience excused him. It was the higher-ups, the really vengeful bastards, who taught him how to act. A normal citizen was helpless before those puffed-up dunces. I took a deep breath, swallowed my pride and excused the boy's conduct. He was but a product of the age. Maybe when he went home and shed the uniform, there was a nice family waiting for him and he became a pleasant young man, like my neighbor's son. And maybe he, too, told himself..." I would like to live in a different world".

Be that as it may, yet another attempt to become masters of our fate had failed. On my walk home, which took about twenty minutes, I concluded that there was no legal way for me to leave and there was nothing else for it but to start looking for an illegal way to do it, and to prove to myself and everyone else that only someone willing to bend to anything could be kept in a cruel regime by cruel means. I was not one who would bend to anything or anyone. I did not know how but I was going to act out of my own free will, and with Alizka's full support turn my determination into reality.

66 How we Prepared for our Journey

In my fit of hopelessness, I did not even realize that not only was any legal exit out of the question but whatever way I did manage to leave the country would mean leaving behind all our property, everything we had gained through our own labor since the end of the war. We inherited nothing from our parents whose modest assets had long been taken by others. Screw it all, I thought. The only thing I would regret leaving behind, the one thing nearest and dearest to us both was our decent book collection. It must be stated: those who were able to emigrate legally, could fill a container with their property and belongings, and ship it to the owner's new address, except for art objects.

The main thing now was not to worry about our earthly goods but plan a way to get out. One thing was for sure – we would never again be given permission to travel to a free country from which we could continue our journey to Israel. We had tried for that openly and one could not suspect the StB of sleeping on the job and forgetting their "watchfulness and vigilance". Though I can reveal this in advance: they were not very watchful and vigilant in our case...but I get ahead of myself. I will start at the beginning and will explain as well as I can. I am not sure I am able to put my thoughts into writing as precisely as I would like. I am not educated in sociology, philosophy and even my historical knowledge, though better than those other disciplines, is still pretty limited.

I guess what I am trying to say is this: a two-thousand-year exile, persecution, proscriptions and prohibitions, pogroms, exclusion from normal everyday life throughout many periods of history, confiscation of property, arbitrary regulations, inquisition and who knows what other decrees and catastrophes – all of that had been the Jew's lot from the moment he had been chased out of his ancestral home, from the promised land. And so, he wandered from land to land, from a place where he was persecuted to a place where he would be temporarily tolerated, even if limited in his daily life. Out of the self-preservation instinct, a need to cling to life, to family, to community, a sense of duty for mutual assistance had developed and one could not let those who were unable to help themselves fall and perish. Do I need to write at length about the period before, during and after the Holocaust? Let us simply observe that many actions of many people were motivated by these tragic experiences. Self-preservation was the motto of most Jews.

Not just to survive but also to be able to communicate with far away folks, not just in one's own country but other lands as well. The means of communication was language. What language? The language of the Bible! A unique phenomenon in history. The only dead language that has ever not just risen from the dead but has become a modern language. One in which books, scientific papers, medical journals and textbooks are written, a language used in everyday life and in technical disciplines...I could go on forever.

The State of Israel was a new factor in the period I write about. The state was created not only because every prayer contains the same motif: a return to the promised land, to Jerusalem – a name that appears in the bible hundreds of times. It was created so that there would no longer be pogroms, inquisitions and another Holocaust – or even events less tragic. As the state was born, it proclaimed the right of every Jew to return to his historic homeland. Help was available for anyone who wanted to return "home", even if the regime of the country where the person lived did not make it easy or outright forbade it. Once we reached Israel, we learned that had been the case with hundreds of thousands of Jews who had resided in Arab and African Muslim countries, and who had been given every assistance to find any possible or almost impossible way to Israel. In the meantime, it was us, in Prague, who had no idea how and when we would be able to leave.

We could see no way out, but we had heard about cases of folks who had taken a vacation and never returned. We had no idea how they did it. Someone, somewhere, must have helped along the way. It most definitely could not be done the way those French charlatans had tried to contrive it recently.

A year earlier, at the time Alizka visited the Israeli Embassy in Prague, on Voršilská Street, to secure visas for her trip to Israel, she had struck up an acquaintance with an aide by the name of Yaaron. (The Communist Party newspaper, *Rudé Právo*, "Red Justice", made sure to publicize the fact – just like during the Slánský trials – that Yaaron had been born in Slovakia with the not-very-Slovak sounding name Grünwald. In other words – a Jew. This was after the Six Day War, when Czechoslovakia severed its diplomatic relations with Israel. His Hebrew name was a translation of the German *wald* – forest – into the Hebrew *yaar*, therefore Yaaron. It turned out that *Rudé právo* was correct in other aspects as well. This former Slovak, Yaaron-Grünwald had a hand in helping applicants who were refused permission to reach Israel.)

We decided it would be a wise move to visit secretary Yaaron at the embassy. Alizka was chosen to be our emissary. She had met him previously and it was safer for her to go than for me. Karol (that was his given name and that is how we addressed him later in Israel when we were friends) did indeed give us hope. The only question he had was – did we have a car? We did not. He recommended we get one if possible and once we got it, we were to get in touch with him and he would instruct us further. In the meantime, he said, keep your hopes up, this can be done. Well, what do you know...?

Millions of brain neurons started flying. All the millions of cells that enable us to think, to dream, to conjure things up, to imagine things...they were all engaged in a single task now: a vehicle, no matter how small. My driver's license – acquired through a driving course I had taken through the hospital – lay in my pocket, still unused. All we needed was permission to travel to Bulgaria. I could not imagine which task would be more difficult. To get wheels, this year, next year or maybe in five years, or somehow to hoodwink the all-knowing, all-powerful authorities into giving us exit permits. Well, things moved faster and easier than I could have hoped.

I never expected anyone's help and never asked for it. By that I mean material help. But about a year before, after mom had come back from

Israel, we got a visit from my sister Šarlota (Charlotte) from California. This was mother's first meeting with her in twenty years. It looked like she was doing better financially. So, what would happen if, once in my life, I would ask for help? I knew of people who were receiving financial help from abroad via *Tuzex* (stores that carried Western merchandise, unavailable to buy in Czech stores and purchasable only with foreign currency). The money people received could be converted to a currency called *bon* with which you could buy anything in a *Tuzex* store, including cars. The conversion rate was the real rate, not the artificial rate set by the regime. I found out the cheapest car *Tuzex* carried was a Fiat 600 (yes, the engine was 650 cc's).

Drafting a letter to my sister took a long time. First, I did not keep regular correspondence with her, now I needed to explain why her dear brother suddenly needed a car. Plus, I needed to use a lot of gentle hints to circumvent the censor. But I also knew that when it came to *Tuzex*, the authorities were considerably more lenient. They were dying financially and would be willing to get castrated for each dollar that found its way in. The country was veritably flooded with foreign chocolate, coffee, nylon overcoats, wool coats, French and Italian cars, and rumor had it, even family homes – all bought with *Tuzex* money. Those who had *bons* constituted a special caste in society. Today you would call them celebrities. I did not want to be a celebrity, but I did need a car, the means to realizing my resolve. That was what I was after.

One day I pointed my steps towards the main Prague post office in Jindřišská Street with the letter in my breast pocket. Perhaps I was deluding myself, but I thought: so many letters are sent out from here to the West, a letter full of little hints and clues only understood by close relatives would slip through. It took scores, maybe hundreds of hours drafting the letter to Šarlota, in such a way she would definitely understand what I needed: a loan (yes, a loan!) to her brother, that would cover the purchase of a Fiat 600. I fully intended to get out, get rich quick and effortlessly return the money. I needed to buy it immediately, without being put on a years-long waiting list. But how to explain to my little sister (in reality, to my brother-in-law) that a tiny car had suddenly become my life's dream? It had been almost twenty years since we shared experiences and situations, and I was not sure that was enough for her mind to figure out and understand that the car was a means of escape, possibly to Yugoslavia, from where my big brother would take over and help.

After more than forty years I do not recall details of the letter. There were plenty of hints, fantasy, clues about our shared experiences from decades before, asking her whether she remembered how we had traveled to various locations and the circumstances of our journeys and how great it could be to replicate, relive those experiences. To sit behind a wheel and drive across mountains, rivers, and borders, to meet family you have not seen for years, to show off your own family, your beautiful daughters and to share experiences again. Who knows what else was in the letter but I had a hunch that if a censor were to read it, he would have considered the writer to be kooky and he would wonder what help could be given to this kind of beggar (censors must have read scores of such letters, judging by the thousands of cars *Tuzex* was selling, bypassing the waiting list and the queue). The car would be in front of the house almost the day the money arrived in *Tuzex*. It was symptomatic of the regime at that time – no one was asking who had sent the money and why.

Apparently Šarlota and my brother-in-law understood my letter very well. Despite all my skepticism and mistrust, it only took four or five weeks and I got a registered letter from *Tuzex* asking me to come to their main office. When I went, I was told they had received a sum of money sufficient for the purchase of a Fiat 600 in my name. They led me to the showroom, apologized and said they only had it in white but if I wanted it, it could be delivered in three days. And indeed, three days later, I was the proud owner of a white Fiat 600, plate number AD-71-89.

My Fiat, Ivana and Zuzana.

The first person to be told we had a car was Yaaron-Grünwald. When Alizka told him during a personal visit to the embassy in June or July 1964 – it was during her time as a tour guide at *Čedok* – he revealed his cards and instructed her about our next steps. As a *Čedok* employee she was able to glean information about when exit permits for two-week tours of Bulgaria, via Yugoslavia, would be issued. These trips were advertised as holidays by the Black Sea. The trips were structured in a way that would permit one day's stay in Yugoslavia on the way to the Black Sea, and one day's stay in Yugoslavia on the way back home. Yaaron emphasized "via Yugoslavia"! And if not that year, try again next year. They agreed on another meeting once exit visas were granted. In the meantime, he warned us not to talk to anyone and not to engage in overtly suspicious behavior, such as selling our possessions. From that day on, even when she was not guiding a group, she would show up at her *Čedok* office every day and ask every colleague and acquaintance to inform her if there was any action regarding tours to Bulgaria via Yugoslavia. Such action was pretty thin on the ground.

I will never know if an event that occurred a few months prior had an effect on the course of our adventure. One day, the Bulgarian embassy in Prague reached out to our pediatric surgical ward in the Krč hospital, requesting our help in taking care of the child of an "important" Bulgarian party official; my mother would call him a Big Mister Comrade. The child, his seven-year-old daughter, was diagnosed in Sofia with a tumor on the lung (it turned out to be a mediastinal tumor in the chest). Our ward was recommended to them by the Ministry of Health, specifically by the Institute for the Care of Mother and Child, whose director was none other than Dr. Olga Štolová, our department chief's wife. We performed the operation, the tumor turned out to be benign, the child's recovery was quick. In short, happiness on all sides, including the happiness of the attending physician – myself. After the child's discharge, I was sent a letter of thanks, signed by the Ambassador. There was another letter, more personal in tone, sent by the child's parents, stating that should we ever find ourselves in Bulgaria, it would be their family's privilege to put at our disposal the recreational facility of the Bulgarian Foreign Ministry in Sofia. I kept the letters in my desk – just in case.

Not too much Vltava (Prague river) water had flowed under Charles Bridge (a very famous bridge in Prague) until the day in July 1965, when the phone in my office rang and Alizka's excited voice told me that a few exit visas for travel to Bulgaria via Yugoslavia would be allotted soon but a request must be put in immediately. I did not tarry. I hopped in the Fiat and half an hour later I was in a *Čedok* office with Alizka. We filled out our application right there and then, and added those letters of thanks for extra security. I returned to work and started getting mentally ready for the inevitable disappointment. The authorities must have been aware about our recent moves, our travel, our failed application to emigrate, plus

Alizka's frequent visits to the Israeli embassy. It turned out that the "vigilant ones" were not all that vigilant after all.

We got our exit visas, plus dinars for two days in Yugoslavia and *levs* (the Bulgarian currency) for the two weeks in Bulgaria. The exit visa had immediate validity, leaving us almost no time to prepare and think about it, a fact we actually welcomed. Since we had the papers, I thought let us get the heck out of here, so no one has time to change their mind, to analyze our recent activity and stop us from going. One immediate, unavoidable problem was the need for Alizka to pay another visit to the Israeli embassy. We feared that if the authorities had been lax in observing us before, now they had an extra reason to be watchful and monitor our every move. Or perhaps the authorities were not all THAT watchful... Perhaps we were scared of our own shadows. And so Alizka went there. Yaaron expressed his satisfaction at how things were turning out, and this time he was completely open and explained the process of how to get to Israel in the most expedited way. Was it safe? None of us – Yaaron, Alizka or myself – had given that aspect of it much thought, judging by events that were about to take place in the near future. But I get ahead of myself.

The instructions at the Israeli embassy had been given to Alizka in a special room, perhaps because of the fear of bugging. That is not important: after all, I am not writing a detective story, even if my story would certainly provide great material for that genre. We knew from the start that we were initiating a dangerous undertaking and risking potentially unpleasant situations that could land us in jail, and the family in jeopardy. The kids were in the greatest danger since there was always the risk of their separation from the family for a long period of time. And the kids were the most precious thing we had!

When Alizka came home, she told me all the details of her fateful embassy meeting. It had begun with a warning that we needed to commit everything to memory, and we must not write anything down. No talking to anyone, not the closest family and not the children, about our plans or intentions – nothing that could give us away. There should be no hint of any kind of what was being planned for the near future. We should go to work as usual and act as if we were convinced we would be back in three weeks, and continue normal life. I should put in for vacation time, tell my secretary to set out-patient appointments for August 26th. Leave all documents and papers as they were at home and at work. We should not carry anything out of the apartment, we should bring our clothes to the dry cleaners and our shoes in for repairs, saying we would pick them up a day after we got back from vacation. And the main thing: pack up and take along only the items needed for a seaside vacation: bathing suits, light summer clothing, a couple of sweaters for cool nights, raincoats, sandals etc. No personal or professional documents, most definitely not the diploma – these were the things that were stressed most emphatically. If we were to be searched while crossing the border, it would be impossible to convince the border guard that a diploma and board certification credentials were essentials for our tanning time on the shores of the Black Sea. "But how will my husband find work?" Alizka asked. "Who will hire him without documentation proving he is indeed a physician?" Yaaron replied, "All they need to do is ask us (whom? how?) and there will be no problem at all." That was all we needed to hear.

I am again running ahead of the events: In this most sensitive aspect, the aspect of our documents, I behaved truly recklessly. In fact, I unwittingly endangered our escape and the whole family. I had been hypersensitive and cautious about documentation ever since the war. I began the year 1945 without a single-family document, a single photograph, a single memento. I learned later in life that unlike folks who were able to keep their homes, we, who had lost ours, would never be able to get certified copies of any document. After the war, trying to retrieve something from my hometown or county, which, as you recall, was no longer a part of Czechoslovakia, trying to get a document from Soviet Big Brother? Do not make me laugh! But that was not all. I correctly suspected that Czechoslovakia would not allow me to retrieve a personal or official document either. After all, I had left both countries illegally as far as they were concerned. Old timers will know: this was not just some misdemeanor, some administrative offense – this was a crime, this was treason! And now that traitor would like to obtain a personal document? As I stated, I had suspected correctly, completely correctly, that without documents life would be tough. Later, when I started looking for work in Israel, the first thing they wanted to see was my diploma – which I did not have on me – I would hear sarcastic remarks like "Well, you know, anyone can say they're a doctor."

And so, I decided to take a risk. On the morning of our departure, as we were leaving Prague, we stopped in Karlín at mother's house. We came to say good-bye. Under my coat, I was holding a tube containing my diploma, both my board certifications, a letter from the head of the ward which testified as to the length of my employment and mentioned the courses I had taken, and my evaluation. I do not remember how I had induced him to write such an official report – he did not seem to care much. I had prepared some fictitious story to tell him, but it was not necessary. I also had a large envelope including Alizka, the children's and my birth certificates, citizenship certificates, marriage certificate and my homesteading certificate. I believe that was all. I put it all on the table and asked my mother to hide it well (she might be interrogated, and her apartment searched after it became obvious we were not coming back). My mother looked at it all and she was not a stupid woman – she asked if we did not intend to return. She continued moaning until I was able to summon enough eloquence to convince her that summer vacation time – and people were indeed being warned about this – was prime time for burglary and theft, and I could not risk leaving all my documents at home, since they were the most important possessions we had.

We left Mom in great trepidation. I knew her well and knew it was only a question of time before she started panicking and going crazy. We learned later that she went to the police (sorry, to the StB) during the period when we were still officially on vacation and began yelling at them, telling them it was all their fault that her son and his family had abandoned her, because they had denied an application to emigrate. We also learned that the police entered our apartment that very day and left nothing of value or beauty in there. By the time the apartment was officially opened following a court order, it was practically empty. All that was left for the state to confiscate was useless bric-a-brac. Somehow, I do not know how, we managed to evade a total fiasco, a catastrophe, by a hair. I guess that we had not made any mistakes throughout the whole period of planning our escape. Our caution had paid off and the family got away clean.

Let us pick up where we left off. Another instruction we got was to plan our route from Czechoslovakia through Hungary in such a way as to arrive in Belgrade on a workday. We were to spend a night in some hostel and first thing in the morning we were to head for the Israeli embassy on Zmaj Jovina Street. The best strategy would be for Alizka to go in – a woman is less suspicious – and for me to wait in the car with the kids, a certain distance from the building. The person who would deal with Alizka would be told the Moťovič family had arrived, and we would head to Trieste in Italy with new documents in our pockets. Once we reached Trieste, we would be safe, we would be in a democratic country. At that point we would be handled by the *Sochnut*, a Jewish agency that used to be called the Palestine Office before the Communists had taken over Czechoslovakia. Everything perfectly planned to the letter. All one needed was to write a screenplay for a movie titled, let us say, "From Prague to the Holy Land in an elegant, smooth, triumphant way". One could shed a tear! The Israeli aide Yaaron's words were so encouraging when he said we did not even need to buy Bulgarian currency since we would go straight from Belgrade to Italy, and from there we would sail on to Haifa on the first available boat. Still, he said, "Buy a few levs, in case they check as you leave Czechoslovakia. It would be tough to convince the border guards you are leaving for Bulgaria for two weeks without any local currency. Now go, travel safely and be careful. We cannot help you at this point. We cannot risk blowing your cover and ours, and you would be easy prey for the Czechoslovak authorities." He wished my wife safe travels and said he hoped we would meet in Israel in the future.

I put in for vacation time between August 4th and August 25th. I fixed a rack to the roof of the car to put two suitcases on (there was no room inside the tiny car for a family of four), and I bought a spare tire. We packed according to the instructions: summer clothes, bathing suits, a couple of sweaters and summer dresses and other clothes for the girls (Ivana was eleven and Zuzana five and four months). We put in some reading material for us and story books for Zuzana – and that, I believe, was all. We left literally everything behind in the apartment. Everything was clean, tidy, folded, and neat. We put some sandwiches and some drinks into two small travel cases, one between the girls in the back, one between Alizka's legs in the front. We checked to see that the electricity, water, and gas were turned off. We locked the apartment and I put the keys in my pocket (they are still in the drawer of my desk till this day) and, as I have written, we piled into the car and started the 650 cc engine on August 4th 1965, Alizka's thirty seventh birthday. We began our possibly very risky journey into the unknown.

Our hearts were heavy as we took one last look at Prague, flooded with morning sunshine. Prague, I am not ashamed to say, that had wormed its way into our souls and had become our true home. Prague, where I graduated from high school, where I completed my university studies, where I got married, where we brought children into the world. Prague that had given me everything that only a native city could give. The city we loved so much and still do, a city we have missed every moment since our departure. Luckily, we were able to go back and visit in our old age and we were – and are – able to do that which we could only dream of for twenty-five years: visit with love and joy and even live there a few months each year. We were able to wait it out and we got our reward: no longer could some young police sergeant spit an arrogant sentence in my direction about not being obliged to explain to me where I could and could not travel. No one could any longer dictate to me whom I could or could not be in contact with, be it my brother whom I had not seen or written to in twenty years and whose family I did not even know, or someone else. But, like I said: any future path to a good career was hermetically closed to me – not because I lacked the know-how or the ability but because I had a brother in Israel. I had a brother who, like me, had been able to survive the worst hell on earth ever devised. I had a brother who had run via Austria and Italy illegally to Palestine, had gone through another deportation by the British to Cyprus and then, again illegally, back to Palestine before it became the State of Israel. And the authorities, the all-powerful ones, had decreed that this brother, who had left places that had wounded him so deeply, now found himself in the wrong place at the wrong time.

We drove non-stop from Prague to Bratislava, the first section of our route. We stayed overnight and early the next morning, as the first sunrays danced on the surface of the Danube, we headed for Komárno. The border inspection on the Slovak side must have taken a fairly long time. To be honest, my concept of time was foggy at that moment, to say the least, due to my bad conscience. All I could do was stare at the other side of the bridge. The language spoken on the other side was different, though the people's nationality was the same... At any rate, I could not wait to be there already. Finally, the border barrier lifted. I could not see anything suspicious in my rear-view mirror: no one was following us. We left Komárno, crossed the bridge slowly and arrived in Komárom. I do not even remember anyone checking us at the border station. That was something too! We had no *forints* (Hungarian currency) of course, and we drove just a few meters into the country, pulled over on a side street, got out of the car and stretched our legs. We used the restroom in a small tavern nearby, pulled some snacks and drinks out of one of the bags and, after a short rest, we continued across Hungary to Yugoslavia. I do not know that I felt anything special in those moments. Perhaps just the realization we were no longer at home, in Czechoslovakia. Looking at a map told me there was no time for long analysis or rumination. We could not tarry. We had no Hungarian money to stay in the country for any length of time and the way to Yugoslavia was long. Not long, though: our little Fiat was able to traverse it in a day.

We arrived in Belgrade in the afternoon, still in full daylight, happy, though with mixed feelings. Along the main road in a Belgrade suburb, we found a schoolhouse that for the summer had been converted to a tourist hostel. They had a vacancy, we got a clean room with a bathroom, and we were able to buy a cheap, modest dinner. We were tired but took a refreshing shower and after dinner we went to sleep early, eager to face the big day. Actually, only Alizka and the kids went to bed. I started studying the map and decided to explore our surroundings – mostly to find Zmaj Jovina Street, where the Israeli embassy was situated, so that we did not waste time searching for it in the morning. It was also a way to prepare myself mentally, to see what the starting point leading to our new life would be. That way, we would head out bright and early, knowing exactly where to go. We would tell the first person we met at the Embassy that Dr. Moťovič's family from Prague had arrived. I saw ourselves being greeted with joy and jubilation, handed a thick envelope from a safe, given instructions for our trip to Trieste, told who to speak to there and, naturally, expecting a dinar or two in the envelope as well. After all, we had to eat, and the gas tank was almost empty after crossing all of Hungary and a part of Yugoslavia! It was a good thing we had filled the tank with our last Czechoslovak crowns in Komárno! I already saw in my mind's eye all of us getting into the car and heading down what they called an *autostrada* here (inter-city highway) towards Trieste, to Italy. Let us get out of here, who knows if the hand of Czech justice could reach into Yugoslavia too. (It should be said that the girls suspected nothing at this point, especially Zuzana who was still very young and innocent.)

It is unlikely the night was calm. Our thoughts wandered, imagining highways and cities alongside, their names that I had committed to memory, all the words a driver needed to know, words that were the same for all the nationalities contained within Yugoslavia, though some written in the Cyrillic alphabet – I did not care. Everything was clear and understood. I do not remember if we had anything for breakfast, but I do remember we made an effort to look the best we could, put on our best clothes, loaded up the car, paid for our stay and thankfully accepted the manager's offer to stay again, on our way back from Bulgaria.

I parked the car about two hundred meters away from the embassy, at a spot I had scouted the previous night. I had a clear view of the entrance where Alizka would walk in and after a few minutes' walk out with the thick envelope in her hand. (Why did I imagine it precisely that way? I do not know. I cannot answer that.) Alizka walked with confidence towards the gate of the building. With a familiar movement of her right hand, she pressed the bell. It surely took only a few seconds for the huge gate to open, but for me, in the distance, it seemed like an eternity. I calmed down a little bit once the gate had shut behind her. We had reached our goal, and everything would go smoothly from that point on. A brief look at the back seat calmed me down even more – the girls were relaxed, and Ivana was reading Zuzana's favorite stories to her. "Your kids are relaxed, calm down as well", I told myself. But it was not easy.

It could have been seconds, it could have been minutes, it could have been hours. Time flowed heavily, like thick molasses. My nerves were like taut strings from the moment she disappeared inside the gate and until the gate opened. Only a person who knows his wife well, who's been living with her for eighteen years, could tell immediately by her slow and uncertain gait, by her body language, that something was amiss. As she came closer and I could observe her facial expression and saw the disappointment, it was clear that she would have nothing good to say. She got in the car and told me what the embassy staff had told her. No one from Prague had contacted them. No one had told them anything about "Dr. Moťovič's family". They knew nothing about us and could do nothing for us. Still, they did tell her to come back the next day. Logic would dictate – and that is what I tried to convince my crushed and disappointed wife about – that they probably needed the time to contact the Israeli embassy in Prague, to verify who we were and what our situation was. I told her, "Look, anyone could just waltz in there and say my name is such and such, from such and such a country. I need to get to Israel. Please help me". For all they knew, it could be an agent provocateur and it could create an international incident. And so, we assumed that Prague would send a positive response and we checked into a guest house we had noticed on our way to Zmaj Jovina Street. We were afraid of our own shadow and thought it safer not to return to our previous hostel. We counted our remaining dinars. We had only been given a very modest allotment since we were only supposed to be in Yugoslavia a total of two days: one day on the way to Bulgaria and one on the way home. We must have been hoping for a miracle because we had no money left for food and another overnight stay except...except if we continued on to Bulgaria.

The next day and the one after that – a drive to the embassy, me in the car with the girls, Alizka walking to the gate, me immediately knowing that we are in deep trouble when she walked out. One look at her as she walked towards the car said more than a thousand words. Her embassy visit was a bust – yet again. I decided that the next day I would go in myself. I wanted to see the faces of the people who considered the fate of my helpless family unimportant. I wanted to find out what that aide at the Prague embassy meant exactly when he said that all we needed to do was mention our names here in Belgrade and everything would be taken care of, and we would be on our way to the Promised Land that very day! And I wanted to stress the fact that here was a family with two little kids, without a penny in their pockets, and most definitely in danger because we were not supposed to be in Yugoslavia more than a day in each direction. Who knew how many secret agents in Yugoslavia were observing Czech tourists' every move? (I have written about the one I had uncovered in Romania.) The relations between Czechoslovakia and Tito's Yugoslavia were not exactly very warm at the time.

The situation had become totally hopeless. The thought of failure had begun sneaking into my mind. I decided to throw caution to the wind and walk into the embassy to see the people who had made our lives complicated and who had basically left us hanging. We were broke, and our stomachs, but mainly the girls' stomachs, were crying out for food, not to mention the empty gas tank. It was no farther from the car to the embassy gate than from one side of Wenceslas Square to the other but traversing the distance seemed endless. My brain was spinning feverishly, and our desperate situation really came into sharp focus for me. I felt hopeless, fearful – not so much for myself but for the family left back in the car. I got to the gate in a stupor. My hand reached for the buzzer without aiming. I pushed the button and waited. My legs were about to give out. I was looking around constantly to see if I were being followed, if someone already stood behind me, perhaps, about to put his hand on my shoulder and remind me I was about to betray my socialist homeland and would be severely punished. I had not yet committed a crime but even the intention already constituted a punishable offense. That was the regime's philosophy.

I can only guess how long it took to hear steps on the other side of the gate. It is hard to know exactly after forty-four years (yes, yet another long pause in writing, it is now the fall of 2009). The sound of shuffling steps interrupted my dark thoughts, a little window opened, and part of a tanned face appeared in the twenty by twenty-centimeter frame. All I could see was a nose, eyes, and a bit of forehead. I could not see the mouth, but I did hear the voice and an incomprehensible language. I will not strain my senile, eighty-two-year-old brain and the question of what I said and in what language shall remain unanswered.

All I recall is that the window slammed shut, the gate opened, and I found myself standing in front of a short man wearing a crumpled checked shirt, jeans and tattered sandals on bare feet.

Later, when I was a regular Israeli citizen, I learned this was the normal "uniform" of lower government and municipal employees, who were kibbutz members in the main. Wearing a suit with the obligatory tie, I immediately felt like the foreigner I was. In time I got used to the local mores and the tie was pulled out of moth balls only for professional trips abroad. A tie was not needed for conferences inside the country, except when delivering a lecture or chairing a session. The country was still in diapers, all of seventeen years old. It had already gone through two wars. It was built on rocks and sand and so pretty much everything was informal when it came to social settings. The country had to fight for every little thing, it was surrounded by enemies, it was under embargo from many sides and its inhabitants were people from all over the world who had gone through hell and back. The population was young. Everyone spent a huge chunk of their time on reserve duty. They had not forgotten what they had gone through to get there, the fact that they were put into active service the second they disembarked from their ships, many went straight to a battlefield and perhaps were killed in the line of duty because they could not understand the language their orders were in. When the Czechoslovakian weapons stopped flowing, they fought bare-handed and later, with the help of those weapons they had won and defeated the well-armed Arab armies. It was no time or place for raising kids to European standards of etiquette.

The guy who received me at the embassy could speak some English or another European language, but I forgive his appearance and even his manner: he had never had the need to ascribe much importance to social niceties and in my stressed-out frame of mind I found it hard to just accept the person the way he was.

67 Go back to Czechoslovakia and come back in a Month

The person I was led to was called Tabori. I do not know what his job was at the embassy. His exterior looked rather diplomatic, but I really had never imagined I would meet a nitwit of such magnitude on Israeli territory! We communicated in a language you could describe as a mix of Yiddish and German, but the sum of his knowledge about life in a communist regime was zero. In fact, what he thought he knew was erroneous and dangerous, and his advice reflected it. Mr. Tabori would have caused a personal catastrophe for anyone reaching out to the Israeli embassy for counsel and help. Listen to what he advised: "Go back to Czechoslovakia and come back in a month". The aide who took care of issuing the *laissez-passer* had been involved in a car accident somewhere in Europe and would only return on September 1st. I stood there in shocked silence. I was not able to respond to this "advice" in any way. It was unbelievable that an Israeli mission would have no idea about conditions in a communist country, and that its representative could make suggestions like that was absurd. Or perhaps Mr. Tabori was a total ignoramus and an irresponsible man. Most likely he was just your typical Israeli government grunt whose favorite byword was (and still is) *it'll be alright*. In the years that followed I had plenty of opportunity to get used to this phrase and I learned that it was most frequently used with new immigrants. I did not know it back then but, in reality, this empty slogan really means "get out of my face, you're wasting my time". I tried to explain to Mr. Tabori that he was living in fantasy land. An exit visa the next year (and for many more years afterwards) was simply not going to be issued. Ivana had to go to school on September first and my last vacation day was the last day of August. He was living in a fool's paradise and his ignoring of Czechoslovak reality and political practice was a dangerous fantasy.

When I was back out on the street and heard the heavy gate shut behind me, I realized the precariousness of our situation even more keenly. I kept hearing the words of that clueless embassy aide who had just left us hanging and even before reaching my little Fiat, I had decided there was no way we were going back to Czechoslovakia. We would travel to Bulgaria, and we would return to Belgrade on September first. Following this decision, we made another one: we planned to notify Alizka's brother-in-law in Israel about the situation we found ourselves in and tell him about our plans. We knew the main post office was not far off and assumed it would be possible to phone Israel from there. They told us it was indeed possible but when we learned what the price was going to be, we abandoned that plan. All we could do was send a card, describe our situation in a few words and, importantly let him know we would be back in Belgrade at the beginning of September. We asked him to send a note detailing how he could help us, which we would collect from the main post office. (At that time there was a system called *Poste Restante* or General Delivery as it was known in the USA, where those traveling could receive their post.) We were unable to write many details and we did not want to criticize the embassy staff in whom we had completely lost confidence. We used our last dinars to fill the tank, spent one more night in the hostel and we set out for the Black Sea in Bulgaria at the crack of dawn.

The original decision to leave our homeland was more daring than our decision to travel to Bulgaria and return to Belgrade on September 1st. It was dangerous. On the road to Sofia, the girls on the back seat stopped chattering and, tired after the long night and short rest, they fell asleep. Alizka and I began to dissect the situation and we gradually realized that our plan had not really been completely thought through, and that we were entering an adventurous and dangerous phase. We whispered as we did not want Ivana in the back to hear anything. We hadn't told her of our plans. Zuzana was only five and so she was not really comprehending much of what was going on, but Ivana was already eleven, a very intelligent girl and already, back in Belgrade, she had begun suspecting something was afoot. She became anxious and started asking questions, and as long as we could not be certain our plans would work out, we did not want to contribute to her anxiety any more.

We realized we did not even know where we were going! Bulgaria, as I said, was never in the plans. We had little Bulgarian currency, just that little bit I had exchanged prior to departure to allay the possible suspicions of border agents who would have wanted to see the currency of the country of our destination. We did not know where we were headed, whether we wanted to get to the sea, how far it was and whether we had enough gasoline. Another important factor: September first was already beyond our allotted time, I was supposed to be back at work at that point, Ivana was supposed to begin her fifth grade and it was almost certain that a search for our whereabouts would have begun.

We were approaching the capital. It was around noon when we stopped at a gas station in a suburb of Sofia. Between bites on a sandwich and gulps of lukewarm water (all carefully prepared by Alizka prior to our morning departure from Belgrade), I remembered that there was one Sofia address among all the addresses in my notebook. I reached into the glove box and found not just the address but also the phone number of the family of Big Mister Comrade, the important Bulgarian party official, whose seven-year-old daughter I had operated on the previous year. The family was extremely happy with the treatment. I had to promise to get in touch with them if I should ever find myself in Sofia. This is a good place to state that I have received tens, perhaps hundreds of telephone numbers from my patients' delighted parents – working folks, artists, businesspeople, car mechanics and so on, and I declare that I have never taken advantage of nepotism in any way!

But now we were in a hopeless situation and so when I found a phone in the gas station office, I asked the attendant sitting there to dial the number for me. He was very helpful, called the number, spoke to someone for a few seconds, then passed the receiver to me. The person on the other end of the line must have recognized my voice – or perhaps my Russian – and he let the gas station attendant explain to him where we were. He let us know he was not too far away and could be with us in half an hour. It did not even take that long. A Soviet limousine (ZIM, build to serve mid-rank Soviet functionary) pulled up and the man I knew from Prague recognized me and greeted me in a very friendly manner. We sat down in a somewhat generic restaurant, ate a light lunch, a good dessert and had some drinks. The girls had ice cream cones. Out of courtesy I asked him how his daughter was feeling, he smiled widely and answered *normal'no* (fine)! We told him we were on our way from Prague to the Black Sea, whereupon he expressed disappointment we had not notified him. From where we were sitting on the patio, we saw our host's limo, with the driver pacing around it. I do not know if the driver got some sort of signal, but he came up to our table and conversed with our host. We did not understand the conversation but when the driver left, we had been invited to stay at a Bulgarian government run recreational facility in a forest not far off.

The place was fabulous! Comfortable, modern villas dispersed around the complex at a decent distance from each other, with what looked like larger buildings around them, likely clubhouses. Adults and children came and went, dressed in bathing suits, in an out of a swanky looking mansion, which we assumed was the swimming pool. We also espied a good size lake in the wood. In a word – paradise on earth. We reached it in our little Fiat, with the limo leading the way at a good clip. We stopped in front of a two-story building which contained a luxurious hotel type apartment, equipped with every possible convenience. We did not need to unpack anything – not even toothpaste or shaving cream. After a short while, our host showed up (sadly, I do not remember his name or in what capacity he worked for the state or the Party) "I'm sure you'll want to rest and get refreshed after your long trip. We will pick you up later and it would be our pleasure to treat you to dinner".

68 A Royal Two-day Stay, then a Poor Fisherman Village

At the appointed time, our host and his wife came up to our room. I remembered her from the time she had sat by my little patient's bed on the pediatric surgery ward in Krč (I had not seen the girl – according to her parents she was at a young pioneer summer camp in Crimea). It was apparent to us immediately that we had stumbled upon a type of place one would see in Hollywood movies. The hospitality was regal. The festive atmosphere was as different from what we were thinking and feeling as it could possibly be. We were playing a dangerous game. We had to take care not to drop a single hint that we were on the run. The girls were in the dark though they were smart enough to know something was up, especially Ivana. We felt bad about deceiving those nice, friendly people.

When they asked for our address and phone number in Prague, we were embarrassed. It was not likely they would ever find us there. They asked where we were going to stay at the Black Sea. Again, clearly, we did not know because we had not planned to get there in the first place. After a moment's hesitation I answered that once we reached Varna, I would contact the local *Čedok* office for directions to our lodgings. There were a few such unforeseen and awkward moments.

We stayed a couple of days and notified our hosts we were going to continue our journey, wishing to enjoy the beach for as long as possible. We told them we would be getting up very early, there was no point in them coming to see us off, we should have a nice dinner and say our good-byes in the evening prior to our departure. They accepted and brought a little bag of sweets for the girls, and we were given a nice wooden box painted with Bulgarian folk motifs. It is still in my display cabinet at home, along with other artifacts.

The only witness of our early morning exit was the sun as it struggled to peek through the dawn mist, starting its daily journey. We reached Varna in the early afternoon. We felt quite carefree after our road trip and had not really discussed our lodging plans. As we approached Varna, there were more frequent rest areas along the highway. We pulled into one of them and were not too surprised to see many cars with Czech license plates: *Škoda MB 1000*'s, East German *Trabants* and *Wartburgs* and a couple of Soviet *Pobědas*. There was even the odd Fiat 600 like ours. We were not surprised because in those years, thousands of Czechs traveled around the highways and byways of Bulgaria and Romania. On the one hand, we were happy to see fellow Czech travelers but on the other hand we suffered from a not unreasonable feeling of paranoia: as if there was a sign on our forehead announcing to the world, we were no ordinary tourists but rather fugitives in the process of committing a crime. (A short aside now: it is now January 2011, forty-six years since the events I am describing and after a break of a few years when I have not written a single line.) It has been so long and so much has happened in my life in the interim that now I cannot recall, no matter how hard I try, why we decided not to drive into Varna. We agreed to find some small, ordinary village by the sea and spend the few remaining days till the first of September in quiet anonymity. I may have spoken to some of the drivers or perhaps I had overheard people talking about potential places to stay – I am not sure. I started studying a map of the coast and chose a name of a village completely at random. We got into the car and started on the last leg of this part of the journey.

With the map spread on Alizka's knees (as she had done the whole trip) and with her navigation abilities we arrived at a small, poor looking hamlet on the coast. There seemed to be a tourist car parked in front of every ramshackle hut, but we did not need to pull over and ask anyone. The local women and children were offering room and board to the new arrivals. We struck a deal with one of the women. Not just the village but the home of this Turkish (not Bulgarian) fisherman family was very poor. Our room was clean and large enough for a few days' tourist stay. It was furnished with a large armoire, two beds and two chairs. We sat on the beds and on the chairs. We could park the car in their small yard which was fenced to let a small goat graze there. There was a fireplace in the yard which became Alizka's kitchen central for the next few days: she would prepare the tastiest dishes there, out of practically nothing. We had fresh fish daily, caught by the man of the house. To his credit, he first fed his family and us, and only then took what remained to sell at the daily market in the neighboring village. He would come back home towards evening, pulling various necessities out of his sack. Bread was baked at home and all vegetables were grown in their small garden. Occasionally, he would give his wife a few coins. This was the daily routine of that very kind, modest and friendly fisherman family. I do not recall if they had their own children, but the lady of the house absolutely adored my daughters and they loved her in return. The girls had a sweet or treat in their hands at all times.

You must be asking yourself (assuming anyone's reading) how we were able to pay the family. The few Bulgarian levs we had taken out in

Prague – far short of what we could and should have taken, had we indeed been planning for a Bulgarian stay – were gone. It had never been in our plan to spend a single night there, never mind a few days' worth of food and lodgings, plus all the gas money that was needed to get to the Black Sea and then back to Belgrade. Well, since no one has asked the question, I will answer it without being asked. It is the polite thing to do in case there are readers who would like to know. Those old-timers who remember the time before the "Velvet Revolution" need no explanation. They remember the conditions of foreign travel in those days – for the few lucky ones who could travel at all. And today's generation, which travels wherever and whenever, with as much money as is needed and in total comfort – they would not understand anyway. I know from personal experience that when I try to describe the conditions back then, I am not believed! There were times when one traveled to "friendly countries" (pretty much the only places one could travel) armed with incredibly detailed knowledge, strategy, and tactics of how to get money for fuel, money for food and entertainment and have enough to buy a small present. Organized tours were slightly better but, even there, an individual had to hustle like crazy to make sure they had enough foreign currency for their personal needs. The government and the Communist Party had generous billions to spend on shady governments the world over, as long as they battled "international imperialism and Zionism". But it only gave ridiculously tiny sums to its own citizens who wanted to travel abroad. The lucky ones permitted to travel to the West had to produce proof that they would be financially taken care of (sponsored) while out of the country, by those who had invited them. Then they would get the sum of ten pounds sterling, without regard to the length of their stay! (This was the situation in 1964 when Alizka went to Israel with the kids.)

Back to business: the locals – decent, modest, and very poor people, had their beds, their fish, some vegetables, a bit of milk and some bread they baked in the oven in their yard. But they had no money for clothing, for example. As regards money, we were in the same boat: we had none, either. What we did have, although in modest quantities, was clothing, and specifically one highly desired commodity in those days: a nylon raincoat, colloquially called "the rustler" (it made a rustling sound as you moved). These coats were hard to get, even in Prague. One could get them in *Tuzex*, the foreign currency stores, and occasionally the House of Fashion (a well-known department store in Prague) would stock them but you needed to know someone on the inside to help you get it. We also had some shirts and blouses, sweaters, and other textiles which we were able to swap for room and board. True barter economy. One of our suitcases emptied out and itself became a part of a transaction. Even the second suitcase was lighter and flatter towards the end of our stay with those humble, fine people, since we needed some money for our trip to Belgrade. We took short side trips in our car to explore our surroundings, and I will describe one such outing that made our stay more "colorful" because we still chuckle as we remember it. We found ourselves in some small town, perhaps it was even a suburb of Varna. Our stomachs rumbled and we noticed a garden restaurant, clearly frequented by tourists from less well-to-do countries. There was only one dish on the menu, and we ordered it. Even before we were served, we had noticed a knife and fork sticking out of the waiter's back pocket. When he brought us our dinner, he whipped out the cutlery from his pocket, walked around the table to tend to each plate. He cut up our food and stuck the knife and fork back in his pocket. He then walked over to the next table and repeated the procedure. No one said a word, no one seemed surprised. I guess they had bad experiences with tourists or perhaps cutlery was a scarce item.

69 The Belgrade Sojourn, Fear and Hope

All in all, we did not want for much during those fourteen days. We had a roof over our heads, decent food, plenty of rest. It was only towards the end that we had begun realizing we needed to inform Prague that our return might be delayed due to Zuzana's illness. We were supposed to be back in Belgrade on September 1ˢᵗ, which was the very day Ivana was supposed to start fifth grade and I was supposed to be back from vacation and resume work. We decided to send telegrams from Bulgaria and not wait till we got to Belgrade. That way, there would have been no suspicion about our intentions. We set out for Belgrade on August 30ᵗʰ, and we planned the trip in such a way that we would arrive in Belgrade in the early morning hours of September 1ˢᵗ. During the following forty-eight hours, the Fiat became our home. During the day it clocked miles on the highways and byways. At night, the back seat was the girls' bed and Alizka and I tried to grab a few hours of shut eye however we could. Since we were now completely penniless, we always pulled into a highway rest stop during the night, always one that already had some cars parked in it. Other cars meant more security. As she had since the beginning of our fateful journey, Alizka was responsible for our nourishment. The deep bag on the floor always contained the most necessary modest sustenance.

Our last rest stop – on the night between August 31ˢᵗ and September 1ˢᵗ – was close to Belgrade so we could be at our destination at eight in the morning. Our first steps led to the main post office. We were hoping for an answer from my brother-in-law to the letter we had sent before heading for Bulgaria. We went through a whole pile of mail under the letters "A" (for my first name) and "M" (for my surname) but there was nothing. We never thought to look under "D" for "doctor". My brother-in-law's note that had indeed been sent, addressed to Dr. Moťovič, was returned to him in Israel. In that note he had notified us that he would come and get us in Belgrade. By the time he got the returned note, we were already in Israel.

I do not need to tell you that our mood dropped to below freezing point, though we still clung to the hope that the Israeli embassy would have good news and notify us that we were indeed going to Israel from Belgrade, and nowhere else. Our paranoid state of mind was not helped by seeing Yugoslavian and Egyptian flags displayed all across the city, along with huge portraits of the two close friends – Yugoslavia's Tito and Egypt's Nasser. The Egyptian president was on a state visit there. Not the most appropriate time to visit the Israeli embassy. I was certain that the embassy would have been in the crosshairs of all the secret services. Czechoslovak citizens would ordinarily not be suspect, but we were a family now officially on the lam! As the saying goes: the thief's cap is on fire. Still, we had no other alternative and so we repeated the well-rehearsed procedure from before: park the Fiat on the now familiar Zmaj Jovina Street at a certain distance from that heavy gate. As you will recall, the routine had the girls and me stay in the car while Alizka walked to the gate. The gate opened after about a minute and Alizka disappeared inside the building. To my surprise, her visit was quite short this time. It was hard to tell from her body language what the score was and whether she had good news or bad news. She sat down and told me the news was both good and bad, and which did I want to hear first? I do not recall what my preference was, but the crux of the matter was this: there were no travel documents for us to get to Italy. It had something to do with Nasser's presence in the country (was the relevant embassy official too busy?). The good news was that my Haifa brother-in-law was in Belgrade already. He would be at the embassy at noon, and we would meet him there. Finally, one positive piece of news after a very long time.

There were a couple of hours left till noon and we took a walk through the busy streets to kill time. We passed a dairy store and had the worst experience a parent can have: our five-year-old, Zuzana, asked for a glass of milk and we had to tell her we did not have money to buy it. As we were trying to explain this to the poor kid, Alizka told me to turn around and there, a few steps behind me stood a tall blond man, my brother-in-law Chaim. I had never seen him before and only knew him from photographs, but Alizka and the girls knew him from their visit to Israel the year before. Naturally all three jumped up to hug him and the very first thing we did was buy Zuzana her milk.

It was not the most auspicious spot to be celebrating our reunion, or at least that is what we thought, in the vicinity of the Israeli embassy, during Nasser's visit in the country – the four of us consisting of an Israeli citizen and an illegal Czech family. We found a nice park in the neighborhood with some unoccupied benches and a kiosk with a decent selection of food and refreshments. Alizka ordered and my brother-in-law paid, and so we all sat together and organized our first picnic. There were a few more like it in the following five days. Chaim checked into a nearby hotel and when we were told our documents were not ready yet, he booked a room for us as well. A man who had come from a free country found it all difficult to understand why we could not book a room in a hotel, or why the brew of Nasser, an Israeli citizen, Czechoslovak citizens illegally present in Yugoslavia and visiting the Israeli embassy, was so toxic! He finally understood, and we decided to go back to the hostel we used when we had first arrived in the city. It was still in business and we took a room there. When we were asked for how long, we said our child was ill – indeed, Zuzana had an allergic cold. Apparently, their school year did not start on the first of September, the day our sojourn had entered the home stretch. Our schedule for the next four days was simple. A visit to the embassy in the morning, now done by my brother-in-law, not my wife. Each day he would come back with disappointment written on his face. From there we drove to the outskirts of town, to a small, wooded area where we would sit on a bench almost till nightfall, chatting, planning, and destroying any written document that bore even one word in the Czech language.

70 The Home Stretch

After four days in Belgrade, on September 4th, 1965, precisely a month after leaving Prague, we finally hit the home stretch. The long-coveted document, our *laissez passer* with all the necessary stamps, was in our trembling hands. The documents bore our real names (without the Czech diacritical marks), it stated we were from the kibbutz Khanita in Northern Galilee and that I had spent time in Czechoslovakia in the function of a "mohel" (a rabbi who performs ritual circumcisions).

As they say, there is a bit of truth in every rumor. I am not sure if my presumptive profession was a fluke or if some paper-pusher at the embassy had a sense of humor. As a pediatric surgeon in Prague, I had indeed occasionally been approached by a Jewish family to circumcise their newborn boy. Naturally, this was done in the hospital, under general anesthetic in one of our operating theaters. I should state here, that to make the situation more amusing I was promoted to rabbi for the day by the chief surgeon and, as long as the newborn was in our hospital, that is what the staff called me. Just fun, friendly ribbing. I will now admit, more than half a century later, that those were the only instances when I faked the diagnosis. For whatever reason, probably just to be safe, I would usually put on the child's chart a diagnosis of phimosis – a condition where the foreskin is too tight to pull back over the glans and which requires surgery. It was nobody's business why I did not perform the Schloffer procedure, the gold standard for such a problem, but rather a ritual circumcision. My conscience is clear. The small deceit was performed with the chief's knowledge, and I believe that after all these years my misdemeanor is past the statute of limitations.

There is an interesting aside to this: in several cases some non-Jewish parents actually requested a written certification that their child had indeed undergone the Schloffer procedure for purely medical reasons and not a ritual circumcision, to explain the unusual look of their son's foreskin. I was glad to give them the certificate. That way, the person in question could prove throughout his life that he was not – God forbid! – a Jew.

A few decades later I performed similar surgeries on a not negligible number of immigrants from the Soviet Union, again under the guise of a phimosis diagnosis. They could not be circumcised as infants for obvious reasons but later wanted to be thought of as "kosher" Jews. If diagnosed with phimosis, they were entitled to receive surgery covered by their insurance. After a long period of time, the news had reached the Chief Rabbinate, the body in Israel that has the exclusive right to determine who is and who is not a Jew. They did not like the fact that they were losing oversight. I defied them for as long as I could and continued performing the surgery and charging the insurance company. In the end, the Rabbinate exerted a huge amount of pressure on the insurers, who finally balked and stopped covering the procedure. I am not sure what bothered the Rabbinate more: the fact that I was not religious and not performing the surgery according to their instructions, or the reasons listed above.

Let us return to the embassy in Belgrade. Before we were handed the desired documents, we had been given instructions to travel to Trieste in Italy. We were warned not to speak Czech while crossing. We were supposed to put an item on the dashboard that would point to our Israeli origins (we found a bag of Nescafe with Hebrew letters on it for the purpose). The most brilliant suggestion – like the previous genius instruction to drive back to Prague and return to Belgrade later – was truly beyond belief: "If the customs people on the Yugoslav side start questioning you and you feel they are suspicious, leave the car, grab the kids and run towards the Italian side." I could not believe my own ears. It was incredible that a person working in such an important position at a diplomatic mission, would dispense such idiotic and dangerous advice, which would put the whole family in danger.

We drove back to our little bench in the forest, ripped up all remaining papers written in Czech and we discussed with my brother-in-law our next steps. We already had an address in Trieste. It was a place my brother-in-law had escaped to with a group of young Jews after the *Anschluss* of Austria. He was going to meet us there the following day. My brother-in-law bought us some food for the long trip to Trieste, about 600 km (almost 400 miles), gave us money for gas and for our overnight stay and then late in the afternoon left for the train station.

We were orphaned again. We tried to rest a little, but our minds kept spinning, thinking about the next day, the day that would fundamentally change our family history, our whole life; the day when no one, not even the wisest person, could answer the question whether leaving our past for an uncertain future was the right thing to do. Yes, it was true, that if everything went smoothly I would be able to hug my brother for the first time since 1944, when we hugged on the *Appelplatz* in Auschwitz, twenty-one years earlier. I knew his wife and two sons only from black and white photographs. It had been even longer since I had any news of uncles, aunts and cousins, who had survived ghettos and death camps but who had lost their families, then bid good-bye to the places they loved.

I had not seen my sister for sixteen years. She was nineteen when she married a man who had family in America. His family sent them their "papers" and they were planning to depart. They were caught by surprise by the "Victorious February" and America remained a dream. As I mentioned earlier, one day in 1949, the young couple showed up in Prague. They were on the way to Bratislava hoping to be smuggled across the border to Austria. They succeeded and soon my mother received a note telling her they were on their way to the USA. My sister visited my brother in Israel every three years or so. I had no doubt that once we were "out", she would travel there to visit us as well (I was correct!). We thought of her every hour, especially at that point because without her help, our whole trip, the whole crazy trek would not have been possible. As I have mentioned before, we were able to buy our Fiat with the dollars she had sent.

We had the necessary documents for crossing into Italy with the permission of the Yugoslav authorities, we put our remaining suitcase up on the roof rack and we returned to our room (a classroom during the school year). No loud words were spoken. The girls still did not know that our route the next day would not lead back to Prague and that they would not be able to tell their friends of their adventures because they would likely never see them again. They would not even be able to visit their birthplace as tourists (unless a miracle happened, which it did in 1989!). We were getting ready for the penultimate stage of our anabasis. The girls fell asleep, but my wife and I did not get a single minute of shut eye, and it is impossible to describe our thoughts even today, after fifty years (yes, the pauses in writing are getting incredibly long: I am writing this in 2015).

71 The Belgrade – Trieste Highway

And so, early in the morning of September 5th, 1965, we got into the Fiat and drove down the good highway in the direction of Italy – to Trieste, to be exact. The trip was going smoothly until we stopped at a rest stop and I began thinking about the advice given to me by the embassy employee, regarding the possible over-curious probing of Yugoslav customs officials. I did not like the idea of running to the other side. I was suspecting that a similar situation had arisen before with other families, or else why give such advice? Truth be told, it would not have taken much to be suspicious. All they had to do was look at our license plate, complete with the letters ČS on it and even an inexperienced official would have been highly skeptical. Alizka and I thought of the most likely culprit in our family to give us away: our five-year-old Zuzana could start babbling. She could say something in Czech, like "Uncle, what's your name?" We estimated that we were about a two-hour drive away from the border and the most sensible thing was to give her something to make her sleep. I do not remember what we gave her, but she was asleep within minutes. We were rested but our mood was foul. We squeezed ourselves and two large bags of food into the Fiat and continued our journey.

Why the bad mood? The younger generation will not be able to understand but older folks will remember that a citizen of a socialist country could not move freely in the vicinity of international borders, especially those of western countries. And soon we began seeing signposts and notices warning us that we were approaching the border. I slowed down inadvertently. We were being passed by scores of other cars with license plates from all over western Europe. And there we were, advancing slowly among them, the one car with a ČS tag on the back, our progress halting and hesitant. Then we saw a barrier, about 50 meters away, and it was lifted. Two uniformed men, one on each side, waving drivers through, urging them to speed up and not to delay the dense traffic. They glanced at the license plates only infrequently as the cars passed them without slowing down.

By now I was so close to the point of no return that I had no choice but to merge with the stream of traffic. But I was driving slowly, and the two uniformed men looked at the tag and probably realized that I was some kind of intruder. One of them motioned to me to pull over, which I did, of course. The sentence that flashed through my mind was "leave the car, grab the kids and run for the Italian side" but I did nothing of the sort. I obeyed the man in uniform and stopped where I was asked to. The man gestured for me to turn the engine off. He approached the open window, scanned the inside of the car briefly and uttered a single word: "Passport". I was busy pulling out our documents with its various official stamps and did not notice Zuzana stretching and waking up in the back seat. The very second the man took my precious document, we heard Zuzana's little kid voice: **"Are we back where they speak 'Pragueish' already?"** I am sure I turned pale (or beet red) or fainted (or just got angry) I was not mad at Zuzana, after all she was a tiny girl who could not know better. Maybe she was missing her school and her friends. Or maybe she had had enough of the endless trip in an unairconditioned car. Be that as it may, the man towered over the car, looked inside again, now especially at Zuzana. He then checked the documents – our faux passports – and finally ordered me out of the car and told me to follow him to the office.

Right inside the building there was a desk behind a glass partition. A man who sat behind the desk began conversing with the uniformed man who had brought me in. He lifted his head, looked me in the eye and pointed at my document, saying loudly: "Passport". I guess the adrenalin kicked in and I used the same tone of voice he did, and also pointed a finger at my document and exclaimed with loud emphasis: "Passport". The man did not say a word. I could say that he even gave me a scant smile. He pulled a round stamp from a stand on the desk, gently impressed it on my document and handed it back to me. Perhaps no other unforeseen development could happen now. We would be at the Italian border barrier in a few seconds and a short time later in Trieste, at the address we had been given in Belgrade.

Accompanied by the same guard (I had probably been seen by his superior) I returned to the car. I started the engine having nodded to my crew that everything was alright. I glanced at my rearview mirror and noticed the two guys pointing to the rear of my car (ČS?). I stepped on the gas and a few seconds later, without any further inspection, we were on Italian territory. There was a right turn in the road and when I could not see even the Italian border station in my mirror and noticed a small parking lot, I pulled over and turned off the engine. I must have been in shock. I could not say a word. The girls were quietly inspecting our demeanor and they began to truly understand. Especially Ivana, who was eleven, an intelligent, bright girl. She understood she had been deceived, kidnapped, in fact. Her unease spread to her sister, the five-year old Zuzana who began fidgeting in her seat.

This was the moment for me to speak with the children and explain the situation. I did so, using simple words. "Girls, we are not going back to Prague. We are going to visit Auntie Maňka!" "Going to visit Auntie Maňka" had been our code for going to Israel. The girls had visited there a year previously and they had just met their uncle in Belgrade – and would soon see him again in Trieste, as I explained. Zuzana remained unimpressed but Ivana grasped the gravity of the situation, and she began sobbing bitterly. She only said two things: "I won't see Ivan Dudek" (a classmate, neighbor and faithful friend), and "I won't see or hear my Zíma. Will I be able to get my collection of his photos back?" (She collected his photographs like many of her contemporaries). What could we tell her? She would not talk to us for hours and seemed not to react to her surroundings.

We got a small map of Trieste at a nearby gas station. We marked the spot we needed to get to (I still have that little map among my old documents). The only unexpected difficulty was a steep hill the Fiat had to conquer. We reached our destination and found ourselves in the presence of smiling people. We regained our confidence and could breathe freely again.

We were told we were being impatiently anticipated by some gentleman from Israel. The brother-in-law showed up, drunk as a skunk fell down on one of the beds in our room and started snoring. The alcohol proved more powerful than his eagerness to welcome us. It took hours before he was able to describe the events of the preceding hours. He had started being nervous and impatient because it seemed to him, we were taking too long to arrive. To kill time, he sat down in a little garden café and basically nodded every time the waiter came by and offered something. Even after many years he could never remember what he had consumed. He did not know what he had eaten or drunk. But I tell myself today: That week in Belgrade, during the Egyptian president's visit, that must have been a real hit for the nerves! It must have played a role in the whole business. Be that as it may, our joy was tremendous.

72 The Final Stage of our One-Month Road Trip

One or two hours later, as evening approached, we all calmed down, had supper together, and the brother-in-law departed for Rome to catch a flight to Tel Aviv. The gentleman who had been taking care of us during the preceding few hours invited us to his office and gave us instructions for the next day. The day when we would board a ship and permanently leave Italy and Europe, the day that would start a journey for us to become inhabitants of Asia and citizens of Israel. The calendar showed the date to be September 6th, 1965. We understood the essence of what he was saying, despite the mixture of various languages being used. He told us an Israeli ship was anchored in the port of Mestre (in essence, Venice). We had to make sure to arrive there on time before the ship sailed for Haifa. "One of our people will be there", he said, "and he will take it from there".

We did not get much sleep that night. We got down to the parking lot at dawn. I started to drive, Alizka was next to me with the little map of Trieste and the girls were dozing in the back seat. I had written down the names of all the towns we would be passing through on the back of it. I was watching the signposts and the names of each town as I drove, as well as the remaining distance to Mestre – Venice.

Kilometers were passing quickly and at a certain point we hit a high point from which we could see the port with a huge number of vessels of various sizes. I nudged the brakes and started slowing down. All around me, I was hearing brakes screeching and people yelling and cussing. I felt bad but what could I do? I was looking for a pedestrian to ask for directions to the passenger ship port. I was getting desperate, horns honking and people yelling all around me. Not far, in the middle of a busy intersection, I noticed a policeman directing traffic. I had no other choice. I drove to the intersection, stopped the car right next to the policeman's stand. All hell broke loose around us. I had never heard such a din and so many voices cussing and swearing. It seemed like I was about to be lynched. The cop stepped down and started walking towards me, looking determined and angry. He stopped to look at the car, probably noticed where it had come from and shouted *Emil Zátopek* (a famous Czech long track runner). He smiled and began directing traffic again, calming down passers-by and the screaming honks of automobiles. He pointed to a spot in the far corner of the square where I could pull over without disrupting traffic. Still smiling, the cop walked up to the car and began speaking to me, though of course I did not understand a single word. I took a chance. Having seen a lot of cars with the letter "D" on their plates, I yelled in German: *"Das Schiff Theodor Herzl?"* Whereupon the nice policeman yelled another name, even better than the first one: "Ah! Moshe Dayan!" His arms and his whole body gestured in the direction of the Israeli ship we needed to reach. He stopped all traffic to make room for me and we continued.

In a few minutes we were driving along a quay where several large ships were anchored. Alizka suddenly jumped up and yelled, pointing to the Israeli flag on the mast of one of the ships. We found ourselves alongside the giant vessel in a single hop (yes, it is possible, even in a car). On the ship's side I saw the large letters *Theodor Herzl*. An invisible hand started pulling up the passenger ladder. A man appeared out of nowhere, he asked our names, muttered something into his walkie-talkie and gestured for us to get out of the car. A crane pulled up the Fiat which disappeared in the bowels of the ship. The ladder was lowered again, and we were asked to board. There is a black and white photograph that I have somewhere, documenting our entrance into that modern, luxurious ship, still silent and reticent, as if afraid of something. The pleasant sailing lasted three days, with a stop-over in Piraeus. Many people disembarked and ran into the harbor, coming back with bags of nuts. We remained on board. We were still afraid of something. We could not get used to the fact that we had left fear behind and we were free!

After a three-day sail, the ship dropped anchor in Haifa and our new life began.

The date was September 9th, 1965.

73 Instead of a Joyful Epilogue – A Painful Obituary

It has taken me almost a quarter century to write these few dozen pages. Breaks in writing took years, sometimes up to three years. During the time of writing, all the friends and classmates near and dear to me, have left this world. At any rate, all the ones I have written about or mentioned in this narrative.

The last break took four years. Perhaps it is just an excuse if I say it was caused by Alizka's three-year grave illness, to which she succumbed half a year ago. I am terribly sorry I was not able to finish writing this work while she was still alive. She tried to impress upon me all the time that we are all mortals, and it would be a shame not to write about certain episodes in my life. In OUR life, I should say. She even ended up agreeing with my decision not to write about the ghettos and the concentration camps, but I did accede to her wish and the reader can sense hints in the background, hints of something horrific, inhumane and beyond all belief that befell us in our lives.

Despite the illness that she suffered from being rare and incurable, she did not keep it a secret, she knew what the end would be, down to the last detail. And yet she was always ready, at the drop of a hat, to offer help. I do not wish to repeat myself. I have written about a lot of her troubles and her joys. She lived to a blessed old age, she was happy and grateful for every moment she could spend with us. The mutual love between her and our children and grandchildren was the essence of her life. She was overjoyed to be with them and there was no better mother or grandmother. And permit me to write a less poetic sentence: I have never eaten better food than the dishes she made. For myself, I can say one thing in this context: she gave everything a person could give, so that I could have a rewarding surgical career. She was the creator of all that was beautiful, pleasant and rich in our lives. She ran an amazing household, she raised two great girls and then was a pillar of support to their families. Her relationship with her grandson and two granddaughters would form a whole independent chapter. As far back as I remember, there were always people or institutions whom she helped and supported. No one left empty-handed if they came asking for help. Aside from all that, she had a job and was helping to support the family financially – mainly after we arrived in our new homeland. I worked endless hours from the very beginning and therefore the whole burden was on her shoulders.

I am not writing all of this only to comply with the famous Latin saying *De mortuis nil nisi bene* (nothing but good words about the dead). It is all from my heart. Many things happen when two people spend sixty-six years together, but I can declare with a clear conscience that even as I stood at Alizka's grave, I did not feel the need for abject apologies. And if there had been some things...the fact that we lived together and remained together all those years, speaks for itself.

Finally, the road trip is over -- In Venice, boarding the ship to Israel, September 6th, 1965.

I cannot come to terms with her not being here. I cannot even say life goes on. Yes, it does go on, but it is not the same and never again will be.

I am sorry if these words sound very sad. There's nothing I can do. The sorrow is overwhelming.

Let these words be our good-bye. I am sorry that she left us at a time when Nov, her first granddaughter, is completing her physical therapy studies at Tel Aviv University, her grandson, Jonathan, is a freshman at Beer Sheva University, and Maya, the second granddaughter – with whom I am staying now – is starting medical school on October first. She is starting medical school at the Faculty of Medicine at Charles University in Prague, the faculty from which I graduated sixty-two years ago. She would have been so happy to have lived long enough to see these milestones.

And so, I bring this chronicle to an end here, in Prague. Looking at the calendar, I see the date is September ninth, two thousand and fifteen. I have been writing, with shorter and longer pauses since nineteen ninety-seven. A full eighteen years.

And it was on this day, this month fifty years ago, when I took my first steps on the soil of my new homeland.

Prague – Kfar Saba, 2015

© Antonín Moťovič
Translated from the Czech by George Jiři Grosman
Unless otherwise noted, all photograph and pictures in this publications are author's personal collection.

Translator's Remarks

I have endeavored to stay as close to the original as possible. In some cases, I took the liberty of using a well-known English place name such as "Wenceslas Square" for the original "Václavské náměstí". I have changed some Czech spellings to the commonly used English spellings, especially for geographical locations ("Dněstr" in Czech "Dniester" in English). This was done in accordance with current Google Maps usage. Czech diacritical marks are preserved in some instances but not in all. I have preserved the author's voice as much as possible, though I have inserted an occasional explanation of a specific term.

George Grosman
Winter Haven, FL
August 2018

Editorial Input

The editors have made certain editorial amendments to the translated text, especially with regard to its accuracy, historical events, geography and literary references, in order to make it more accessible for today's reader.

MO and TD, February 2022

With Alizka in 2004.

Me in 2017.

Zuzana's family in Prague in 2018: Hagai, Nov, Zuzana and Maya.

Ivana, Zeev and Jonathan

With Nov, Jonathan and Maya.